GENDER AND EDUCATION

GENDER AND EDUCATION

Ninety-second Yearbook of the
National Society for the Study of Education

PART I

Edited by
SARI KNOPP BIKLEN AND DIANE POLLARD

Editor for the Society
KENNETH J. REHAGE

Distributed by THE UNIVERSITY OF CHICAGO PRESS • CHICAGO, ILLINOIS

The National Society for the Study of Education

Founded in 1901 as successor to the National Herbart Society, the National Society for the Study of Education has provided a means by which the results of serious study of educational issues could become a basis for informed discussion of those issues. The Society's two-volume yearbooks, now in their ninety-second year of publication, reflect the thoughtful attention given to a wide range of educational problems during those years. In 1971 the Society inaugurated a series of substantial publications on Contemporary Educational Issues to supplement the yearbooks. Each year the Society's publications contain contributions to the literature of education from more than a hundred scholars and practitioners who are doing significant work in their respective fields.

An elected Board of Directors selects the subjects with which volumes in the yearbook series are to deal and appoints committees to oversee the preparation of manuscripts. A special committee created by the Board performs similar functions for the series on Contemporary Educational Issues.

The Society's publications are distributed each year without charge to members in the United States, Canada, and elsewhere throughout the world. The Society welcomes as members all individuals who desire to receive its publications. Information about current dues may be found in the back pages of this volume.

This volume, *Gender and Education*, is Part I of the Ninety-second Yearbook of the Society. Part II, which is published at the same time, is entitled *Bilingual Education: Politics, Practice, and Research.*

A listing of the Society's publications still available for purchase may be found in the back pages of this volume.

Library of Congress Catalog Number: 92-063305
ISSN: 0077-5762

Published 1993 by
THE NATIONAL SOCIETY FOR THE STUDY OF EDUCATION
5835 Kimbark Avenue, Chicago, Illinois 60637

First Printing, 4,500 Copies

Printed in the United States of America

Contributors to the Yearbook

SARI KNOPP BIKLEN, Syracuse University, Co-editor
DIANE POLLARD, University of Wisconsin—Milwaukee, Co-editor

DEBORAH P. BRITZMAN, State University of New York—Binghamton
JOAN N. BURSTYN, Syracuse University
MEG CAMPBELL, Expeditionary Learning Project, Cambridge, Massachusetts
PATRICIA CAMPBELL, Campbell-Kibler Associates, Groton, Massachusetts
MICHELLE FINE, Graduate Center, City University of New York
SELMA GREENBERG, Hofstra University
MAXINE GREENE, Teachers College, Columbia University
ELISABETH HANSOT, Stanford University
DIANA LAM, Dubuque Community School District
PAT MACPHERSON, Germantown Friends School, Philadelphia
HEATHER MCCOLLUM, Policy Studies Associates, Washington, DC
JANET L. MILLER, National-Louis University, Beloit, Wisconsin
ELOIS SCOTT, U.S. Department of Education, Washington, DC
NAN D. STEIN, Wellesley College
CHRISTINE E. STREETER, University of Wisconsin—Parkside

Acknowledgments

Professors Sari Knopp Biklen and Diane Pollard, editors of this yearbook, have brought together contributions from a number of authors who have deep concerns about issues with respect to gender and education. The National Society for the Study of Education is grateful to the editors and to the other contributors for their work in preparing chapters for this stimulating book.

The Society is also indebted to Professor Margaret Early, a member of the faculty of the College of Education, University of Florida, for her competent assistance in the editing of this volume. Her editorial talents and her wise counsel have been of immeasurable help.

KENNETH J. REHAGE
Editor for the Society

Table of Contents

Section One
INTRODUCTION

CHAPTER I

Sex, Gender, Feminism, and Education

SARI KNOPP BIKLEN AND DIANE POLLARD

Put very simply, we might say that one's sex is involved in every activity connected to education. Since every interaction involves a male or a female, sex is everywhere; we must take it into account. When to take it into account looms as a big question because it may be central even when it seems to have no relation to what is going on. But being male or female carries few meanings in and of itself; its most potent meanings come from the social and cultural meanings attributed to it. These meanings we call gender, the social construction of sex.

Listen to talk during the lunch period in a teachers' lounge, watch students engage with each other over texts or on the playing fields, attend a school board meeting and you will see men, women, boys, and girls engaged in both cross-sex and single-sex interactions. How they act, both with each other and across sex boundaries, is constructed not only culturally but also by gender. Gender, as a category of analysis, suggests that to understand female—or male—experience each must be analyzed in relationship to the other in order to see how each is shaped by the other. Patriarchy, for example, is a central part of women's lives even when men are not around. That is why this book, even though it is mostly about women, focuses on gender. We want to explain more about this, and about the feminist perspective on gender that each of the essays takes.

Sari Knopp Biklen is Associate Professor in the Department of Cultural Foundations and Curriculum, School of Education, Syracuse University. Diane Pollard is Associate Professor in the Department of Educational Psychology, School of Education, University of Wisconsin—Milwaukee.

Gender

Gender is a category of analysis that refers to the social construction of sex. What we have come to identify as belonging to men's or women's behaviors, attitudes, presentation of self, and so on is produced by social relationships and continually negotiated and maintained within cultures. The chapters in this volume explore the production and maintenance of gender relationships in different areas of education. While gender could refer to the social construction of men's or women's lives, it does not have to refer to both at the same time except insofar as the category is relational. That is, what we know as masculine has been defined in relation to what is feminine, and vice versa. At some level, therefore, it is impossible to talk about gender without this relational frame.

We want to emphasize gender as this kind of category of analysis in this book, even though all the essays focus on women. A comparison to other categories illustrates how you might think about gender. If you were to use the category of "class" in a title, you would not demand that the book be about working-class people and middle-class people and upper-class people. The book could focus on one class; this would not be unusual because we see so clearly that class is a category of analysis. If you were to use the word "race" in the title of another book, you would not have to write about all races. The book could focus solely on African-American people. Or it could center on European-American people. The use of these categories as descriptors communicates that class or race will be an issue in the book, but it does not limit which classes or races will be considered. The same is true with gender. The title suggests that the authors are using gender as a category of analysis, a category which can be used to analyze the lives of women and/or men—not necessarily both at once.

The opening sentence of this introduction suggests that all experiences are gendered; that is, we experience everything we do as men or as women. But we are not simply neutral men or women. We are also African-American, or Latino, or European-American men or women. We are working-class or middle-class or homeless men or women. We are men and women with different disabilities and with different sexual preferences. Today, these other intersections cannot be ignored; the way we experience gender also rests on other aspects of our identities. This way of understanding gender is connected both to questions current in feminist theory and with the development of multiculturalism.

Toward a Multicultural Feminism

For many years feminist scholarship in different fields has assumed that we cannot understand the world without understanding the everyday experiences of girls and women. The unity and purpose represented in this view, however, have been diminished in recent years by the growing awareness that the everyday experiences of girls and women can differ dramatically by how their identities are otherwise constituted. Class, race, and ethnicity also position girls and women so that the earlier commonalities that feminists represented are less obvious. Any feminism that hovered only around the norms of experience of European-American, middle-class women would be too narrow to account for the complexity of gender.

So as we near the end of the twentieth century we must speak of feminisms rather than feminism because of the many differences between perspectives on gender in feminist theoretical positions. These feminisms are categorized in different ways by scholars. Some people use political labels such as socialist feminism, liberal feminism, and radical feminism to categorize different feminist perspectives. Others refer to the theoretical orientations of materialist feminists, cultural feminists, postmodern feminists.

Theorists ask different questions about gender and about which contextual issues need to be considered. The French feminists ask, "Is there any such thing as a woman?" Cultural feminists assume that there is and ask what she is like, what her way of looking at the world is. Materialist feminists study how material conditions, particularly the sexual division of labor, shape gender relations. Liberal feminists wonder how we can change social conditions to make women's lives equal to men's or to make life better for all. African-American feminists both criticize European-American feminists for not taking their perspectives into account (for assuming that black and white women experience the world in the same way) and conceptualize a feminism that makes "race" central.

While these theoretical and political positions vary on many planes, they can be categorized according to how they respond to and consider difference. Two major perspectives corral these positions.

One perspective emphasizes commonalities among women and minimizes differences. Views which represent this perspective cluster around the understanding that gender links all women together. The work of Carol Gilligan on women's moral development, of Nel Noddings on caring, of Mary Belenky and her colleagues on women's ways of knowing might be classified in this perspective. While this perspective recognizes differences between women in Southeast Asia, for example, and women in North America, or between rural farm women and urban white-collar working women, or between African-American and Latina women, it attends more to what is shared: underneath those differences women share common threads of experience. These threads emerge both from the discrimination and oppression that women face as a group (no matter how privileged) as well as from the culture of resistance and shared realities. Views anchored in this location suggest that what it means to be a woman is more powerful and cogent in explaining situations of women than are other identities.

Another group of feminist perspectives clusters around what we might call a multipositional or multilocational view. These perspectives represent a way of considering gender that argues that other identities (of race, class, ethnicity, relationship to colonialism, for example) cannot be subsumed under the category "woman." Rather, these perspectives represent the argument that, for example, in the intersection of gender and class, class shapes the experiences of gender in particular ways. Jean Anyon's work on working-class girls represents such a view, as does research on themes of cultural capital. There is no "classless" or "raceless" gender; in other words there is no generic gender. Identities relating to social class or ethnicity are so important that they separate women from each other. From this standpoint, one's identity as a woman cannot be separated from these other identities. The work of Patti Lather on research and empowerment might also be located here. This perspective less clearly articulates commonalities among women because it recognizes and pays attention to difference and its representations. How did feminism get here?

When the press represents the recent women's movement in the United States, the movement is said to have begun in the early 1960s, when the economy was in an upswing for certain segments of the population, pinpointed particularly with the publication of Betty Friedan's *The Feminist Mystique* in 1963. This volume identified what Friedan called "the problem that has no name," a term which referred to the situation of middle-class housewives and mothers who had been well educated in American colleges and then experienced malaise because they had no way to put their educations to use. The work they did in the home was work that needed daily repetition. They made beds only to have them unmade. They cooked meals only to have them immediately eaten. They played with their children and talked with other mothers who played with their children and felt somehow dissatisfied with what their lives had brought them. The women to whom Friedan referred tended to be economically comfortable, well educated, and they wanted more out of life. Compared with many other women in the United States they were privileged.

These women said that they wanted equality with men, that they wanted men to share child care with them, and that they wanted work in order to have more meaningful lives. Women began to meet together to discuss their lives, the meetings taking the form of "consciousness-raising groups" to talk about how those aspects of their lives that they had always considered personal and private were really related to questions of power relations between women and men. And they began to talk of women's oppression. They examined how conditions that harmed women were part of the institutions of American society. Schools received serious early attention because of their role in socializing future generations.

The rise of the feminist movement and its resistance to oppression did not occur in a vacuum. Connections to the civil rights movement, which provided both strategies and a language to speak about justice, and to the movement of resistance against the Vietnam War, created frustrations among a new generation of young American women who went to college in the 1960s and experienced there the contradictions between a language of equality and the experience of inequality. These connections provided a context for feminist activity in which personal oppression could be articulated and described. Feminists created cultural space for politicized discussion and legal change around issues relating to rape, beauty, physical and sexual abuse, property and financial rights so that these issues would never be the same again.

How little was known about women from their perspectives created an agenda for scholarship among women who were active in community women's movements and among those who were students or professors in universities. Feminists who wanted to know what kinds of work were particularly exploitative of women studied women who worked on assembly lines, women who worked as domestics in people's homes, women who worked as prostitutes. What happened to girls in school classrooms that made them lose some of their expectations for independent lives for themselves? These early studies unleashed an extraordinary array of feminist scholarship which assumed that one could not understand the world if the everyday experiences of so large a chunk of the population were excluded.

So far, this history of the feminist movement in the United States has been represented as linear and uninterrupted. This portrayal distorts changes in American feminism which reflected the growing numbers of women for whom feminism was an issue. The very questions which had earlier seemed to describe women's place did not pertain to the situations of all women. Hence, some women whose locations were not explained by feminist principles questioned the relevance of feminism for them.

Some examples will show this. The idea that women need to work in order to have meaningful lives, and that women's depression was due to the lack of self-esteem they felt when they were "just housewives," emerged from a strong class and ethnic perspective. That is, these women who experienced what Friedan talked about in *The Feminist Mystique* were identified predominantly as European-American and also, often, as middle-class. Even though these feminists pointed to a major social problem, they had located themselves in the center, benefiting from racial and class prejudices that went unrecognized (at least by them), as many feminist scholars have since pointed out.[1] In some ways they were the least oppressed of any group of women in the United States if you measure it by their privileges. In fact, it was because of their education and what we might call privileged positions that they had the energy to develop a women's movement.

As those for whom the feminist analysis seemed inadequate challenged feminism, conflicts existing within feminism (for example, over pornography and sexuality) expanded to challenge feminism itself. Some of the very explanations which had triggered such strong responses among the population first drawn to feminist ideology alienated others. African-American women who had always had to work to support their families did not feel dependent on their husbands; they were more independent as women than the European-American, middle-class women. Additionally, as bell hooks has shown, women were not silent in black communities: "[O]ur struggle has not been to emerge from silence into speech but to change the nature and direction of our speech, to make a speech that compels listeners, one that is heard."[2] The experiences of women from differing backgrounds, in other words, suggested that the women's movement was too closely connected with the experiences of white middle-class women. In the process (not without struggle) of expanding to face the sometimes contradictory, sometimes intersecting experiences of different women, the question of decentering the experiences of women who were privileged in order to address the perspectives of all women revealed some of the tensions within feminism. Feminists' contemporary vocabulary constructs feminism to read experience in the following way: there is not a woman's perspective, but rather many women's perspectives shaped by how gender interfaces with race, ethnicity, class, and geography.

So at the end of the twentieth century we can no longer speak about *a* woman's movement or *a* feminist movement. Now we must speak in the plural. In the United States we speak of feminisms rather than feminism because there are many differences in the perspectives taken by feminist theoretical positions regarding the situations of women and their relationships to other women and to men. Women from differing multicultural locations have taken the leadership to help feminists address the experiences of women for whom earlier feminisms lacked integrity. As Tania Modleski notes, "It is up to white middle-class women to make sure that their own uses of terms like 'identity' and 'experience' do not work to shut out the experiences of people of various colors, classes, and sexualities."[3] Then, it is hoped, we can articulate what is common among us.

Gender and Education

In the field of education, feminist scholarship on gender has reflected similar changes as it has moved away from a scholarship that reflects the privileges of only some women. These changes have affected how different questions have been conceptualized, demonstrating that gender is not a seamless category. It operates differently as it is mediated by questions of race, class, and nation; hence, any exploration of gender in the working lives of teachers, for example, must pay attention to the ways the social construction of sex is positioned by race and class. While middle-class European-American women, for example, saw teaching as an ordinary occupation for the ordinary woman during much of the twentieth century, African-American women viewed teaching as an occasion to serve their people for racial uplift as well as for professional opportunity.[4] And teaching provided social mobility for working-class women.

Contemporary feminist scholarship on gender and education ranges over a wide terrain. This volume represents some of the newest work done in the field, but because of constraints misses the work of other important scholars. Your familiarity as a reader with current feminist work in education will shape how you read the essays collected here. One of our assumptions is that all scholarship emerges in a contextual framework structured somewhat like a conversation. It is like a conversation in that articles are often written either as a positive or a negative response to the work of others. It is also like a conversation in that all the participants do not get equal opportunities to speak and be heard. In this sense, then, all writing takes the form of "writing against." That is, the writing of others forms the backdrop against which each of us writes.

The construction of this book is somewhat analogous to a sustained conversation that began between the two editors and then was taken up, expanded, and enriched by the writers of each of the chapters. As editors, we began the book by identifying various topics that we felt would provide readers with a sense of the breadth of issues that can be considered under the rubric of gender and education. Although we are aware that we have left some areas uncovered, our goals are to familiarize readers with the pervasiveness of issues of gender throughout education and to suggest the range of work being done today.

Another goal was to recognize the importance of the diversity that exists within and among gendered experiences. In particular, we emphasized that issues regarding ethnic, socioeconomic, and other aspects of sociocultural diversity should be interwoven throughout the text rather than relegated to a single chapter or section, as so often happens in discussions of feminism.

As our conversation expanded through the responses of the individual authors of chapters, it became clear to us that we were dealing with *diversities* rather than *diversity*. Each chapter recognizes that contexts of social class, ethnicity, and race must be considered in any discussion of gender. In addition, however, each chapter demonstrates diversity in the writer's interests, conceptual orientation, ways of approaching the topic, and ways of reporting information. For example, some writers employ a more personal narrative form not only to suggest how important gender was to them, but also to argue, through the form itself, the importance of where the author is placed in relation to knowing. Others conducted empirical studies and reported their analyses of their informants' behaviors. Still others turned to the existing literature in their focus and provided reviews as well as critiques of the ways in which gender has been considered and constructed. These diversities, we feel, add to the richness of the text.

Although the authors of each chapter demonstrate the various ways in which gender is presented in educational contexts, it is important to note that there are also some themes that serve to provide unifying threads across chapters. Throughout the book, for example, the theme of struggle is engaged, particularly in terms of women's collective struggles to be heard and taken seriously in formulating theory, policy, and practice in education. In addition, the theme of equity, especially when contrasted with the continuing experiences of inequity faced by women, emerges throughout the chapters. Finally, each chapter emphasizes, in some way, a theme of alternatives, that is, alternative ways of framing questions, investigating problems, and interpreting data. These alternatives are sorely needed and can be used to inform not only issues of gender but also issues of race, class, different abilities, and other areas that educators have traditionally had difficulties coping with.

This book is organized into six sections, of which this introduction is the first. Section Two, "Locating Gender and Education," consists of three chapters. Elisabeth Hansot provides a historical perspective on gender and education. Deborah Britzman presents a theoretical overview of multiculturalism and shows how gender and multiculturalism must be considered in relational terms. Janet Miller discusses connections between experience and theory in curriculum and notes the artificiality of separating them.

In Section Three, "Gender in Research, Achievement, and Technology," the authors offer alternative perspectives for understanding how gender frames each of these topics. Patricia Campbell and Selma Greenberg critique research methodologies that obscure or misinterpret gender issues, and they point out the fallacies of focusing on differences without considering how methods themselves influence results. Diane Pollard discusses perspectives and myths concerning the academic achievement of women. She indicates shortcomings in the literature on this topic and analyzes two perspectives which have been advocated to improve achievement in diverse sociocultural groups. Joan Burstyn describes how technological advances in education have ignored the needs and abilities of women. She analyzes popular views of the uses of technology in schools and shows where these viewpoints conflict with reality.

The two chapters in Section Four, "Gender at Work among Adolescents and Adults," describe studies their authors have conducted. Michelle Fine and Pat Macpherson listen to four adolescents from diverse communities as they discuss the factors that constrain their lives and empower their resistance. Sari Knopp Biklen discusses how mothers' and teachers' interactions are carried out on the terrain of the children they share. In particular, Biklen points out how gender, class, and race combine to shape teachers' interpretations of mothers' roles as well as teachers' interactions with mothers.

In Section Five, "Gender in Classroom and School Policy," the authors demonstrate how schools have perpetuated gender inequities and offer suggestions for change. Elois Scott and Heather McCollum describe classroom practices that have thwarted gender equity in schools despite Title IX legislation. They use change theory to demonstrate what must be done to transform these practices. Nan Stein discusses how schools have ignored or denied the existence of sexual harassment and how this position affects students, especially adolescents. She demonstrates how harmful sexual harassment is to students as well as to faculty and suggests ways to confront this problem. Finally, Meg Campbell and Diana Lam write about school policy from the standpoint of administrators and demonstrate how gender frames these roles both as they are filled by women administrators and as others react to them.

In Section Six, "Power, Multiplicity, and Voice," issues regarding diversities within feminism are explicitly addressed in terms of how they relate to educational philosophy and policy. Christine Sleeter provides a critique of the white middle-class orientation which characterized feminism for many years. She also describes a number of alternative and more inclusive perspectives which have been espoused as feminism has multiplied into the various feminisms viable today. Maxine Greene uses historical, literary, and philosophical frameworks to explore how the multiple voices of women emerge in different forms in narrative. She tells us that, despite the availability of this literature for many years, our lack of recognition of what these voices of women were saying about diversity has hindered our perspectives on gender.

The variations illustrated by the essays in this volume do indeed emphasize the pervasiveness of sex in education and in our lives. Many writers have pointed out that schools simply mirror the societies of which they are part. To the extent that inequity remains entrenched in this society, it will be evident in its educational institutions. To the extent that issues concerning gender continue to raise controversies in the broader society, they will also be debated in schools. Traditionally, these and related issues have been treated in covert ways, denied, or viewed as less important than other aspects of education. As these writers have indicated, however, questions and concerns regarding gender will not disappear. Over time, however, there are changes in how we construct the important questions and concerns. The essays in this volume suggest that gender identities are embedded in other identities such as race and class, which mark different ways that identities emerge and count. These new constructions provide a prominent lens through which we analyze individual and institutional behaviors.

A number of people helped to get the essays in this volume in their present form. We would like to thank Suzanne K. Damarin, Linda Street, Patricia Russo, and Melissa Keyes for reading chapters and making helpful suggestions. We also appreciate Sue Kelly's typing.

Notes

1. See, for example, bell hooks, *Feminist Theory: From Margin to Center* (Boston: South End Press, 1984) and Patricia Hill Collins, *Black Feminist Thought* (Boston: Unwin Hyman, 1990).

2. bell hooks, *Talking Back* (Boston: South End Press, 1989), p. 6.

3. Tania Modleski, *Feminism without Women: Culture and Criticism in a "Post-Feminist" Age* (New York: Routledge, 1991), p. 19.

4. Linda Perkins, "The Black Female American Missionary Association Teacher in the South, 1861-1870," in *Black Americans in North Carolina and the South*, edited by Jeffrey J. Crow and Flora J. Hatley (Chapel Hill: University of North Carolina Press, 1984).

Section Two
LOCATING GENDER AND EDUCATION

CHAPTER II

Historical and Contemporary Views of Gender and Education

ELISABETH HANSOT

Historically, disagreements about the nature of women have abounded. From Republican mother to suffragist, people have argued about whether women's humanity would be best served by expressing their nurturant abilities in home and family or whether their humanity requires access to the more combative "male" world of jobs and careers and politics. Much of this debate has focused on the question of whether women are basically different from or similar to men. But despite disagreements about what the "true" nature and abilities of women are, these understandings of women's nature have tended to share a common assumption: that human nature is more or less a coherent construct, stable over time. In other words, most such attempts to say what women are, no matter how various, share a common belief in the stability of the subject.

The 1970s liberal feminists and the 1980s cultural feminists continue the debate about the nature of women. Should women share all the opportunities of men because they share a common humanity, as many liberal feminists argue, or are women in some way distinctive, for instance, in the way they approach moral questions, as many cultural feminists argue? And if they are different, what sort of environment will best sustain these characteristics?

Within the last decade another group of theorists has once more changed the terms of debate by exploring a poststructuralist perspective that dissolves the postulate of a stable gender identity and

Elisabeth Hansot is Senior Lecturer in the Department of Political Science at Stanford University.

substitutes for it a notion of multiple selves. Although, as in any school of thought, there is difference and debate among its members, it is, I think, fair to say that this group has profoundly challenged the notion of personal gender identity as a coherent and stable construct over time. And although much of the poststructuralist debate has sources in psychoanalysis and literary theory, its potential to alter the terms in which feminists have debated school reform is considerable.

Even when people agreed about the stability of "woman's nature," they differed over gender policies and practices in public schools. In this essay I will look at three such reform efforts: the "boy problem," identified in the Progressive era when critics charged the schools with being too "female"; a concurrent discussion of the "woman question," when critics worried that women were not being adequately prepared for their adult vocations of wife and mother; and the critique of coeducation in the 1960s and 1970s, when feminists argued that the curriculum and training of girls was intentionally or inadvertently sexist. Despite the very different assumptions about the nature of boys and girls espoused by these reformers, they shared a belief that their understanding of human nature was the right one, and that the schools would be permanently improved by reforms based on their gender assumptions. I will then return to the new gender issues raised by poststructuralist theorists.

The Origins of Coeducation

It is of consequence that the common school developed at a time when there was considerable unanimity about women's nature and future destiny. Education was to prepare women for their sacred tasks as adults: marriage and motherhood. Adult institutions reflected these understandings: marriage was the proper vocation for the female; only a few paid jobs, such as teaching, were regarded as an acceptable interim occupation, to be relinquished when the more important vocation of bearing and rearing children occurred. Paradoxically, one may argue, the very certainty and stability in conservative societal understandings of female nature made it a matter of some indifference whether they were educated in coed schools.

Other conditions were also important: the schools were predominantly rural and poor; clearly it was more economical to school youngsters together than apart. And unlike the schooling of blacks and whites at the time, there was no compelling reason to segregate the sexes. Boys and girls could learn the three Rs together just as they might go to church together. Parents assumed that boys and girls could effectively learn together and still be prepared for their separate futures in the adult world.

As schools became more comprehensive in the late nineteenth century they took more of their pupils' time, and they differentiated more between them. In cities children were classified into grades, by academic achievement and by age; they were promoted when they demonstrated by examination that they had learned the curriculum. Clearly, age and academic achievement were more important than gender in this reorganization of schools.

In the Progressive era, in response to increasing concerns about preparing students for the adult workplace, vocational education, differentiated by gender, became more widespread, especially for older children. Schools, then, did come partially to reflect a pattern of gender differentiation in the larger society. But the core activity of the school—a group of children being taught by a teacher in a classroom—remained remarkably like its predecessor; with respect to gender, boys and girls continued to be taught the same subjects together. And until the larger societal pattern of gender inequality was challenged by feminists as unfair, coeducation was generally not seen as problematic, at least for girls.[1]

For much of the public school's history, then, gender arrangements were rather more taken for granted than not. Other issues loomed larger: organizing schools by age and proficiency, school consolidation, the "Americanization" of immigrants, to name only a few. And it is striking that when gender issues did intrude, historically the "boy problem" was as salient as the "woman question." At the turn of the century critics claimed that the problem of the schools was that they were doing all too well by their female students while they risked feminizing the boys.

The "Boy Problem"

In some senses the "boy problem" was real even though much of the rhetoric about it was exaggerated. Its other face was the "woman peril," that is to say, the fear that there were too many women teachers and that they were creating a feminized environment in the schools in which boys could not prosper.

Examples abounded: girls learned to read earlier, got higher grades, and were made class valedictorians more frequently. They also attended school longer and in greater number. By the first decade of the twentieth century, concern over male dropout rates increased. In a study entitled *Laggards in Our Schools*, Leonard P. Ayres found that 17 percent more girls than boys completed elementary school. While boys outnumbered girls in the earlier grades because they were held back more often, by the sixth grade girls began to predominate and by the twelfth grade they constituted a clear majority of 61 percent.[2]

These figures mask considerable variability in dropout rates by social class, nationality, and locality. Social class was a key factor in school retention for both sexes, but as John Rury points out, fewer working-class boys than working-class girls continued in school, suggesting that the males dropped out more often to go to work. Ethnic and racial differences were also important. While the small number of black secondary schools in the South severely limited schooling for both sexes, more African-American girls than boys attended high school, in part because attendance enlarged their chances of entering the increasingly feminized occupation of teaching.[3]

The "boy problem" became exacerbated during the period from 1900 to 1930 as the percentage of boys in the paid labor force dropped. In part this was due to compulsory schooling and child labor laws; equally important were technological and organizational changes in the workplace itself, which eliminated many jobs boys had traditionally held and created new white-collar jobs that required further schooling. Some boys, forced to remain in school well beyond what their patience or interest counseled, reacted by forming a male counterculture in which the school figured as a place for sissies and for girls.[4]

The "boy problem" was an amalgam of alleged feminization by too many women teachers, a working-class, antischool male counterculture, male underachievement, and the high male dropout rate. Reformers reacted by attempting to change the school system. One proposal was to separate the sexes in academic subjects. They did not argue for separate schools—coeducation was too firmly fixed for that—but rather for separate classes for boys and girls and in certain required subjects like English and mathematics. Such experiments were short-lived and there were both practical and ideological explanations for this failure. Segregation by sex encountered the same conditions that had initially influenced the schooling of boys and girls together: there were relatively few high schools with a large enough population to support the expense of shuffling of teachers and students that such a reform entailed.[5]

Sex-typed academic electives fared somewhat better. Rather than being mandated, electives were voluntary and could be more easily designed at the local level. And such electives were buttressed by proponents of vocational education who argued that the process of selecting an occupation and preparing for it in school would motivate the student, particularly the new working-class child who could no longer so easily find alternate employment in the labor market.

The track record of vocational education is too complex to be evaluated here. Suffice it to say that despite the claim that training for future jobs would powerfully motivate boys, questions arose about how effectively vocational programs prevented dropouts and promoted mobility into skilled jobs. But the adoption of vocational education helped defuse the criticism that the schools were not a sufficiently stimulating environment for boys. The creation of a distinctively male and "hand-minded" niche in the curriculum showed schools to be responsive, at least symbolically, to the "boy problem." Since vocational education was accompanied by competitive athletics, which was institutionalized at about the same time and was deemed to create manly character, reformers could claim that they had seriously attended to the problem of making schools work for boys.

The "Woman Question"

When reformers turned to the "woman question" they were less concerned with how women were doing in school than how school was preparing women for their adult vocations of wife and mother, or, for feminists, for access to the workplace. From one perspective, public schooling had always been vocational for women. The claim of the common-school crusaders was that education made women better mothers. The products of women's labor were to be healthy, literate, moral, and disciplined offspring. And as the country became increasingly urban and industrialized, home economics programs were seen as providing the training that earlier had been the purview of the family.[6]

The proponents of home economics wanted it to go well beyond training in the cooking and sewing that had been the staples of some schools in the nineteenth century, and to become the science of household management and child raising. Advocates of home economics linked their cause to a thorough analysis of the "woman question." They saw home economics as holding the key to pressing social problems; knowledge of nutrition and hygiene would variously reduce the high rates of infant mortality, improve child health, and lower the divorce rate. Educated to be skilled consumers and managers, women would manage to offset the effects of low income and poverty. By making homemaking into a profession based on science, home economics would attract back to the home those women who had been lured to an outside career and, at the same time, stem the drop in the birthrate in native-born families.[7]

In the high school, home economics did become a part of the schools, but not usually as the required subject that reformers argued for. In the 1920s, even in commercial tracks, girls still took about 70 percent of their courses in academic subjects. Race, however, made a difference. In the South, 85 percent of black high school girls were required to take home economics, compared to only 30 percent of white girls, no doubt an attempt to train them for domestic labor and laundry work. Across the country, elective home economics courses were far less popular than commercial or academic subjects.[8]

Home economics secured a modest place in the high schools, by and large as an elective for older students. Like vocational subjects for boys, it was a place to put girls who did not do well in more academically oriented subjects. And most important, home economics was a visible sign that the schools had done something about the "woman question" and reaffirmed the institution of motherhood through the appropriate instruction of the young women in their charge.

Recent Gender Reforms in the Schools

Both the "boy" and the "woman" problems suggest that the American high school, rather like the Catholic church, had a remarkable capacity to blunt criticism by incorporating reforms at the periphery while continuing business as usual. And many feminists in the Progressive era believed that the coeducational public school, for all its faults, was already more egalitarian than the workplace or the family.

In the 1960s and 1970s, reinvigorated feminists took a fresh look at the school and found the legacy from their predecessors wanting. Broader changes in adult society prompted activists to generate an agenda for educational reform, and in turn schools institutionalized these changes in differing degrees without, however, radically changing their customary patterns of instruction.

The starting point for these later feminists was not primarily education itself; rather, it was the inequality adult women encountered in legal, economic, and political domains. But they believed that the lack of power and opportunity of adult women could be traced back in part to what they were taught and the way they were taught in school. Thus, when feminists redefined women's grievances as a public rather than a personal problem, sexual discrimination in schools became a prime target.[9]

Whereas opponents of coeducation in the nineteenth century had claimed that high schools were too virile for girls, in the Progressive era critics claimed that they feminized the boys. In the 1970s, the new feminist reformers reversed the charge, arguing that public education made the girls too feminine and the boys too masculine. The schools, they argued, were bastions of male dominance and female subordination because, appearances to the contrary, boys and girls did not really learn the same things in school. By sex equity in education, feminists in the 1970s meant the elimination of sex bias and a reduction of sex stereotyping.

This reformulation of sex discrimination in the schools was based on the conviction that schools could not be observing gender-neutral policies if their female graduates fared so poorly in the workplace in adult life. The schools were the sites where many of the attitudes that held women back were learned; hence the schools were an important target of the larger reform effort to produce a society where women enjoyed equal opportunity with men.

Convinced of the hidden injuries of coeducation, activists in the women's movement had several tasks: persuading people that there was a problem by documenting gender discrimination; finding legal and political remedies; and raising the consciousness of educators about bias in everyday activities that they took for granted.

Like their nineteenth-century predecessors, many of whom had been abolitionists, a number of the leaders of the modern women's movement had taken part in the campaign to secure equality for blacks. But in important respects, sexual discrimination differed from racial bias in education. Disproportionate numbers of blacks were poor, whereas gender cut across all social classes. Discrimination against blacks, therefore, was compounded by class bias.

The law, also, was used differently. In the South and in some parts of the North, racial segregation in the school system and unequal resources for schooling resulted from clearly racist laws and deliberate public policy. But law and conscious policy had not been major contributors to sex inequity in public education. Statutes and district regulations of the Progressive era that distinguished between the sexes in coeducational public schools were few in number and could trace their origins as reforms, not discrimination. These regulations became ready targets for a statute like Title IX that banned single-sex access to vocational subjects, for example.[10]

There were ways, however, in which race was similar to sex. Beyond the bias built into law and policy, blacks faced a more amorphous, unconscious kind of discrimination which became labeled "institutional racism." Feminists argued that in similar ways schools discriminated against females. They called this "institutional sexism." In public education, civil rights groups targeted biased behavior of teachers, negative stereotypes in textbooks, bias in counseling, and the use of unfair tests.

While the concept of sexism owed much to this discovery of institutional racism, sexism in public schools was not nearly as visible to most people as racism. Many educators thought gender distinctions natural and hence regarded sex stereotyping as a nonissue. Whereas blacks were not well served by schools, girls were not seen as suffering significant academic or social disabilities.

The concept of institutional sexism spread rapidly among feminists, however, for it captured the silent, often unselfconscious character of sex conditioning. Feminist researchers labored to expose the schools' hidden curriculum, partly to convince educators and parents that sex bias was a reality. They attacked biased institutional practices through demands for policies explicitly requiring open enrollment for both sexes, equal funding, and affirmative action.

Feminist organizations like the National Organization of Women (NOW) used a variety of political-legal strategies to eliminate sex bias in the schools. They pressed for legislation at the federal and state levels but realized they would have to lobby local leaders to see these laws implemented. They worked to write sex equity into legislation like the Equal Pay Bill of 1963 and Title VII of the Civil Rights Act of 1964. But passing legislation is not tantamount to implementing it, and organizations such as the Women's Equity Action League (WEAL) and NOW publicized continuing inequalities by bringing sex-equity suits, lobbying officials, and testifying at congressional hearings.[11]

The major tool for implementing equal coeducation was Title IX of the 1972 Education Amendments. Its controlling provision read as follows: "No person in the United States shall, on the basis of sex, be excluded from participation in, be denied the benefits of, or be subjected to discrimination under any education program or activity receiving Federal financial assistance." Despite its sweeping language, Title IX aroused little controversy as it passed through Congress, which was then preoccupied by the controversy over court-ordered busing to accomplish desegregation.[12]

Passed by a Democratic Congress, the statute was neglected in the Republican administrations of Presidents Nixon and Ford. The then Department of Health, Education, and Welfare (HEW), charged with devising regulations, stalled for two years before issuing them. The lobby for strong enforcement of Title IX, called the Educational Task Force, was composed largely of sympathetic educational organizations and groups interested in feminist research and in legal and political action. Their strongest opponents were representatives of organized college sports who feared that sex equity would endanger their programs. After vigorous political fighting, the women's lobby, aided by the support of black congressmen concerned about the potential for a similarly laggard enforcement of civil rights provisions, managed to get Title IX regulations put into effect, fully three years after passage of the bill.[13]

Title IX was a hard-won battle for feminists. It required every school system to evaluate its policies and alter them to comply with the new regulations. Every district was to appoint a Title IX officer responsible for coordinating compliance and hearing complaints about sex discrimination. With some exceptions, the regulations banned separate-sex classes in health, physical education, and vocational subjects as well as banning sex-segregated vocational programs and schools. Equal treatment of boys and girls in athletics was affirmed with the exception of contact sports. Discriminatory counseling and sex-biased guidance tests and materials were banned.

Title IX, perhaps more than any other piece of legislation, exemplifies both the triumphs and the frustrations of the feminists' battle for equal treatment of the sexes in the schools. Ambiguous language in the statutes on sex equity in sports provided grist for lawyers. Federal implementation was stumbling, erratic, and bogged down in red tape. The HEW civil rights office was at best an indifferent ally. And despite the fact that some school districts openly challenged Title IX, the federal government never imposed the ultimate sanction, the cutting off of federal funds.[14]

The U.S. Supreme Court added its level of complexity to Title IX in the case of *Grove City College v. Bell* (1984) by narrowing the coverage from entire institutions to particular programs that discriminated against women. Some of that damage was undone in 1988 when feminists united with other equity activists to secure passage of the Civil Rights Restoration Act.[15]

Space does not permit a detailing of the history of other important initiatives such as the Women's Educational Equity Act, nor an assessment (at best provisional) of the extent to which federal and state statutes affected practice in the schools. Although the scoreboard of feminist reforms shows mixed results, it is possible to argue that the schools proved to be a more responsive target for feminist reformers than many other institutions, in part because both the public and educators themselves expected the schools to be fair, and in part because schooling has been increasingly viewed as a path to adult equality of opportunity. The 1980s were to see this assumption challenged both by some cultural feminists who wondered whether girls benefited by having the same education as boys and more radically by those who from a poststructuralist perspective questioned the link between childhood experience and adult behavior.

Conclusion

Coeducation became a defining characteristic of American public schools very early in their history. And despite vast political, ideological, and social changes in the society, the coeducational classroom has persisted. At first, the practice of coeducation did not imply a commitment to equalize adult roles. On the contrary, coeducation appeared at a time when Americans were busy drawing lines between adult gender spheres. Many of the sex biases that this coeducational legacy entailed have been successfully challenged in recent decades; schools have become more gender neutral in their formal procedures and practices.

The reformers of the 1960s and 1970s mostly took it as given that coeducation was a good; the problem as they saw it was that the schools had not examined the ways their curriculum and extracurricular activities advantaged girls over boys. Once the schools could be made to provide truly equal opportunities for boys and girls, the latter would not be handicapped by forms of sex-role socialization that limited the development of their abilities and aspirations.

The critique of this liberal feminist position predictably came from many quarters. Feminists of many different persuasions would criticize liberal feminists for not being sufficiently critical of the class and racial nature of male-dominated American institutions. But the group whose writings posed perhaps the greatest challenge to the coeducational character of the schools were the cultural feminists.[16]

The variety among cultural feminists is great. What they have in common, however, is a revaluation of women's socialization and of their moral and cognitive processes. The special ability of women to show caring behavior or the special perspective from which they engage in moral questions, it is argued, importantly differentiates women from men. Embodied in this perspective is an often explicit critique of mainline masculine institutions and the values that are central to them. If women's ways have been undervalued in the past, they risk being impoverished in the present, cultural feminists claim, if attention is not paid to their nurture.[17]

Both the liberal feminists of the 1970s and the cultural feminists who built on and criticized their work raised a host of new issues about how females are treated in school. In part the impetus for change has rested on a venerable American faith that reform of the schools would be a powerful contribution to the solution of adult social problems. Liberals believed that if children were not taught to behave in sex-stereotyped ways, the adult world into which they would graduate would be a more equitable place for both sexes. Cultural feminists, many of whom espouse a socialization paradigm, believe that schools should be refashioned to honor and reinforce feminine values as well as masculine ones. For both groups the adage "As the twig is bent, so grows the tree" might stand as a homely summary of their concerns about the schools.

Both liberal and cultural feminists, despite their differences, assume continuity in human development. Adults become consistent products of their history. But recently a new group of feminists, often called poststructural or postmodern feminists, questions such assumptions. To rephrase the adage, they might say, "A bent twig has no demonstrable connection to a grown tree." In other words, there is no necessary link between childhood socialization and adult behavior. Humans respond differently to different contexts; it is a mistake to explain behaviors that are context-driven as continuities in psychological development.

Like cultural feminists, poststructuralist feminists have challenged some of our deeply embedded assumptions about the objectivity of Western cognitive systems and the neutrality of social institutions. But these thinkers have gone further and used linguistic and psychoanalytic constructs to question the very notion of personality itself as a stable, coherent entity. By and large, poststructuralist thinkers have not focused their attention on how their understandings of human nature might affect our thinking about schools. They have, however, explored a perspective that dissolves the postulate of a stable gender identity created in large part by early socialization and substitutes for it a notion of multiple selves. How these selves are constructed, according to what contexts or discursive traditions they are formed and reformed, is very much open to debate. Even the extent to which such critical notions as "political" and "reform" continue to make sense or be actionable under this new dispensation is ambiguous. Clearly, this latest revisiting of women's nature has the potential to redefine not simply that construct but also the terms of discourse in which the debate about her nature (and of course her male counterpart's) has taken place.[18]

What might this new perspective about human nature mean for institutions like the school? Its imperatives for reform are far less clear than those of liberal or cultural feminism. Let me suggest some very tentative conjectures. The twig of sex socialization may not become a rigid tree, but rather a flexible bush of many branches. Or perhaps even a variety of different branches, loosely if at all connected to a bush. Put more prosaically, the poststructuralist perspective does not seem to entail that any one period—such as childhood—is critical for adult socialization. The schools, then, would not be in a privileged position with respect to their shaping influence on adult lives. To the extent that "reform" continues to hold its conventional meaning in a universe as unstable and variegated as the poststructuralist one, school reform would have to be justified in terms other than its presumed benefit for adult lives and institutions.

Gender policy in public education has been shaped by diverse groups that had quite distinct notions about the ideal gender order for American society and how schools should contribute to it. The schools have proved resilient and adaptive on the periphery while retaining the basic forms of coeducation. Given the variety of different and sometimes conflicting gender critiques of the schools over the past 150 years, this is perhaps quite a reasonable mode of response.

Notes

1. David Tyack and Elisabeth Hansot, *Learning Together: A History of Coeducation in American Public Schools* (New Haven: Yale University Press, 1990), pp. 1-27.

2. Leonard P. Ayres, *Laggards in Our Schools: A Study of Retardation and Elimination in City School Systems* (New York: Charities Publication Committee, 1909), p. 7; F. E. De Yoe and C. N. Thurber, "Where Are All the High School Boys?" *School Review* 8 (1900): 234, 240.

3. John L. Rury, "Urban Enrollment at the Turn of the Century: Gender as an Intervening Variable," *Urban Education* 28 (1988): 68-87.

4. Harvey Kantor, *Learning to Earn: School, Work, and Vocational Reform in California, 1880-1930* (Madison: University of Wisconsin Press, 1988), 132-34, 114; Selwyn K. Troen, "The Discovery of the Adolescent by American Educational Reformers, 1900-1920: An Economic Perspective," in *Schooling and Society: Studies in the History of Education*, edited by Lawrence Stone (Baltimore, MD: Johns Hopkins University Press, 1976), chap. 10; William D. Lewis, "The High School and the Boy," *Saturday Evening Post* 184 (April 6, 1912): 8-9.

5. Edward L. Thorndike, "A Neglected Aspect of the American High School," *Educational Review* 33 (1907): 254; U. S. Commissioner of Education, *Report for 1907* (Washington, DC: Government Printing Office, 1908).

6. Eleanor Flexnor, *Century of Struggle: The Woman's Rights Movement in the United States* (Cambridge: Harvard University Press, 1975); p. 255; William J. Reese, *Power and the Promise of School Reform: Grassroots Movements during the Progressive Era* (Boston: Routledge and Kegan Paul, 1986), chap. 2.

7. John L. Rury, "Vocationalism for Home and Work: Women's Education in the United States, 1880-1930," *History of Education Quarterly* 24 (1984): 21-33; Ellen Richards, "The Social Significance of the Home Economics Movement," *Journal of Home Economics* 3 (1911): 116-122.

8. Kate Brew Vaughn, "Some Colored Schools of the South," *Journal of Home Economics* 8 (1916): 583-589; Jane Bernard Powers, "The 'Girl Question' in Education: Vocational Training for Young Women in the Progressive Era" (Ph.D. diss., Stanford University, 1986), pp. 163-165, 175-178; Kantor, *Learning to Earn*, p. 61.

9. Barbara Sinclair Deckard, *The Women's Movement: Political, Socioeconomic, and Psychological Issues* (New York: Harper & Row, 1979).

10. David Tyack, Thomas James, and Aaron Benavot, *Law and the Shaping of Public Schools, 1785-1954* (Madison: University of Wisconsin Press, 1987), chap. 5, epilogue.

11. National Organization of Women, "NOW Bill of Rights," in Deckard, *The Women's Movement*, p. 348. See also, pp. 342-349.

12. Title IX, *Education Amendments of 1972*, Public Law 92-318, 92d Congress, S. 659, June 23, 1972; Andrew Fishel and Janice Pottker, "Sex Bias in Secondary Schools," in *Sex Bias in the Schools: The Research Evidence*, edited by Andrew Fishel and Janice Pottker (Rutherford, NJ: Fairleigh Dickinson University Press, 1977), p. 92.

13. Anne N. Costain, "Eliminating Sex Discrimination in Education: Lobbying for Implementation of Title IX," *Policy Studies Journal* 7 (Winter 1978): 189-195.

14. NOW Legal Defense and Education Fund, *Stalled at the Start: Government Action on Sex Bias in the Schools* (Washington, DC: PEER, 1977), pp. 5, 21-25, 33-39, Appendix E.

15. *Grove City College v. Bell* (1984) 465 U.S. 104 S. Ct. 1211, No. 82-792; Nancy Duff Campbell et al., *Sex Discrimination in Education: Legal Rights and Remedies* (Washington, DC: National Coalition for Women and Girls in Education, 1984).

16. Alison M. Jagger and Paula S. Rothenberg, *Feminist Frameworks* (New York: McGraw-Hill, 1984), Part 2; Alison M. Jagger, *Feminist Politics and Human Nature* (Totowa, NJ: Rowman & Allanhead, 1983), Part 2.

17. Nel Noddings, *Caring: A Feminine Approach to Ethics and Moral Education* (Berkeley: University of California Press, 1984); Carol Gilligan, *In a Different Voice: Psychological Theory and Women's Development* (Cambridge: Harvard University Press, 1982).

18. Chris Weedon, *Feminist Practice and Poststructuralist Theory* (Oxford: Basil Blackwell Ltd., 1987); Stanley Fish, *Doing What Comes Naturally* (Durham, NC: Duke University Press, 1988), pp. 315-341.

CHAPTER III

Beyond Rolling Models: Gender and Multicultural Education

DEBORAH P. BRITZMAN

It is comforting to think that individuals are the authors of their identity rather than the bearers and even the effects of its conflictive meanings. Many educators, administrators, and curriculum developers persist in their belief in the uniqueness of the individual. The myth of individual uniqueness is often the foundation of what many take as multicultural education, and consequently the practice of multicultural education is typically reduced to the sole concern for developing positive self-image. According to this approach positive self-image is fashioned by encountering positive role models and by valuing individual differences as something "unique" and "special." This formula fails to address the disruptive question of whether it is even possible for persons to imitate a role—that is, to take on the characteristics of the dominant group—given the fact that role models themselves are the result of social standards and conventions. Can a copy be unique?

The concept of role models is both safe and comforting. No educator in her right mind could be against these official looking creatures. It is even rather flattering to be mistaken for one because this status is thought to produce rightness, clarity, completeness, and stability. Role models arrive preassembled. They are not only larger than life; they are rolled out precisely because they have rolled over all that stood in their way. Put differently, educators seem to be rolling the controversy out of these essential folks. Neglected in this simple version is the fact that idealized identities do not lend insight into the mobile and shifting conditions that make identity such a contradictory place to live.

When multicultural education valorizes the abstracted individual, all that makes identity both meaningful to the self and others *and* the

Deborah Britzman is Associate Professor in the School of Education and Human Development at the State University of New York, Binghamton.

site of conflictive meanings is erased. The use of role models in multicultural education as *the* transitional object becomes especially problematic in the context of gender, since gender is one of the most policed and surveilled categories in which each of us attempts to live. One need only think about places like bathrooms, shoe stores, and clothing stores, or even about where one places one's wallet, to see the normative force of gender. Or one need only think about issues of address: what to call strangers and the qualities one calls upon to distinguish between females and males. Exploring the cost of maintaining this category of gender, then, is not a matter of recovering some fictive uniqueness. Instead, we are detoured by the uncomfortable and contradictory fact that individuals are neither in charge nor in control of their identities. At the same time, this discomforting recognition of identity as social rather than individual is crucial to the changing of identities.

In this chapter, then, I argue for a deeper and more complex understanding of multicultural education by attending to the particularities of gender. I explore the damaging effects for students and for educators when the meaning of gender is reduced to the category of sex-role stereotyping and when multicultural education dissipates into an endless celebration of uniqueness. There is nothing unique about racism, sexism, heterosexism, and Eurocentrism, nor in the way that these dynamics visit identity without an invitation. My argument is that gender, as a significant category where each of us lives, needs to mean more than what Bronwyn Davies terms "category maintenance work"[1] or the push to fix one's identity and the identity of others in normative ways. Those sets of gendered directions can only result in the maintenance of domination and subordination. Our understanding of gender, then, needs to move beyond singularity, taking into account the reality that each of us embodies a wide range of categorical commitments such as race, sexuality, generation, class, and so on; the shifting meanings of these social markers arrange the experience of gender. Consequently, in investigating the conceptual framework which multicultural education offers to the study of gender and which feminist concepts of gender offer to multicultural education, I begin with the controversial.

Warning: Multicultural Education Requires Identity Work

If multicultural education is to make a difference both in terms of how individuals relate to one another and what these relations do to the self, *and* to attend to the forms of sociality which identities create, educators must become open to complicating not just their conceptions of and practices in this field but also their own identities. This is because multicultural education requires educators to explore not just the identities of others but to consider how the meanings of one's own identity are contingent upon the conflictive meanings of race, gender, sexuality, generation, ethnicity, and so on.

In a provocatively titled article, "What Not To Do in the Name of Multicultural Education (Or, If You Can't Stand the Heat, Get Out of the Kitchen)," Caroline Sherritt says this to educators:

> Don't presume that you can become multicultural without addressing issues of oppression and discrimination. Don't focus on cultural plurality if you are unwilling to deal with sensitive issues, such as religion, gender roles, standardized testing, poverty, and politics.[2]

Simply put, multicultural education requires engagement with the politics of power.

Years earlier, Stuart Hall posed the basic dilemma educators must confront when teaching about race. Hall underlined the explosiveness of this "subject," reminding educators that everyone—including the educator—carries "strong emotional ideological commitments" and that race "is not a topic where an academic or intellectual neutrality is of much value."[3] Talk about race means talk about racialized selves. Hall reminds us that everyone is "raced" and so talk must include the meanings of whiteness as well as the meanings of blackness.

Finally, Lisa Delpit, directing her advice to majority white educators, writes of the need to be "willing to see yourself in the unflattering light of another's angry gaze,"[4] and thus to cease to exist for a moment in order to understand perspectives that are not theirs. In Delpit's words, teachers must:

> learn to be vulnerable enough to allow our world to turn upside down in order to allow the realities of others to edge themselves into our consciousness. . . . This can only be done by seeking out those perspectives that differ most, by learning to give their words complete attention, by understanding one's own power, even if that power stems merely from being in the majority, by being unafraid to raise questions about discrimination and voicelessness with people of color, and to listen, no, to *hear* what they say.[5]

These warnings mark multicultural education as controversial. The "subjects" of multicultural education do not merely reside between the covers of the textbooks but rather in the bodies and minds of those who populate classrooms. Sherritt, Hall, and Delpit intend more than the familiar mandate to "integrate" curriculum with model "minorities." The educator herself must change. The call is for a persistent self and social reflexivity, a double vision of seeing one's own identity through the eyes of others and looking again at others with lenses that are not one's own. Multicultural education can offer students and educators new identities and critical visions of lives committed to fairness, social equity, and social change.[6] One part of this identity means questioning the effects of the categories each of us embodies.

The category of gender becomes even more controversial when we consider how gendered selves are tied to specific histories of social justice, civil rights, colonialism, economic struggles, social positions, and to the emotional commitments that are built because of these histories. Exploring the contradictory meanings of gender requires a second and more complex look at how received discourses, stereotypes, and social practices make gender a significant site of identity struggle.[7] After all, gender is one of the central ways individuals are recognized, distinguished, categorized, and experienced. Teachers and students enter classrooms with gendered identities and with their own deep convictions about how gender should be understood, lived, and recognized.[8] As with race, one cannot talk about gender without referring to something about social differences, social expectations, social relations, and the acknowledged and unacknowledged inequalities that work within any definition of gender.

Definitions of gender are made from an odd combination of history, popular culture, and cultural socialization; such forces push talk about gender in the classroom in directions that are highly charged and contentious. These definitions tie this talk to a wide range of unwieldy political positions about equality and ability, and about control over the body. In other words, talk about gender, like talk about race, means talk about everyday power.[9] Whether invited or not, when the topic concerns how everyday relations of power are mediated by gender, the discussion opens up the difficult and painful cultural issues of violence against women, domestic violence, control over one's body, and the most misunderstood and disparaged identities of lesbians and gay men. To become open to topics routinely considered "taboo," "political," or "too controversial" for classrooms, educators must come to terms with the messiness of emotional commitments as they work through their own fear that inviting controversies means not being in control.[10]

What conceptions of gender are offered within the field of multicultural education? Do such conceptions recognize the volatile and contradictory meanings of gender and the deep investments many have in "getting gender right," that is, in making sure one is not mistaken for a gender one is not, or in policing the appearance of others so they conform to the norm? How might multicultural education make sense of the ways in which gender is constantly being rearranged by other social markers such as race, size, ethnicity, sexuality, style, age, and so on? What are the possible and given relationships between gender and sociality and between gender and power? When we think about the ways in which education represents gender, what images and questions are posed, modeled, and refashioned? What might it mean to understand gender in feminist terms?

Toward a Feminist Framework for Understanding Gender

Theories of gender attempt to explain the nature and meaning of femininity and masculinity, the social organization of gender into sex roles and social positions, the sexual division of labor, the socialization of females and males throughout the life cycle, the development of desire and sexuality, and the social, political, aesthetic, and historical processes whereby gender becomes a category of domination or subordination yet continues to inscribe desire and pleasure.[11] These theoretical investigations unravel the history of gender, accounting for both institutional arrangements and individual lives. Theories of gender can emphasize questions of origin, such as the implicit qualities that seem to compose gender and the accompanying discourses and practices that seem to make gender a recognizable part of one's identity. Or theories can emphasize the effects of how gender is constructed by social meanings, cultural contexts, and the language that makes it possible to recognize gender as a descriptive, predictive, and inscriptive category. ("Inscriptive" here refers to the process whereby social meanings leave a signature on the body.)

Feminist theories of gender can be distinguished in three ways. First, feminist theories *critique* the gendered practices and structures of male supremacy and patriarchy. They address how these structures and the practices which sustain them arrange gender as a relation of unequal and oppressive power. For example, rather than view behavior in individual terms, feminist theories attempt to explain how the social meanings and histories of masculinity subordinate all that is deemed feminine. On an everyday level, feminist theories are interested in explaining how it is that white males are overrepresented in positions of power. Consequently, these theories of gender express explicit political imperatives.[12] Second, feminists consider gender as a site of power, not only in the ways in which gender becomes the basis for inequality (although this direction has been central to both feminist scholarship and to multicultural education) but still more in the contradictory effects of gendered identities. Feminist theories are concerned with how life choices and social positions become fixed to gender, and what gender has to do with one's sense of entitlement, safety, and possibilities. In terms of everyday practices, such theories would address the prevalence of domestic violence, violence against women, and the ways certain forms of femininity become standards of beauty. Third, feminists address how these dynamics of patriarchy and male supremacy structure social relations between and among females and males. The interest is not just in how males and females relate to each other but also in how normative practices of heterosexuality fashion both intragroup solidarity and conflict and intergroup solidarity and conflict and thus definitions of the gendered self. For example, questions of male bonding, of female-to-female competition, and of female friendship would be of central interest. From feminist perspectives, then, gender does not refer simply to being a male or a female. Rather, gender is about placing oneself and becoming placed in a range of symbolic orders, a series of metaphorical landscapes that are continually being recharted. For feminists, the problem of gender is the problem of directions.

The field of feminist scholarship is quite contentious. In fact, it is more accurate to speak of feminisms in the plural.[13] For example, within feminist scholarship, and thus within the three areas of concern described above, theories of gender can be distinguished by two different orientations.[14] One orientation embraces theories of essentialism, that is, theories that focus on origins. The other orientation derives from theories of social constructivism, or theories that focus on meanings and their effects. While seemingly academic, each theory represents competing sets of social practices, visions of identity, and pedagogical interventions. How one constructs the meaning of gender has everything to do with the kinds of interventions one makes and whether or not one rolls models over and looks at the underside. In moving toward theories of gender, then, feminist scholarship must address not just the received category of gender but, more significantly, the discourses that render this category intelligible and historically persistent.

Are You a Boy or Are You a Girl?

Essentialist theories of gender are concerned with questions of causality and origin. "Essentialism," Diana Fuss explains, "is most commonly understood as a belief in the real, true essence of things, the invariable and fixed properties which define the 'whatness' of a given category."[15] In this view, gender exists prior to the social meanings it generates: that is, gender is a function of nature and thus already contains particular qualities prior to how these qualities become reworked by historical and social meanings. For example, the condition of caring, or a concern for others, is commonly viewed as an inherent female attribute and this then justifies the ways females are socialized to care. According to an essentialist perspective, such an attribute originates with a female's biological possibilities to bear children. Essentialists might argue that the problem resides not in the attribute itself, which in their eyes is unchanging and stable, but rather in the ways society devalues this implicit quality.

The early work of Carol Gilligan,[16] for example, focuses on what she considers the inherent qualities of gender, and how these qualities determine the morality and the psychology of women and men. Reviewing the "masculinist biases" of research done in the name of human development, Gilligan, like the later research of Belenky et al. and Nel Noddings,[17] asserts that women have a "different" voice and thus different ethical imperatives. For these researchers, difference is not the problem. Rather, the problem lies in the ways difference is valued or stigmatized. This line of research depends upon the view that women, because they are women, will be more concerned with the specificity of relationships, feelings, and caring, whereas men, because they are men, will be more concerned with establishing universal rules and laws and hence will be preoccupied with establishing control, order, and their own positions as experts. The argument is that "female" qualities of caring are made subordinate while "male" qualities of making rules and laws are viewed as desirable and, more significantly, as the norm to judge competence and entitlement. Thus these researchers seek to uncouple inherent qualities from relations of domination and subordination.

These directions continue to be central to the disruption of the universal and genderless claims common to social science in general and especially within the field of human development. The work of Gilligan and others has demonstrated that orientations to human development are neither neutral nor innocent of the investments of the researchers and the research apparatus within which researchers work. Yet while Gilligan and others offer empirical data to illustrate gender as central to questions of development, their adherence to the essentialist views of gender as nature ignores how nature is socially ordered and policed. They also cannot address how the insistencies of race, class, sexuality, and generation, for instance, work upon the meanings of masculinity and femininity.

Essentialist views of gender are intricately linked with common sense. Common sense asserts that gender is determined by biology. Each of us, the story goes, is assigned a gender because of our sex and this stability then becomes a rationale for explaining behavior. The repetitive conclusion, "Boys will be boys and girls will be girls," directs the way gender is mistaken as an explanation for inclination, behavior, ability, investments, emotional commitments, and social position. What is normative frames not only how one goes about recognizing the self and maintaining the other but also the more insidious work of identifying deviance because the "norm" is considered the natural. Think how disturbing it is if we rearrange the slogan to "Boys will be girls and girls will be boys." Who would strike this pose?

Theories of social constructivism allow for the last question. They push at the boundaries of common sense and challenge the historicity of normative categories: how they become established, the languages that orient them, and the structures that maintain normality and abnormality. As the term suggests, social constructivism begins with the genealogies of meaning: how meanings work as mimesis and what it is that structures their social currency and their capacity to determine measures of thought and conduct.[18] This orientation is quite controversial because it decenters the subject. Social constructivists argue against the view that identities are stable, natural, or unique. Individuals, they argue, are not the sole authors of the self but rather are authored in language and by social practices.

Within this orientation, Bronwyn Davies's research on the gendered identities of preschool children investigates how children come to distinguish themselves by gender and thus know who is a boy and who is a girl.[19] Drawing on the feminism of Simone de Beauvoir,[20] Davies argues that males and females are made, not born. On the one hand, Davies addresses how children's games, stories, and play objects take on gendered meanings (such as the ways toys and styles of dress come to be thought of as either masculine or feminine). On the other hand, Davies theorizes about why young children are so invested in establishing their identities and the identities of others in normative terms. Given the fact that the women's movement has made gains in opening previously closed avenues for women and girls, and the fact that many of the children who participated in the Davies research live with feminist mothers, why do these children reject feminist identities? Why do they hold on so tightly to normative roles?

The story of how Davies began to rethink the very category of gender is instructive. The research began when Davies observed the difficulties one five-year-old girl had in distinguishing the gender of her peer.

> There was a child [at the picnic] whom neither she nor I had met before. The straw-like unkempt hair, old jeans and checked shirt, the rough way of talking and eating, left us in no doubt that this was a boy. When someone who knew her called her Penny, I was startled, but my five-year-old friend was shocked and outraged. . . . "Mummy, why are they calling that boy Penny?" The disturbance that she felt seemed to be related not so much to the failure on her part to read Penny "correctly," that is, as a girl (since she still presumed that Penny was a boy), but the fact that the others could give a boy a girl's name.[21]

Readers of this passage do not hear Penny's perspectives, what she feels like when she is mistaken for a boy *and* refused as a girl. Does Penny see herself as someone who did not "get gender right?" Thoughtful readers, however, are offered insight into how essentialist views of gender persuade a rigid set of moral imperatives that damage, though in different ways, both the holder of these ideas and those who must receive these directions. We are also privy to the odd contradiction that essentialist views must also be constructed in order to be maintained. Finally, the passage suggests something more: What would be the source of one's identity if gender were no longer a meaningful category? What about imagining a world where the very question, "Are you a boy or are you a girl?" and the normative imperatives that police such distinctions, stopped making sense? The point is to question the stable and limiting ways gender is perceived, understood, and policed and to address the power relations that shape the ways gender becomes lived as a relation of domination and subordination. How can multicultural education move us in these ways?

Gender and Multicultural Education

Historically, multicultural education began in the late 1960s and may be seen as a direct consequence of the civil rights movement.[22]

It began with the push to include in the school curriculum the experiences, perspectives, and histories of those groups of people historically absent, namely, people of color and of various white ethnic groups. While gender is certainly a part of every culture and racial group, women of all groups continue to be marginalized and the study of gender is rarely concerned with the question of masculinity or with the politics of a wide range of feminisms. If addressed at all, the experiences of diverse women—in terms both of the dynamics of inequality and progress and of how groups of women relate to women—are typically positioned as an afterthought in the study of white men. Three related problems emerge from this additive and singular treatment: first, the study of gender has historically ignored race and culture;[23] second, the study of race ignores the complication of gender;[24] and third, even if race and gender are integrated, the complications of heterosexuality and lesbian and gay sexuality are ignored.[25] This last problem—of not acknowledging differences within the category of sexuality—is perhaps the most persistent and widespread.

The first two of these problems were suggested in Sleeter and Grant's review of research[26] on multicultural education in compulsory education. These researchers tallied the goals and commitments that compose parts of the field. They counted articles that contained the descriptor "multicultural education" as opposed to those articles that might lay the foundation for the ways this field could position social differences. Except for those who take the human relations perspective (although this perspective mainly limits the study of gender to the correction of sex role stereotyping[27]), mainstream multicultural education not surprisingly uses neither gender nor feminism as a central category. While in an earlier article Grant and Sleeter argue for what they term "an integrated analysis,"[28] they do not address the more difficult problem of what happens when gender *is* admitted into multicultural education. Clearly the call for adding women of all races to the curriculum and, hopefully, understanding differences within the categories of masculinity and femininity is an important first step. We are obligated, however, to ask something more: What conceptions of gender can push the field beyond role models and additive frameworks? What does the concept of gender do to how knowledge is made? Generally, mainstream orientations to multicultural education do not raise these sophisticated concerns and thus do not require complex thinking from students or teachers.

The Trouble with Models: Cultures of Gender

The work of Michelle Fine, Regina Austin, and Lois Weis all suggest more complicated orientations to the meanings of gender: how gender is inscribed through sexuality, class, and race; prescribed through representations and directives; and uncomfortably lived as a relation of power.[29] Each of these researchers, in different ways, challenges the prevailing assumptions that gender inequality can be "cured" if males and females are presented with positive gendered role models and with a rational argument for why these role models are desirable to emulate. While it is beyond the scope of this chapter to address the dependence of multicultural education on the method of rational persuasion,[30] the problem of gender is not synonymous with rationality. As Leach and Davies point out, the dominant place of sex role theory in the field of multicultural education as a way to explain inequality cannot account for the contradictory ways individual identities are rooted in larger histories and in social structures.[31] Leach and Davies dispute a central tenet of socialization theory—that those acquiring roles are passive receptors or that roles are simply a stable given entity one "naturally" steps into.

> Teachers using sex role socialization theory often think that if they tell students they can be equal and encourage them to act in "nonstereotyped" ways that is enough. They are puzzled by what they see as students' resistance to "equality" [and then] often fall back on biological explanations.[32]

In other words, sex role socialization theory, because it is so firmly grounded in traditions of essentialism and its push to present identity as stable, cannot offer teachers and students insight into either the deep emotional investments people make in normative actions and in committing themselves to living traditional roles, or the deep conflict that emerges when one attempts to live these roles. Moreover, sex role socialization theory cannot explain the conflicts and pleasures of those who define themselves differently. This latter point is especially relevant to the question of how research on gender might understand the circumstances and struggles of gay, lesbian, and heterosexual youth.[33] Sex role theory ignores questions of sexuality.

The recent ethnographic research by Lois Weis on the meanings of race, class, and gender in a working-class community disrupts a range of working assumptions about gender.[34] Weis documents how the larger social dynamics of racism and sexism set the terms for white working-class males as they strive to define their masculinity. Weis argues that in order to recognize the self one must distinguish the self from others. Within this negotiation, the lived experiences and structures of racism and sexism become implicated in the formation of identity. The white male working-class youth of this study define "the other," or what they are not, in terms of blackness and femininity. They practice what Weis terms "virulent sexism," holding tightly to the expectations and beliefs that women are their property, that traditional sex roles must be maintained, and that white men are entitled to control women. They expect to benefit from traditional patriarchal relations and the segregation of races in these relations. These white males are violently opposed to African-American boys dating or even talking to white girls and can only view African-American girls in disparaging terms. They are deeply suspicious of feminists and have a strong investment in maintaining relations of gendered and racial subordination. Basically, school curriculum ignores the violent effects of these white masculinist investments and hence cannot intervene to help any group make sense of the other.

Juxtaposed to the expectations of white males are the rising expectations of white females who understand the importance of establishing a career and the need to support themselves economically. The majority of girls interviewed did not mention marriage in their near future. White boys, however, articulated their desires to marry and be the sole supporter despite living in a deindustrialized community where work is scarce and double incomes are necessary. These conflicting and racialized desires of gender—of white girls who seek more autonomy and of white boys who seek control of white and black girls—Weis predicts, if left alone, will lead to an increase in gendered and racialized violence. On one level, then, Weis points to the necessity of creating school curriculum that can uncouple the practices of white masculinity from sexism and from racism. On another level, this work suggests that the dynamics of gender cannot be understood outside of the other social markers that distinguish identity. Again, role models cannot do such sophisticated work.

In a different context, Elsa Barkley Brown pushes us to think about not just the differences between males and females, but how each position sustains the other.[35] Brown argues that just as women have many races, they have many genders. To understand how each position sustains the other one must take into account, as Weis's ethnography also suggests, that differences work relationally. Brown puts it this way:

We need to recognize not only differences but also the relational nature of those differences. Middle-class white women's lives are not just different from working-class white, black, and Latina women's lives; it is important to recognize that middle-class women live the lives they do precisely because working-class women live the lives they do. White women and women of color not only live different lives but white women live the lives they do in large part because women of color live the ones they do.[36]

And yet, in subtle and in not so subtle ways, gender studies, even if included in school curriculum, do not address the problem of either white supremacy or male supremacy and how this deadly combination works to define differently the imperatives of masculinity and femininity. Instead, gender is approached as if it could be understood outside of history and as if it could be unencumbered by the conflictive and unstable meanings of race, class, and sexuality.

The work of Michelle Fine investigates how gender is studied in the formal school curriculum. She critiques how sex education courses fail to encourage males and females to explore questions of desire, social conventions, and a range of sexual orientations. Her conclusion holds no surprises: as presently constructed, sex education courses perpetuate the victimization of females of any sexuality and victimization of young gay men of all races. Fine outlines three problems:

Within today's standard sex education curricula and many public school classrooms, we find: (1) the authorized suppression of a discourse of female sexual desire; (2) the promotion of a discourse of female sexual victimization; and (3) the explicit privileging of married heterosexuality over other practices of sexuality.[37]

Consequently, girls do not have opportunities to understand and to explore the meanings of their bodies, nor are lesbians and gay males acknowledged and they therefore have no opportunities to explore their identities or even to look to institutional support for intervening in violence against them. Girls, in general, are taught to view themselves as the victims of male heterosexual desire. These "lessons" are intended to "protect" girls, given the assumption that sexuality is linked to disease, promiscuity, and to female victimization. The irony, of course, is that this kind of protection works against a girl's capacity to feel entitled to take action and to negotiate her sexual practices with other people. The essentialist view of sexuality naturalizes male entitlement. After an examination of sex education curricula and discussions with adolescent girls, Fine concludes that for a girl traditional notions of femininity—which value female passivity and self-sacrifice—"may be hazardous to her health."[38] The advocacy of safe and traditional roles neither prevents teenage pregnancies, ostensibly one of the central reasons for sex education, nor provides the space for girls to think positively and critically about themselves and their partners.

Can the mere presentation of role models do the work of multicultural education? And what definitions constitute a role model? These questions are taken up by the work of Regina Austin, who critically analyzes as problematic the representations of African-American girls in the media and in academic research, and the meaning of teenage pregnancy in the context of jurisprudence and daily life.[39] Austin considers the lawsuit of Crystal Chambers, a single African-American woman in her twenties. Chambers, a craft instructor for the Omaha Girls Club, was fired when she became pregnant. The Girls Club maintained Chambers could no longer serve as a positive role model to young African-American girls who participated in this club. When Chambers brought her case to court—an act, Austin rightly observes, that should have helped everyone involved to see that Chambers indeed offered girls a powerful identity—the court ruled in favor of the Club and for the dismissal of Chambers. Austin comments on the irony of firing a single African-American woman in order to protect other young female African Americans. This case illustrates the conflicts produced by legal definitions and enforcement of who can and who cannot be a role model. As Austin points out, role models are typically viewed as an antidote by those who deem a given community as diseased. This is the medical model. "Chambers' condition," Austin writes, "becomes problematic *because of* the enforcement of the role model rule."[40] This opens a central problem with role models: exactly what are roles modeling? Whose version of goodness and clarity are valorized? The point is that, although role models always model a particular version of morality, the way they are handled prevents any critical discussion of how morality becomes constituted.

The mistaken and damaging belief that the condition of teenage pregnancy is merely tied to girls' lack of proper role models shuts out awareness of the real social and emotional forces tied to teenage pregnancy. Moreover, young men are oddly absent in this scenario. As Austin argues, teenage pregnancy does not correlate with one's proximity to good or bad role models:

Teenage pregnancy is the product of the complex interaction of, not only culture and individual adjustment, but also material conditions which present black teens with formidable obstacles to survival and success. . . . Blame for black teenage pregnancy must be shared by an educational system that fails to provide black youngsters with either the desire or the chance to attend college, a labor market that denies them employment which will supply the economic indicia of adulthood, and a health system that does not deliver adequate birth control, abortion, or family planning services.[41]

Austin argues for a view of teenage pregnancy that can take into account the structural effects of racism and sexism. But along with this, Austin critiques the prevailing view in social science and among many white professionals who work with African-American adolescents that they are merely pawns in the system. African-American adolescents who are economically disadvantaged, Austin writes, "create a culture of their own that is weighted with contradictions and ambivalence, promise and peril."[42] The reasons for teenage pregnancy, in other words, are far more contradictory than present explanations acknowledge.

If multicultural approaches to understanding gender are to be effective in moving students and teachers to consider a range of new identities, then they must take seriously the fact that students are neither stable subjects nor empty vessels waiting to be filled with the goodness of essentialized role models. As the studies of Weis, Fine, and Austin demonstrate, students bring to the classroom contradictory desires. Unless they have opportunities to explore these desires as contradictory and in relation to culture, social structure, history, and one another, and in relation to their own proximity to the histories and experiences of racism and sexism, they are apt to continue to dismiss education along with its irrelevant models.

The Real Is Controversial

Multicultural education is controversial because it pushes us to inspect the damage of oppression and invisibility and to repair the structures and practices of inequality and stigma. Our concern should be with the persistency of ideologies that portray social differences as undesirable or that deem subordination inevitable and natural. These imperatives require not just that we critique the bad old past but, more uncomfortably, that we rethink the relation between the past and our present investments and identities.[43] It means bringing to the fore one's own investments in maintaining stereotypical appearances, naturalizing heterosexuality as the only sexuality, and in continuing gendered practices without admitting their stultifying and contradictory effects.

I have argued here that multicultural education must ground itself in the controversies that make this field so necessary in the first place. Three significant directions must be addressed. First, gender in all of its nuances and troubles must become a central concept in the field of multicultural education. This requires educators to engage with a wide range of feminist orientations to scholarship. Second, educators themselves must grapple with how they are tied to, and how they tie multicultural education to, specific histories of social justice, colonialism, civil rights, and economic struggles. Along with their students, educators must create the emotional and analytical means to give critical attention to the orientations and subjective commitments brought to masculinity and femininity. Within this context, educators must begin to understand that masculinity and femininity take on meaning because of race, sexuality, and class. It is this multiple vision that will make it possible to leave behind the literal theory that role models can do the work of education. Third, critical attention must be focused on the perceived and real relations of students, educators, and the curriculum to the experiences and histories of racism, sexism, heterosexism, and Eurocentrism and how these oppressive dynamics direct gendered identities. To engage in the field of multicultural education, then, requires everyone involved to move beyond the myth of the unique self and of unencumbered role models that support this view and address identity in more fluid, controversial, and creative terms. It means as well that any model should be represented as rolling: expressing the tensions, volatility, and slipperiness of identity and its mobile and shifting character.

Notes

1. Bronwyn Davies, *Frogs and Snails and Feminist Tales: Preschool Children and Gender* (Sydney: Allyn and Unwin, 1989).

2. Caroline Sherritt, "What Not To Do in the Name of Multicultural Education (Or If You Can't Stand the Heat, Get Out of the Kitchen)," *Contemporary Education* 61, no. 4 (1990): 215-216.

3. Stuart Hall, "Teaching Race," in *The School in the Multicultural Society*, edited by Alan James and Robert Jeffcoate (London: Harper and Row, 1981), p. 58.

4. Lisa Delpit, "The Silenced Dialogue: Power and Pedagogy in Educating Other People's Children," *Harvard Educational Review* 58, no. 3 (1988): 297.

5. Ibid.

6. Warren Crichlow, Susan Goodwin, Gaya Shakes, and Ellen Swartz, "Multicultural Ways of Knowing: Implications for Practice," *Journal of Education* 172, no. 2 (1990): 101-117; Terry Dean, "Multicultural Classrooms, Monocultural Teachers," *College Composition and Communication* 40, no. 1 (1989): 23-37; Cameron McCarthy, *Race and Curriculum: Social Inequality and the Theories and Politics of Difference in Contemporary Research on Schooling* (Philadelphia, PA: Falmer Press, 1990).

7. Valerie Walkerdine. "Some Day My Prince Will Come: Young Girls and the Preparation for Adolescent Sexuality," in *Gender and Generation*, edited by Angela McRobbie and Mica Nava (London: Macmillan Publishing, 1984), pp. 162-184.

8. Deborah P. Britzman, "Decentering Discourses in Teacher Education: Or, the Unleashing of Unpopular Things," in *What Schools Can Do: Critical Pedagogy and Practice*, edited by Kathleen Weiler and Candace Mitchell (Albany: State University of New York Press, 1992), pp. 151-176; Kathleen Weiler, *Women Teaching for Change: Gender, Class, and Power* (South Hadley, MA: Bergin and Garvey Press, 1988).

9. Patti Lather, *Getting Smart: Feminist Research and Pedagogy With/In the Postmodern* (New York: Routledge, 1991); Magda Lewis, "Interrupting Patriarchy: Politics, Resistance, and Transformation in the Feminist Classroom," *Harvard Educational Review* 60, no. 4 (1991): 467-488.

10. Deborah P. Britzman, *Practice Makes Practice: A Critical Study of Learning to Teach* (Albany: State University of New York Press, 1991); Janet Miller, *Creating Spaces and Finding Voices: Teachers Collaborating for Empowerment* (Albany: State University of New York Press, 1990).

11. R. W. Connell, *Gender and Power* (Stanford, CA: Stanford University Press, 1987).

12. Teresa de Lauretis, "The Essence of the Triangle or, Taking the Risk of Essentialism Seriously: Feminist Theory in Italy, the US., and Britain," *Difference* 1, no. 2 (1989): 3-37.

13. Chandra Talpade Mohanty, Ann Russo, and Lourdes Torres, eds., *Third World Women and the Politics of Feminism* (Bloomington: Indiana University Press, 1991).

14. Marianne Hirsch and Evelyn Fox Keller, eds., *Conflicts in Feminism* (New York: Routledge, 1990).

15. Diana Fuss, *Essentially Speaking: Feminism, Nature, and Difference* (New York: Routledge, 1989), p. xi.

16. Carol Gilligan, *In a Different Voice: Psychological Theory and Women's Development* (Cambridge, MA: Harvard University Press, 1982).

17. Mary Belenky, Blythe Clinchy, Nancy Goldberger, and Jill Tarule, *Women's Ways of Knowing: The Development of Self, Voice, and Mind* (New York: Basic Books, 1986); Nel Noddings, *Caring: A Feminist Approach to Ethics and Moral Education* (Berkeley, CA: University of California Press, 1984).

18. Carole Vance, "Social Construction Theory: Problems in the History of Sexuality," in *Which Homosexuality? Essays from the International Scientific Conference on Lesbian and Gay Studies*, edited by Dennis Altman, Carole Vance, et al. (London: Gay Mens Publishers, 1989), pp. 13-34.

19. Davies, *Frogs and Snails and Feminist Tales*.

20. Simone de Beauvoir, *The Second Sex* (New York: Bantam, 1970).

21. Davies, *Frogs and Snails and Feminist Tales*, p. ix.

22. McCarthy, *Race and Curriculum*.

23. Elsa Barkley Brown, "Polyrhythms and Improvisation: Lessons for Women's History," *History Workshop Journal* 31 (1991): 85-90; Gloria T. Hull, Patricia Bell Scott, and Barbara Smith, eds., *All the Women Are White, All the Blacks Are Men, But*

Some of Us Are Brave: Black Women's Studies (Old Westbury, NY: Feminist Press, 1982); Maxine Baca Zinn, Lynn Weber Cannon, Elizabeth Higginbotham, and Bonnie Thorton Dill, "The Costs of Exclusionary Practices in Women's Studies," in *Making Face, Making Soul/Haciendo Caras: Creative and Critical Perspectives by Women of Color*, edited by Gloria Anzaldua (San Francisco: Aunt Lute Foundation, 1990).

24. Carole Boyce Davies, "Writing Off Marginality, Minoring, and Effacement," *Women's Studies International Forum* 14, no. 4 (1991): 249-263; bell hooks, *Talking Back: Thinking Feminist/Thinking Black* (Boston: South End Press, 1989); Bettina Aptheker, *Tapestries of Life: Women's Work, Women's Consciousness and the Meaning of Daily Experience* (Amherst: University of Massachusetts Press, 1989).

25. Judith Butler, *Gender Trouble: Feminism and the Subversion of Identity* (New York: Routledge, 1990); Audre Lorde, *A Burst of Light* (Ithaca, NY: Firebrand Books, 1988).

26. Christine Sleeter and Carl Grant, "An Analysis of Multicultural Education," *Harvard Educational Review* 57, no. 4 (1987): 421-444.

27. Nicholas Colangelo, Cecilia Foxley, and Dick Dustin, eds., *Multicultural Nonsexist Education: A Human Relations Approach* (Dubuque, IA: Kendall/Hunt Publishing Company, 1987).

28. Carl Grant and Christine Sleeter, "Race, Class, and Gender in Educational Research: An Argument for Integrative Analysis," *Review of Educational Research* 56, no. 2 (1986): 195-211.

29. Michelle Fine, "Sexuality, Schooling, and Adolescent Females: The Missing Discourse of Desire," *Harvard Educational Review* 58, no. 1 (1988): 29-53; Regina Austin, "Sapphire Bound," *Wisconsin Law Review* 3 (1989): 539-578; Lois Weis, *Working Class without Work: High School Students in a Deindustrializing Economy* (New York: Routledge, 1990).

30. See, for example, Elizabeth Ellsworth, "Why Doesn't This Feel Empowering? Working through the Repressive Myths of Critical Pedagogy," *Harvard Educational Review*, 59, no. 3 (1989): 297-324; Michael Olneck, "The Recurring Dream: Symbolism and Ideology in Intercultural and Multicultural Education," *American Journal of Education* 98, no. 2 (1990): 147-174; Walkerdine, "Some Day My Prince Will Come."

31. Mary Leach and Bronwyn Davies, "Crossing the Boundaries: Educational Thought and Gender Equity," *Educational Theory* 40, no. 3 (1990): 321-332.

32. Ibid., p. 328.

33. Eric Rofes, "Opening Up the Classroom Closet: Responding to the Educational Needs of Gay and Lesbian Youth," *Harvard Educational Review* 59, no. 4 (1989): 444-453.

34. Weis, *Working Class without Work*.

35. Brown, "Polyrhythms and Improvisation."

36. Ibid., p. 86.

37. Fine, "Sexuality, Schooling, and Adolescent Females," p. 30.

38. Ibid., p. 38.

39. Austin, "Sapphire Bound."

40. Ibid., p. 553.

41. Ibid., pp. 558-559.

42. Ibid., p. 562.

43. Maxine Greene, *Dialectics of Freedom* (New York: Teachers College Press, 1988).

CHAPTER IV

Constructions of Curriculum and Gender

JANET L. MILLER

I recently sat through countless faculty meetings called in response to accreditation pressures and labeled on our agendas as "final urgent discussions" about curriculum and knowledge bases. Even though I had participated in several years of discussions about our School of Education's undergraduate and graduate programs, I still felt detached from the accreditation agency's reified definitions of curriculum that necessarily guided our deliberations. Within those definitions, I felt encased like the books, shelved according to someone else's categorizations of knowledge, that lined the walls of our meeting space.

And so, in those end-of-semester conversations, I could only watch spring erupting around me in the dogwood blossoms of pink and white that framed the windows of the School of Education conference room, as my colleagues and I wrestled with narrow conceptions of curriculum that emphasized linear and sequential approaches to design, development, and evaluation of courses of study.

Varied Constructions of Curriculum

The curriculum conceptions with which we were grappling in those endless accreditation meetings replicated the positivist and management-oriented nature of the curriculum field, which had emerged in the United States during the 1920s in response to school administrators' needs within burgeoning school bureaucracies, and which quickly had assimilated the prevalent characteristics of scientific management that dominated the field of education in general. Within such conceptions, curriculum was defined as content or subject matter

Janet L. Miller is Professor of Education at the Beloit (WI) Campus of National-Louis University.

or course of study, as a program of planned activities, as intended learning outcomes. The emphasis was on prediction and control of students' educational experiences.[1]

Thus, even though we were working in the early 1990s for this accreditation, we had to ignore recent developments that challenged such technical-rational curriculum conceptions. In the late 1960s and early 1970s, a disparate yet concerned group of scholars who were dissatisfied with the prescriptive and positivist orientations of curriculum work began to analyze, critique, and reconceptualize the field. Initially contributing to this reconceptualization were existential, phenomenological, and psychoanalytic studies of the school and of curriculum, especially from the point of view of the individual. Autobiography was, and continues to be, a predominant mode utilized within this strand of the reconceptualization. Autobiographical work attempts to acknowledge, and to examine as knowledge, the interwoven relationships among one's educational experiences, one's contextualizations and constructions of those experiences within social-political worlds, and constructions of curriculum as both reflecting and creating those worlds.[2]

The other predominant strand of scholarship that emerged within attempts to reconceptualize curriculum studies was neo-Marxist in nature. These studies focus on schools and curriculum as preeminently political realities; from these perspectives, school policies and practices, including curriculum constructions, are analyzed for ways in which they replicate or reify oppressive economic, political, and ideological relations of the larger society.[3]

In recent years, reconceptualization also has included feminist and poststructuralist perspectives that have further expanded definitions of curriculum to include the ways in which bodies of knowledge are constructed and transmitted in the contexts of daily lives.[4] As well, expanded emphases within analyses and definitions of curriculum, drawing from both initial strands of inquiry within the reconceptualization, include the ways in which various individuals interpret, experience, and construct their own meanings of "official" knowledge; the ways in which identities are constructed and reconstructed through schooling contents and practices; and the ways in which social, economic, historical, and cultural forces influence, frame, and construct individuals' interpretations and experiences of education.[5] In these enlarged conceptions of curriculum, the power relationships embedded in language, in social relationships and constructs, and in representations of identities are highlighted.

In all of these rather divergent perspectives within reconceptualized curriculum studies runs the theme of viewing education relationally; that is, curriculum as "content" cannot be separated from the individuals who create, transmit, or receive knowledge, or from social, political, cultural, and historical moments and discourses that frame and influence those persons and processes.

However, rather than working with these reconceptualized versions of curriculum, the faculty members in our School of Education were limited, through the forms and conceptions of this accreditation process, to linear and sequential notions of teaching and learning. Curriculum was conceptualized only as "content" or "course of study," as universally agreed-upon information which could be dispensed by teachers, received by students at predetermined, developmentally appropriate stages, and then returned to teachers in unreconstructed forms—that is, in measurable, testable, and standardized terms.

In those faculty meetings, we all struggled to encapsulate into singular form our myriad academic perspectives and passions and examples of knowledge created *with* our students. We had to squeeze our students' and our own particular wrestlings with specific "contents," which often were challenged and transformed by our classroom interactions as well as by the various social and cultural positionings and perspectives of class members, into the mandated design and appropriate delivery and evaluation systems. Finally, after years of discussion and debate, we had to fill in the agency's boxes and slots and grids with those encapsulated and reduced versions of our varied pedagogical experiences and encounters with contents, with students, with historical, cultural, and social moments and forces that all framed and constituted the curriculums of our classrooms. And as we completed those grids, I was as separated from my own and my students' experiences and constructions of teaching and learning as were those dust-covered and categorized books from the blossoms that cascaded to the sidewalk.

In that conference room, as a feminist academic who works within the field of curriculum theory and inquiry, I once again was confronted with an insistent separation of my own experiences of education from "official" definitions of curriculum. I believe that my experiences always are framed and influenced by social constructions of gender, race, class, and other social positionings, as well as by my varying internalizations of, and struggles with, predominant cultural "meanings" of those positionings. My understandings, interpretations, and struggles are a part of curriculum as social construction. But those "official" definitions of curriculum, reflecting a still dominant positivist orientation to educational policies and practices, also adhere to historically dichotomous realms of private and public that work to separate my understandings, experiences, and wrestlings from "official content."

Such narrow definitions of curriculum thus can perpetuate exclusions, silences, and distortions of various individuals' educational experiences. Those experiences, for example, may include the unequal ways that people are treated or regarded in classrooms because of their gender and sexuality as well as the ways in which people are represented or not represented in textbooks, which constitute a major version of "official" school curriculum. However, the fact that we often construct ourselves and our relationships to others and to bodies of knowledge through a prevailing system, say, of gender, often is erased by supposedly "neutral," "objective," "unitary," and "essential" views of what constitutes our experiences and relationships as males and females to one another as well as to school knowledge, to what is commonly termed "the curriculum."

So, as a student and as a teacher too, I have watched through other windows, and I have wanted to exclaim about the connections between particular "curriculum contents" and my own life. I have wanted to further explore how my connections were similar to or different from those of others whose educational contexts and daily lives and social positionings did not resemble or intersect with mine. And I have paused within the palpable silences that followed those attempted articulations and explorations. I have heard and felt the blank spaces, those same momentary pauses in classrooms and school corridors that signaled the smoothings into sameness or the exclusions or the distortions of my own and others' gendered, "raced," classed experiences and understandings from the often one-dimensional "official" school knowledge found in textbooks and in classroom reenactments of that knowledge.

So for several years during our faculty meetings I resisted such separations, exclusions, and distortions. I argued that the "official" definition of curriculum imposed by the accreditation process contained assumptions of universally agreed-upon bodies of knowledge that were of the "most worth." Further, that definition implied that those content areas were bound, like the shelved books, by testable, measurable, and deliverable categories. That definition also contained assumptions and conveyed implicit values about *whose* knowledges and experiences were considered to be of most worth. And quite often, those knowledges and experiences did not represent the concerns, creations, and investments of women, of people of color, of individuals disenfranchised from mainstream versions of knowledge and culture for varied reasons having to do with their perceived relationships or nonrelationships to those versions.

In contrast to such a definition, I argued that my educational and life experiences, framed by my gender, race, class, age, sexual preference, for example, and influenced by social, historical, and cultural constructions of those positionings, constantly infuse my understandings and interpretations of particular educational contents and processes that are encompassed in those enlarged and reconceptualized definitions of curriculum. And my experiences, understandings, and puzzlements, as well as those of my students, about those frames and constructions often provide us with enough discrepancies to challenge or change dominant constructions and "official versions" of knowledge packaged as "the curriculum."

My attempts to define curriculum as content, as my experiencing of that content, and as both the hidden and overt processes and constructions of identities and knowledges within particular social, cultural, and historical moments, obviously are part of the efforts of those who have worked within the past twenty years to reconceptualize the field of curriculum. And so, in those faculty meetings during the two years that we attempted to avoid the final gridding of our varying educational experiences, we discussed the scholarship of those working within reconceptualist framings of curriculum. And we agreed, within the varying degrees that academics can agree, that curriculum reconceptualized can be thought of as the concrete texts that contain particular bodies of knowledge *as well as* the conceptual and experiential texts of individuals' differing versions of that knowledge, and the processes by which individuals construct and are constructed by their relationships to that knowledge.

Those various personal as well as "official" representations of knowledge can intersect in ways that both reflect *and* continually reconstruct the processes, contents, and contexts of teaching and learning. And because they often reflect dominant versions of what counts as knowledge, those representations can be gendered, "raced," and classed versions of particular social, historical, economic, political, aesthetic, as well as personal contexts. Thus, we agreed in our faculty discussions that we need to constantly investigate ways in which particular versions of knowledge may distort, ignore, or silence the experiences, interpretations, and constructions of educational meanings by specific individuals or groups. We need to investigate the power relationships embedded in the very ways that structures and contents of disciplines get constructed. And, further, we need to examine the situated nature of these relationships—the intersections of gender, race, age, sexual preference, class, and any of the other multiple social constructions and positionings that collide within various and shifting contexts and contents of schooling and thus become part of what we now call curriculum.

Research on Gender and Education

These imperatives that emerged in our discussions of curriculum reconceptualized appear to coincide with research on gender and its relationships to education, in general, especially during the past twenty years. However, those imperatives require the acknowledgment of both gender and curriculum as social/historical/cultural/political constructions. They require the acknowledgment of intersections of such constructions with other social constructions of schooling and of identities and positions within those constructions as those identities are affected, for example, by race, class, and age. Such imperatives, with their emphases on the relational and situated nature of pedagogy and of curriculum conceived of as both content and processes of construction of individuals' meanings and identities, extend and expand the boundaries of feminist and gender research in education.

For example, much of the fairly recent research on gender has continued to analyze sexism and gender-stereotyping embodied in aspects of elementary and secondary schooling especially. Thus, physical settings, textbooks, rules and norms, classroom interactions among teacher and students, official policies, and power structures of the schools have been subjects of analyses within gender framings.

Thus, in analyses of curriculum materials (projects that still assume curriculum defined only as content) researchers found that girls were depicted overall much less frequently than were boys, and when they were depicted, they often appeared as passive, other-directed, delicate, cautious, and dependent. Males were found to be depicted most often as competitive, aggressive leaders.[6]

In their well-known analyses of classroom interactions, Sadker and Sadker and the Sadkers with Susan Klein[7] have demonstrated that elementary and secondary teachers give far more active attention in teaching to boys than to girls; they pose more challenging questions to boys, devote more time to listening and counseling boys, and criticize and reward boys more frequently than girls. These interactions are complicated by racial and ethnic backgrounds, where often both minority males and females interact less with teachers than do majority males and females.[8]

Other researchers have focused their classroom interaction research on how gender operates as a cultural category that affects communication behavior, and how communication and language function to create gender categories.[9]

Educational Strategies

These studies and others have suggested strategies for classroom teachers to incorporate into their pedagogical and curricular perspectives. Certainly, selecting and lobbying for textbooks that present nonsexist, nonracist, and "nonclassist" examples of individuals in a variety of contexts and relationships are among those important strategies. An "inclusion" of women into the "official" curriculum as a strategy also has received much attention in recent years.[10] Such strategies often have assumed that solutions to sexual inequality, especially, include an equalization in the schools of the treatment of men and women, of boys and girls, an equitable representation of both females and males within curricular content, and an equitable division of resources.

Many have argued for classroom arrangements and interactions that reflect interactive and cooperative approaches among students, participatory decision making, an emphasis on dialogue, and a facilitative role for teachers.[11] These arrangements can disrupt the normative balance of power in a classroom, where a teacher is usually defined as the authority, and often members of privileged groups dominate class discussions and interactions. These arrangements, within reconceptualized versions, are part of curriculum and can be utilized to call attention to the lens of gender as it operates in classroom interactions and in pedagogy.

For example, given the research noted above on gendered communication among teachers and students, notions of authority might be made explicit within the classroom; students and teachers could discuss and analyze ways in which they have been socialized to think of authority as antithetical to conceptions of women's roles. Various definitions of authority and discussions of who is "in charge" in the classroom can be examined as students and teachers address the difficulties of forging collaborative and equitable arrangements within classrooms that often traditionally replicate hierarchical and gendered arrangements of power.

For example, teachers can help to make students aware of research that indicates that females tend to report more ease and more discovery in settings where learning is a communal activity shared equally by students and teacher. Male students seem more satisfied with authoritarian educational settings.[12] Given reconceptualized versions of curriculum, these varying student preferences are important in viewing not only how power relationships function in the classroom and how knowledge is constructed but also whose knowledge is prevalent in those constructions.

In the elementary classroom, distillations of such research might form a basis for students' explorations. Students can study frequency of speaking of boys and girls, as well as the nature of the teacher's responses. In secondary classrooms, the denial of the authority of women's experiences, perspectives, emotions, and minds can be approached through historical and literary studies. Teachers could examine ways in which such denials contribute to contradictions that women teachers, for example, often feel as a result of this socialization. Such contradictions might also be explored by administrators in their own relationships with one another as well as with teachers, parents, and students.

In our faculty discussions we agreed that such strategies for addressing, examining, and changing sexism and gender stereotyping within schooling structures are important. However, we also addressed ways in which institutional structures such as schools and structures of knowledge that hold privileged positions in the schools are not deeply challenged by such strategies. In order to challenge the very discourses and structures of power that produce and are produced by the current gender system, reconceptualized curriculum inquiry attempts to illuminate the deeply embedded social and educational production of gender and sexuality. Thus, studies focus on the inherent contradictions in enacting equitable and critical versions of teaching and learning within institutions and structures of knowledge that remain privileged. Moreover, such studies challenge these unified and linear notions of the development of student and teacher "voices" and the equalization of "speaking" privileges, of establishment of easy collaborative interactions among students and teachers, and of "empowered" students and teachers.[13]

Strategies for addressing these deep structural contradictions include situated studies of ways in which unequal power relations are replicated even within approaches that claim to be emancipatory for both students and teachers, for both women and men. Those unequal power relations can best be understood as replicating oppressive relationships if they are examined and expressed in the concrete lives of individuals. Further,

> . . . the inclusion of gender issues poses a specific challenge to any unitary notion of the oppressed; namely, that oppressed people may not all speak with one voice. There is no generalized "oppressed" experience, but rather a multiplicity of human experiences obscured by (and differently exploited by) the dominant ones.[14]

Situated narratives of educational experience and inquiry, expressed in multiple versions and forms, offer ways into examinations of such complex intersections and constructions of both identities and curriculum. Current versions of such studies point to work in autobiography, including dialogue journals, life histories of students and teachers, descriptions and analyses of situated pedagogies and curricular practices, "teacher and student lore," and "teachers' personal practical knowledge."[15]

Autobiographical work within reconceptualized versions of curriculum particularly emphasizes the multiple constructions and readings of one's and others' stories. Such multiple processes potentially can challenge the ahistorical, essentialized, and reified selves that our stories tend to create. Such multiple versions of our stories can reveal knowledge that often conflicts with, or is not reflected in, the dominant stories[16] that educational culture tells about its teachers, students, research orientations, and reforms. Such multiple constructions and readings of our individual and collective stories emphasize the relational and situated nature of education:

> The reading and rereading of our stories create a linguistic bridge between our public and private worlds, between what we know and what we teach to others. . . . And it is not only our social history that we need to understand but our gender history as well. . . . Feminist scholars work to bring together domains of experience and understanding that history and culture have kept apart. For what it means to teach and learn is related to what it means to be male or female and to our experiences of reproduction and nurturance, domesticity, sexuality, nature, knowledge, and politics.[17]

As a faculty, we had discussed and worked with such enlarged approaches and strategies in our efforts to examine constructions of curriculum and gender in our own teaching, research, and writing. However, on that spring day, with the dogwood blooming outside our meeting room windows, we were finally drawn back to the pressures of time and conceptualization that we faced in producing concrete and categorized evidence of the certifiable knowledge produced in this School of Education. As we reluctantly succumbed to the grids and charts that objectified and reified the multiple and constantly changing experiences, voices, and histories within our classrooms, I again felt the contradictions that we all face in challenging structures and practices that often appear immutable within our particular social/political/cultural arrangements and structures of schooling. And as I filled in the mandatory grids for my particular subject-areas of "expertise," I was drawn into remembrances of my own gender history within education that signaled for me the extent to which conceptions of curriculum as someone else's course of study, not my own and my students' intertwined experiences of learning and teaching, pervade standard educational experience.

Constructions of Gender and Curriculum: An Autobiographical Account

As a young female student, I read the official school texts and participated in their reenactments of universal and standardized versions of knowledge and looked in vain for images and descriptions and "facts" that possibly could enable me to conceive of myself as a potential mother, teacher, nurse, or secretary, *and* President of the United States. The ways in which I learned about traditionally defined curriculum as representation of others' knowledge, often presented through male-oriented frames of inquiry and experience and translated through metaphors such as assembly line production or military models, are lodged in my early experiences as a female student. Those experiences took place within educational contexts, with their accompanying expectations and assumptions, that most often reflected gendered mediations and interpretations of curriculum. For students and teachers alike, those courses of study or textbook contents were created and determined and framed most often by males' conceptualizations and interpretations of canons or of historical, social, and political events and forces. Thus, they functioned as simultaneous metaphors for gendered conceptualizations of our possibilities as men and women.

In that world, as a female student, I was positioned as a gendered being who often was silenced, whose gaze was diverted from classroom windows that framed possibilities of other worlds, and instead was directed to the sanctioned curriculum that was devoid of my presence and that neglected my experiencing of that erasure. That particular positioning occurred even within seemingly benign and even encouraging contexts.

I want here to narrate, as a gendered curricular tale, some of my remembrances, triggered by that School of Education accreditation exercise in curriculum as well as professional containment. I will describe an educational context that was, for all intents and purposes, an encouraging and nurturing one. That context, my sixth-grade classroom, was one in which my position as a young girl who was eager to learn seemed reinforced by my supportive and yet challenging teacher, Mr. Brucker. "The curriculum" of Mr. Brucker's classroom, however, as conceived by textbook "experts" and enacted by a teacher who wished only the best for his students, still could not take into account the ways in which I interpreted the interactions of our classroom as part of a gendered reading of how I "should be" in the world.

I write autobiographically in part to describe the ways in which my subsequent expectations for myself as a woman and as a teacher were formed through my responses to "the official school curriculum" and its representations by my sixth-grade teacher. Further, I utilize autobiographical modes of inquiry in order to look again and again at the ways in which my particular constructions of myself reflect dominant social and cultural versions of gender-specific roles and assumptions. I think that autobiographical writing also can invite others to inquire into the ways in which their particular educational remembrances, experiences, interpretations, and understandings coincide or differ from mine. Such forms of inquiry constitute another way of conceptualizing curriculum as interactive, reciprocal, and meaning-making processes, and of challenging the dominant and unified versions of educational experience.

> Through education we enter a cultural conversation, always somewhere in the middle. There we find and form our understanding of ourselves and our communities. . . . Because knowledge and gender both are produced and reproduced against the background of available cultural representations, those who are excluded from or demeaned in those representations are at a distinct disadvantage.[18]

The following tale thus reflects ways in which I entered a gendered cultural conversation, billed as school curriculum, from an identity forged most dramatically in my sixth-grade year and in relation to my teacher, John Brucker. Although Mr. Brucker presented the "official" school curriculum through the textbooks and assignments that were deemed appropriate for our sixth-grade class, the curriculum that I internalized was a gendered version of myself as compliant and passive "good girl," eager to please my teacher and eager to replicate those "official" versions of myself as female.

Thus, finally, this tale also represents, in its retelling and reexamining of such internalizations, my attempts to continually deconstruct that particular identity. In acknowledging that I entered an educational cultural conversation packaged as school curriculum from stereotypic gender-identified perspectives, I also want to work toward versions of myself and of curricular interactions and creations that defy such stereotypes and reifications. This tale also represents, then, a form of curriculum inquiry that acknowledges those attempts as aspects of curriculum criticism, research, and creation, and that recognizes gender as a predominant category of analysis within those aspects.

A GENDER HISTORY

What I already had learned, long before that summer between fifth and sixth grade, was that Mr. Brucker was prized among students and teachers alike, not only because he indeed was a kind, caring, and enthusiastic teacher, but also because he was the only male teacher in Sickman Elementary School. The other three sixth-grade teachers, all women, were supposedly equally as good as Mr. Brucker, or so the neighborhood lore implied. But to have a man as a teacher, in that last year of elementary schooling that still sanctioned childhood play even as it prepared us for the grown-up demands and rigors of junior high school, guaranteed for us the rites of passage into the rules and structures of the disciplines and forms of educating that would lead us into our "appropriate" roles and places as men and women. For, if we learned those roles and forms well (those roles and forms most often shaped by men in social, economic, and cultural contexts), we perhaps could take our places in a society that could well extend beyond those industrial hills of Pittsburgh that sometimes seemed to constrain our parents' and thus our own visions of possibilities.

As I began that sixth-grade year, nervous and excited, I immediately could see why Mr. Brucker's reputation for posing such possibilities was so solidified within our community. We all, boys and girls, were charmed by his spontaneous grin and his willingness to join us in every aspect of our classroom life. In his spontaneity, he did not separate our learning from his teaching, and so, instead of sitting behind his desk, Mr. Brucker would straddle a chair as he coached us in our multiplication and division drills. He would leap from one side of the room to the other, foreshadowing the game show host as he attempted to keep our screams of excitement under a roar level during our spelling bees or math team contests. He was the sixth-grade pied piper, his glasses always slightly askew, and his tall lean body perpetually braced against the crush of students who constantly surrounded him as he tried to lead us through the tangled passageways of childhood and into that clearing known as "real school."

But as much as he talked to us about how junior and senior high school would be different from what we were sharing that year, and how we needed to prepare ourselves for those serious undertakings, I always had the feeling that Mr. Brucker never quite believed that was how it had to be. And so I also experienced in that year some of the disruptive and contradictory positions that Mr. Brucker occupied within our particular elementary school culture. I am still learning about the ways in which those contradictory positions contributed to, affected, and ultimately disrupted many of my own understandings about myself as a female attempting to learn and later to teach.

I was aware, in that sixth-grade year, not only of some of the differences that Mr. Brucker as teacher represented for me, but also of some of the differences that characterized the kids in our class. Even though most of us lived within walking distance of our school, we girls who had known each other for a few years did not walk home with the new girls in our class who were part of the group known as the "hill" kids. Even though most of my friends' fathers worked in the steel mills and most of their mothers worked at home, these new kids were part of a growing community of men and women from Appalachia who had recently moved to Pittsburgh to get jobs in the mills. There was a separation between the "old" and "hill" boys too, and I could see that Mr. Brucker tried to include these kids in every team event or partner activity that he proposed in class. And because this seemed important to him, I too tried to talk with my friends about including these kids in our daily school rituals.

Mr. Brucker also emphasized inclusion of examples, in our studies of history and literature especially, of possible versions of ourselves that resisted stereotypic social roles of males and females. I remember that we girls talked, hanging from the monkey bars during recess on warm afternoons, about what we really might want to do in our lives besides be mothers. I, of course, had already determined that I wanted to be a teacher, just like Mr. Brucker.

But I was also learning that, even if I were to teach and even if I were to explore with my students some of the alternative ways of living and thinking that Mr. Brucker's gentle visions encouraged, I still would not be a teacher just like him. As we worked our way through geography and grammar lessons, and built clay replicas of the Panama Canal—replete with water-tight locks—and recited declensions, I began to notice that the other sixth-grade teachers, the women, would often appear at our classroom door—to plead for our teacher's help in calming two students who were fighting in the lunch room, to ask him to open one of the old and constantly stuck windows in the room down the hall, to watch our class radio productions every few weeks, where we introduced and shared with classmates, through recordings and our own handwritten scripts, our latest research on Verdi's "Aida" or on the coal mining industry.

Mr. Brucker was the leader of Sickman School, whether he wanted to be or not. I think now that he tried in some ways to resist that role, and in our class, he constantly was encouraging us all, girls and boys, to consider possibilities for ourselves that did not automatically occur to many of us as we trudged home each afternoon through the ever-present yet gentle grayness of our steel town's southern hills. He challenged us girls to move beyond stereotypic images of ourselves that we reinforced every recess in our jump-rope and hopscotch play, for example, by insisting that we be part of the class kickball team. I still remember his gleeful yelp when I kicked the ball over the fence for my first-ever home run. On rainy days he insisted that the boys and girls play in the jacks tournaments that he set up for us during lunch and recess times. He pushed us all in class, always asking us for another possible way to figure out the current math problem. But even as he was attempting to disrupt our already deeply internalized conceptions of ourselves as gendered beings, as girls and boys who should fulfill certain socially constructed roles within our public and private worlds, I think that what I was learning in sixth grade had more to do with my desires to please this teacher than with my wishes to emulate the disruptive and challenging perspectives that he perhaps was attempting to enact in his teaching. In my desire to earn his acceptance and approval, I was learning the sanctioned forms of gendered relationships, discourses, and curriculums that structured and framed the lives of both Mr. Brucker and myself.

To please Mr. Brucker meant that I had to take some risks; I had to work to overcome my shyness about speaking up in class and I had to be willing to attempt to move beyond giving only the "right answers." He pushed us all not only to frantically wave our hands in our moments of certainty but also to offer explanations for those answers that we thought might be possible within each of our multiple points of inquiry. With that kind of encouragement, I was able slowly to participate in our class exchanges and debates and to articulate the connections that I could make among the various threads of our sixth-grade curriculum. I was enlarging my own capacities to enter into the official school languages of our textbooks as well as into the unofficial languages and relationships that signaled our connections to one another as we studied and learned together in that effusive sixth-grade community.

As the year wore on, I was becoming aware of those connections among Mr. Brucker, the work of our classroom, and ourselves as his students. Yet I also was becoming increasingly aware, as the "hill" kids kept walking home in their own group and as the boys more and more claimed their apparently rightful priorities in grabbing Mr. Brucker's attention on the softball field as well as in our classroom, of the differences between and among those relationships.

I was aware, certainly before sixth grade, that the official languages of schooling were valued more than the discussions and banterings that characterized much of our interaction in Mr. Brucker's class. Even though I think that he clearly valued our dialogues above the facts that filled our textbooks and our "official" recitations of those disparate fragments of information, Mr. Brucker tried, for our own good, he said, to separate us as well as himself from the personal, intimate worlds that permeated our casual yet interrelated conversations about such topics as the geography of western Pennsylvania, the economic interdependence of the industries that grew out of our steel city, and the work in which many of our parents were engaged.

We knew that we had to settle down when his voice would modulate into the somber lower register, and when he would unfold his long, lean frame into his chair that he positioned in the center of our double-layered, concentric-circle desk arrangement. And then, even though our conversations had been filled with information we had gleaned from parents, siblings, friends, about what it was like to work in the mills, or to forge new communities in those still forested hills, or to worry about how to feed and care for children when lay-offs hit, we began to recite the facts of our textbooks, as Mr. Brucker questioned us in rapid-fire order.

And so, I learned that, even though the stories of our daily lives were the ones that Mr. Brucker asked about on the playground or during our lunch breaks or during the conversations of our class, he gave official recognition, official school praise, for facts about the construction of the Panama Canal or about the geography of western Pennsylvania. Thus, as much as I learned from Mr. Brucker about the value of our connections and conversations, I also learned that, in order to receive the sanctioned merits of schooling, to receive his official acknowledgment and approval, I had to talk with others' words, to speak in the modulated, serious tones of others' understandings, to memorize others' stories, to replicate others' knowledge. And in so doing, I neglected or repressed the unofficial, the desires inherent in our stories, our personal conversations and relationships that were at the heart of Mr. Brucker's teaching, and yet were separated as much from his conceptions of official knowledge as were my replications of it. And in my ironic desire to please, to receive authorization, I became a person only in relation to someone else's versions of how I should be in the world.

MULTIPLE CONSTRUCTIONS

I realize that this story too is only a partial telling, a written reconstruction filled with gaps and silences, a story pieced together from myriad memories that are neither static nor agreed-upon by others as factual recreation of events. And this tale is told, too, through the lenses of my subsequent multiple revisionings, experiences, conceptualizations, and enactments of teaching and learning.

In this particular telling, however, are examples of ways in which dominant educational constructions of gender and curriculum worked to frame my initial understandings and expectations for myself first as female student, and later as teacher, researcher, and writer. I learned, for example, that often men teachers who were competent and caring also were more important, more valid in their associations with and creations and transmissions of official knowledge than women teachers. I learned an "official version" of curriculum that often ignored or distorted or marginalized the contributions and creations of many women as well as other minority groups. And I thought that curriculum itself was only what existed between the covers of my textbooks and only that which was discovered, written, and authorized by others.

In this telling, too, are vestiges of the ways in which those gendered conceptions of appropriate teaching and learning stances and curricular constructions continue to manifest themselves in my educational work. I struggled still in that School of Education conference room, for example, to hear my own voice, my own constructions and understandings of knowledge as emanating, in complex and changing ways, from personal conversations, interpretations, and experiences as well as from public and "official" representations of those knowledges.

As I grapple with those still institutionalized dichotomies, I see Mr. Brucker also wrestling with what he seemed to perceive as artificial separations of our public and private knowledges about our worlds and our relationships to one another. He chose, for many reasons that I guess still substantiate many teachers' transmissions of others' knowledge, to officially support school knowledge, while, in his interactions with us, to offer visions of other possibilities for ourselves. But I was so embedded in my own already internalized gender role as "good girl," seeking approval and thus replicating his official choices, that I missed for years the discrepancies between Mr. Brucker's pedagogical and personal representations of curriculum and learning.

While I do not claim my experiences or understandings as universal for all girls and boys who were educated in the United States during the 1950s, I do think that many educational experiences, then and now, are characterized by gendered renditions of curriculum and teaching. Although the textbook industry, for example, now attempts to publish books that represent a gender-balanced representation of roles and of contributions, many classrooms still encapsulate stereotypic gender-specific roles for males and females. Those classrooms reflect larger social and cultural stereotypes for behaviors, expectations, and assumptions that are reified in media representations and artifacts, in which women often are portrayed only in subservient relation to men. Certainly, these renditions contribute to static role expectations for both teachers and students.

Further, they reinforce notions of curriculum conceived within male-oriented experiences and conceptualizations of the world. Such interpretations often conceive of knowledge-generation as objective and measurable, and of knowledge itself as unitary, as the same for everyone. Such knowledge is presented as primary or at least separate from the knowledge generated by individuals' relationships and interactions. These dominant and thus gendered constructions of curriculum have separated and prioritized educational processes and experiences into those that are considered "objective" and verifiable and those that are considered "subjective" and thus idiosyncratic.

Thus, I endeavor, with others in the field, to transcend traditional definitions of curriculum that focus only on content or course of study and that conceive of pedagogy only as means by which to convey or transmit a particular and predetermined body of knowledge to others. As we attempt to understand curriculum as representation of particular historical, social, economic, and political intersections in individuals' lives, we also view those intersections as mediated by multiple constructions of not only gender but also race, class, age, and sexual preference, among others. Thus, as we engage in debate with those who argue for stable, unified canons that supposedly represent consensus on singular and universal traditions and knowledge, we can point beyond inclusions of women's voices and works as a unitary representation. For example, we no longer can insert several selections from white, middle-class women into a literature anthology and call it a gender-balanced curriculum. We cannot assume that those particular women's voices represent all women's experiences. And we cannot assume that those particular women's literary constructions represent all that is possible in challenging and reconstructing the very structure of the literary disciplines. Instead, we must point toward the multiple and shifting nature of those voices, as well as many other women's voices who speak from varied and different positions of culture, race, class, ableness, or sexual orientation, for example. We must acknowledge those positions across various discourses which historically and currently constitute their lives in and out of schools, in and out of textbooks, in and out of curriculums.

Therefore, I want to read and reread my particular gendered curricular tale as a text of internalized social representations and constructions of myself as female; but, further, I want also to reread this tale as a text that portends multiple possibilities and shifting spaces in which to name myself in various ways and in relationship to contexts and contents that are both similar to and different from mine. And in those namings, I also might move into spaces that, rather than fixing my boundaries, could enable me to name myself anew as I forge fresh connections among the processes, contents, and experiencings called curriculum.

Thus, as woman, teacher, researcher, and writer who studies issues of curriculum, I still struggle to address the complex representations of gender, race, class, subjectivities, and multiple identities that inform and frame not only this particular tale but also its replications, for example, in that School of Education conference room. Even as I worked there to include my experiences of spring as part of curriculum conceptions that represent multiple divergences and similarities of individuals' experiences and contexts, I recognize that, for me, such conceptions first gained informal acknowledgment in John Brucker's sixth-grade class. That acknowledgment, although rendered as separate from our official sixth-grade course of study, still provided me with visions of possibilities for myself and for the ways in which I might understand my own and others' experiences and constructions of personal as well as "official" knowledges as aspects of curriculum. And so, while I still wonder what he might think of this particular curricular version of our sixth-grade year together, and how he might construct his own stories of that year, I no longer need John Brucker's permission to tell this particular tale.

Notes

1. Franklin Bobbitt, *How To Make a Curriculum* (Boston: Houghton Mifflin, 1924); W. W. Charters, *Curriculum Construction* (New York: Macmillan, 1923); Ralph W. Tyler, *Basic Principles of Curriculum and Instruction* (Chicago: University of Chicago Press, 1949).

2. Madeleine R. Grumet, "Autobiography and Reconceptualization," *Journal of Curriculum Theorizing* 2, no. 2 (1980): 155-158; idem, *Bitter Milk: Women and Teaching* (Amherst: University of Massachusetts Press, 1988); Janet L. Miller, "The Resistance of Women Academics: An Autobiographical Account," *Journal of Educational Equity and Leadership* 3, no. 2 (1983): 101-109; Jo Anne Pagano, *Exiles and Communities: Teaching in the Patriarchal Wilderness* (Albany: State University of New York Press, 1990); William F. Pinar, ed., *Heightened Consciousness, Cultural Revolution, and Curriculum Theory* (Berkeley, CA: McCutchan, 1974); idem, ed., *Curriculum Theorizing: The Reconceptualists* (Berkeley, CA: McCutchan, 1975); idem, " 'Whole, Bright, Deep with Understanding': Issues in Autobiographical Method and Qualitative Research," *Journal of Curriculum Studies* 13, no. 3 (1981): 173-188; idem, ed., *Contemporary Curriculum Discourses* (Scottsdale, AZ: Gorsuch Scarisbrick Publishers, 1988); William F. Pinar and Madeleine R. Grumet, *Toward a Poor Curriculum* (Dubuque, IA: Kendall/Hunt, 1976).

3. Jean Anyon, "Elementary Social Studies Textbooks and Legitimating Knowledge," *Theory and Research in Social Education* 6, no. 3 (1978): 40-55; Michael W. Apple, *Ideology and Curriculum* (Boston: Routledge and Kegan Paul, 1979); idem, *Education and Power* (Boston: Routledge and Kegan Paul, 1982); idem, *Teachers and Texts: A Political Economy of Class and Gender Relations in Education* (New York: Routledge and Kegan Paul, 1986); Henry Giroux, *Ideology, Culture, and the Process of Schooling* (Philadelphia, PA: Temple University Press, 1981); idem, *Theory and Resistance in Education: A Pedagogy for the Opposition* (South Hadley, MA: Bergin and Garvey, 1983); idem, *Border Crossings: Cultural Workers and the Politics of Education* (New York: Routledge, 1992); Linda McNeil, *Contradictions of Control: School Structure and School Knowledge* (New York: Routledge and Kegan Paul, 1986).

4. Madeleine R. Grumet, "The Politics of Personal Knowledge," *Curriculum Inquiry* 17, no. 3 (1987): 319-329; Magda Lewis, "Interrupting Patriarchy: Politics, Resistance, and Transformation in the Feminist Classroom," *Harvard Educational Review* 56 (1990): 457-472; Janet L. Miller, *Creating Spaces and Finding Voices: Teachers Collaborating for Empowerment* (Albany: State University of New York Press, 1990); Jo Anne Pagano, "Teaching Women," *Educational Theory* 38 (1988): 321-339.

5. Deborah P. Britzman, "Decentering Discourses in Teacher Education: Or, the Unleashing of Unpopular Things," *Journal of Education* 173, no. 3 (1991): 60-80; idem, *Practice Makes Practice: A Critical Study of Learning to Teach* (Albany: State University of New York Press, 1991); Elizabeth Ellsworth, "Why Doesn't This Feel Empowering? Working through the Repressive Myths of Critical Pedagogy," *Harvard Educational Review* 59 (1989): 297-324; idem, "I Pledge Allegiance: The Politics of Reading and Using Educational Films," *Curriculum Inquiry* 21, no. 1 (1991): 41-64; Michelle Fine, *Framing Dropouts: Notes on the Politics of an Urban High School* (Albany: State University of New York Press, 1991); Patti Lather, *Getting Smart: Feminist Research and Pedagogy with/in the Postmodern* (New York: Routledge, 1991); Magda Lewis and Roger I. Simon, "A Discourse Not Intended for Her: Learning and Teaching within Patriarchy," *Harvard Educational Review* 60 (1986): 467-488; Marilyn Orner, "Interrupting the Calls for Student Voice in 'Liberatory' Education: A Feminist Poststructuralist Perspective," in *Feminisms and Critical Pedagogy*, edited by Carmen Luke and Jennifer Gore (New York: Routledge, 1992); Lois Weis, ed., *Class, Race, and Gender in American Education* (Albany: State University of New York Press, 1988).

6. Judith Stacey, Susan Bereaud, and Joan Daniels, eds., *And Jill Came Tumbling After: Sexism in American Education* (New York: Dell, 1974); Marjorie B. U'ren, "The Image of Women in Textbooks," in *Woman in Sexist Society*, edited by Vivian Gornick and Barbara K. Moran (New York: Basic Books, 1971), pp. 318-328.

7. Myra Sadker and David Sadker, *Sex Equity Handbook for Schools* (New York: Longman, 1982); idem, "Is the O.K. Classroom O.K.?" *Phi Delta Kappan* 66 (1985): 358-361; idem, "Sexism in the Classroom: From Grade School to Graduate School," *Phi Delta Kappan* 68 (1986): 512; Myra Sadker, David Sadker, and Susan Klein, "The Issue of Gender in Elementary and Secondary Education," in *Review of Research in Education*, edited by Gerald Grant (Washington, DC: American Educational Research Association, 1991), pp. 269-334.

8. Jere Brophy and Thomas Good, *Teacher-Student Relationships: Causes and Consequences* (New York: Holt, Rinehart and Winston, 1974).

9. Linda A. Perry, Lynn H. Turner, and Helen M. Sterk, eds., *Constructing and Reconstructing Gender: The Links among Communication, Language, and Gender* (Albany: State University of New York Press, 1992).

10. Verdelle Freeman, "The Gender Integration Project at Piscataway Township Schools: Quilting a New Pedagogical Patchwork through Curriculum Revision," *Women's Studies Quarterly* 18 (1990): 70-77; Elizabeth Higginbotham, "Designing an Inclusive Curriculum: Bringing All Women into the Core," *Women's Studies Quarterly* 18 (1990): 7-23.

11. Susan Stanford Friedman, "Authority in the Feminist Classroom: A Contradiction in Terms?" in *Gendered Subjects: The Dynamics of Feminist Teaching*, edited by Margo Culley and Catherine Portuges (Boston: Routledge and Kegan Paul, 1985), pp. 203-208; Frances Maher, "Classroom Pedagogy and the New Scholarship on Women," in *Gendered Subjects: The Dynamics of Feminist Teaching*, edited by Margo Culley and Catherine Portuges (Boston: Routledge and Kegan Paul, 1985); Nancy Schniedewind, "Feminist Values: Guidelines for Teaching Methodology in Women's Studies," in *Freire for the Classroom: A Sourcebook for Liberatory Teaching*, edited by Ira Shor (Portsmouth, NH: Boynton/Cook Publishers, 1987), pp. 170-179.

12. Chris Kramarae and Paula A. Treichler, "Power Relationships in the Classroom," in *Gender in the Classroom: Power and Pedagogy,* edited by Susan L. Gabriel and Isaiah Smithson (Urbana: University of Illinois Press, 1990), pp. 41-59.

13. Britzman, *Practice Makes Practice*; Ellsworth, "Why Doesn't This Feel Empowering?"; Madeleine R. Grumet, "Retrospective: Autobiography and the Analysis of Educational Experience," *Cambridge Journal of Education* 20, no. 3 (1990): 321-326; Lewis, "Interrupting Patriarchy"; Janet L. Miller, "Exploring Power and Authority Issues in a Collaborative Research Project," *Theory Into Practice* 31, no. 2 (1992): 165-172.

14. Frances Maher, "Pedagogies for the Gender-balanced Classroom," *Journal of Thought* 20, no. 4 (1985): 49.

15. Joyce Antler and Sari Knopp Biklen, eds., *Changing Education: Women as Radicals and Conservators* (Albany: State University of New York Press, 1990); D. Jean Clandinin and F. Michael Connelly, "Teachers' Personal Practical Knowledge: What Counts as 'Personal' in Studies of the Personal?" *Journal of Curriculum Studies* 19, no. 6 (1987): 487-500; idem, "Narrative Experience and the Study of Curriculum," *Cambridge Journal of Education* 20, no. 3 (1990): 241-254; Elizabeth Ellsworth and Marilyn Orner, *Present But Not Here: Power and (Re)presentation in Education* (Albany: State University of New York Press, forthcoming); Robert J. Graham, *Autobiography in Education* (New York: Teachers College Press, 1992); Grumet, "Autobiography and Reconceptualization"; idem, "The Politics of Personal Knowledge"; Janet L. Miller, "Seeing *Guernica*," in *Reflections from the Heart of Educational Inquiry: Understanding Curriculum and Teaching through the Arts*, edited by William Schubert and George Willis (Albany: State University of New York, 1991), pp. 239-243; William H. Schubert and William C. Ayers, eds., *Teacher Lore: Learning from Our Own Experience* (New York: Longman, 1992).

16. Sandra Harding, ed., *Feminism and Methodology* (Bloomington: Indiana University Press, 1987).

17. Madeleine R. Grumet, "Women and Teaching: Homeless at Home," in *Contemporary Curriculum Discourses*, edited by William F. Pinar (Scottsdale, AZ: Gorsuch Scarisbrick Publishers, 1988), pp. 537-538.

18. Pagano, *Exiles and Communities*, pp. xiv-xvii.

Section Three
GENDER IN RESEARCH, ACHIEVEMENT, AND TECHNOLOGY

CHAPTER V

Equity Issues in Educational Research Methods

PATRICIA B. CAMPBELL AND SELMA GREENBERG

"Is it a boy or a girl?"

The answer to that question asked immediately after birth, or increasingly before birth, forms the basis for much of a person's life. The influence of gender, or people's expectations of gender, affects every aspect of one's life. This influence is equally strong for whites and people of color; however, the expectations and impacts may differ because gender is refracted through a prism of race.

Issues of gender, race, and their interaction have permeated research and research methods, especially in education and the social sciences. Gender and race have affected research as often by their absence as by their stereotypic or stylized presence.

With an increasing awareness of the impact of gender and race on research and researchers has come a reexamination of basic assumptions behind the very concept of research. Simultaneously, alternative research methodologies are increasing in number and popularity.

In this chapter we explore equity issues in educational research methods. We cover these issues and examine how a view of females and males as "opposite" challenges the legitimacy of using

---

Patricia B. Campbell is Director of Campbell-Kibler Associates, an educational consulting firm specializing in educational research and evaluation, with an emphasis on science and mathematics education and on issues of gender and ethnicity. Selma Greenberg is chairperson of the Department of Curriculum and Teaching, Hofstra University, Hempstead, N.Y.

"difference-based research" in studies of gender. We also consider ways that equity concerns are being addressed through the rethinking of the uses of traditional methods as well as the development of new methods.

An underlying premise of this chapter, a premise most strongly associated with present-day ethnographers, is that we are all influenced and biased by what we are, who we are, and what we believe. This is as true for the authors of this chapter as it is for anyone else. Both authors are white and have been feminists for many years. Patricia Campbell's work focuses on balancing research and advocacy in education and on making research accessible and usable to as wide a population as possible. She is particularly concerned about how gender issues interact with issues of race and class. Selma Greenberg's work has centered on examining the sexual myths and metaphors into which we are all socialized and which influence our lives and work.

The New Scholarship on Women

The many equity issues that have arisen in educational research since the 1960s are directly related to the emergence of the civil rights movement and the second wave of the feminist movement. The feminist scholar emerged after the feminist movement was in motion. "Amateurs" had begun to challenge scholarly theories and practices that resulted in women's alienation and denigration. Early feminists' epistemological moves were in large measure antitheoretical—the work of women who were often amateurs at analyzing and criticizing research and theory but who could tell a bad idea when they read one.

The early feminists' high level of general education and intelligence coupled with a sophisticated view of politics permitted them to see issues with more clarity than their more specially and narrowly trained sisters and brothers. The climate created by early feminists prompted women scholars to review major theories in their fields. The founding of a Special Interest Group (Research on Women in Education) in the American Educational Research Association (AERA) in the early 1970s signaled that such revisions had begun within the education community.

One consequence of these revisions was the finding that theory was inadequate and unhelpful at best and harmful and defamatory at worst. The creation of a body of evidence which casts doubt on the disinterestedness of theories in both the social and biological sciences is perhaps one of the greatest successes of feminist scholarship.

When early feminists asserted that mainstream gender research and theory served to create and maintain women's inequality they called into question the claims of objectivity and disinterestedness, which we had all been socialized to believe are the hallmarks of the "hard" sciences and the goals of the "softer" ones. The doubt cast on orthodox theories included the research methods as well as the content and conclusions of the research.

Thus, beginning in the 1970s new methods of doing research emerged. "Objectivity" having lost much of its power to enthrall, many scholars, especially women, began exploring ways of knowing that were more openly and admittedly subjective. "The personal is political," a feminist motto of the early 1970s, announced that the individual experiences of women needed to be seen as having a political context. Women scholars not only began to see research and theory as enmeshed in a political context but saw the importance of valuing the personal.

The new scholarship on women eschews the distancing of subject and researcher and the distrust of individual self-reported experiences. Rather, the researcher tends to "extend affection and esteem toward her subject, . . . to assume that women are sincere, not chatty fibbers of legend, but reliable witnesses of their own experience."[1]

Rather than separating the researcher and the subject, in this methodology researchers and subjects work in different ways to explore a truth they mutually create. Focusing on the experiences of individual women, these new methods look to phenomena embedded in context, putting women at the center of the inquiry. These methods involve a shortening of the distance between the observer and the observed and a consideration of the complex interactions of the two.

With the new scholarship on women came a series of methodologies and a way of thinking that can be combined with objective application of rules to produce better research—research that can provide insight into the complexity of women's lives and can be used to help us better understand the human condition. By looking at women we learn about women and we also learn about men.

The implications of the new scholarship on women are beginning to be felt in and out of research. In education, participant observation and qualitative research on such topics as women teachers' lives have brought out new information about education.[2] In both education and psychology, with the assistance of Gilligan,[3] we have begun to rethink what is meant by moral development and issues of justice and responsibility.

The challenge to conventional "ways of knowing" raised by feminists is echoed in current debates fueled by a growing body of academics who identify themselves as postmodernists. Mistrusting the entire body of knowledge developed through the positivist, rationalist, modern tradition, the postmodernists call into question the notion of an "objective" reality which gives up its "truths" to an "objective" observer in possession of the "right" techniques and tools. "Postmodernism accepts multiplicity, randomness, incoherence, indeterminacy and paradox which positivist paradigms are designed to exclude. Postmodernism creates distance from seemingly fixed language of established meanings and fosters skepticism about the fixed nature of reality."[4]

Early feminists' work was antitheoretical as was much of academic women's scholarship. Yet, from the start, the hope has been that discredited theories would be replaced by theories of human evolution, association, culture, development, socialization, growth, education, and behavior that are formed and reformed by the insights, experience, and perspectives of people of both sexes and many races.

Bias in the Application of Research Methods

The new scholarship grew out of a dissatisfaction with traditional research methodologies and their emphasis on objectivity. As early as the 1740s, wise women and men were aware that research and researchers were not objective and "value free."[5] More than 240 years later, it was still being said that "it's about time we outgrew the notion that science is value free."[6]

The subjectivity of researchers and the impact of their beliefs on their work is still an issue to be addressed. Who we are and what we believe influences what we study, how we study it, and even what we conclude from our results and the results of others.

Our gender and ethnic or racial background are important components of who we are and affect our work and our findings. For example, an analysis of 148 studies on how people are influenced found male researchers were more apt than female researchers to find women more easily influenced than men. Similar results were found in studies of people's skills in understanding nonverbal behavior. Female researchers were more apt than male researchers to find women better at decoding nonverbal behavior.[7]

While there are great similarities in the research topics covered by women and by men, most of the researchers working on topics directly related to women and girls are women.[8] Whites are equally as apt as people of color to do research on racial issues;[9] however, the data they collect may be different.

In qualitative research the impact of "who the researcher is" is even greater. The traditional concern for bias in qualitative research has been how to render the work of the single onlooker as "objective" as possible. Stratagems and devices have been offered to reduce the participant researcher's "subjectivity." In the postmodern world, objectivity has lost not only its charm but its prestige. No longer is it held that there is a "truth" out there to be revealed by those with the best tools. Rather it is thought that we construct ourselves and our world in interaction, that we learn much about ourselves when we do research, and that each view is partial. Thus, as researchers our responsibility is to label ourselves as best we can and provide readers with a description of ourselves, which of necessity is incomplete. We are not aware of how our status influences our perceptions; we simply don't know. As Geis et al. explained, "Our experience of perception is actually an interpretation of reality in terms of meaning supplied by our own previous beliefs and values. The process of interpretation is unconscious. The product is perception."[10] This concept of research as a collection of personal, partial descriptions of self-referenced reality is particularly problematic when we look at who the researchers are.

WHO ARE THE RESEARCHERS?

Most researchers in education are white and male. A 1982 survey of educational researchers found 60 percent of them were male and 88 percent were white.[11] A more recent survey of the membership of the American Educational Research Association (AERA) found 53 percent of the members were male and 88 percent were white.[12]

A look at recipients of doctoral degrees in education, who are most likely to do educational research, shows a somewhat similar pattern. Although education is a field stereotypically labeled as female, as late as 1977-78 most (60 percent) doctorates in education were earned by men. However, there has been some change. By 1988-89, when women were earning 36.5 percent of all doctorates, they were earning 57 percent of the doctorates in education. About 30 percent of all the doctorates earned by women are in education.[13]

While the percent of all women being trained in educational research through doctoral study has increased, the percent of doctoral degrees earned by blacks in education has decreased from 9 percent in

1976-77 to 8 percent in 1988-89.[14] As too often happens, the data have not been broken down by gender and ethnicity. Therefore we cannot explore the pattern in education for minority women.

Not only are more educational researchers white men; white male researchers tend to publish more than women.[15] Although women make up 48 percent of the major presenters at annual meetings of AERA, women are only 31 percent of those whose work appears in AERA publications.[16] The AERA "Annual Report" for 1988-89 gives the number of minority authors in AERA publications but does not give a breakdown of that number by sex. However, in 1988-89, the total number of minority authors in AERA publications was ten (4 percent) out of a total of 236 authors.[17] It is thus clear that the number of minority authors who were women was very small.

Along with being more likely than women to publish and present, white men are more apt to be those who make decisions about what research is published or funded. For example, in 1988-89 six of the ten editors of AERA publications were men, all of whom were white. Of the eighty-one members of AERA editorial boards, fifty-six (69 percent) were men. Seventy-one members (88 percent) of these boards were white.[18] Similar patterns have been found in other professional organizations.[19]

WHAT RESEARCH IS DONE?

The small and decreasing number of researchers of color has implications for both qualitative and quantitative research, but the most serious implications are for qualitative research. If qualitative researchers can only view research from the perspective of who and what they are, and if all of them are white and middle-class, then they provide the only research lens through which education is viewed.

When the researcher and the researched come from groups that differ in power and status, there are serious implications for the research that is done. And when most researchers are male while most practitioners (i.e., teachers) are female and when the percent of people of color who are teachers far exceeds the percent of people of color who are researchers, there are differences in power and status.

This practitioner/researcher status differential is not found in other fields such as medicine and the law where research rarely focuses on the attitudes, knowledge, and abilities of its practitioners. Rather it seeks to find and solve issues identified as problems in the field. Research serves as a support service for those engaged in practice. While educational research often serves this function, it also emphasizes studies of the attitudes, knowledge, and abilities of those engaged in practice. Through quantitative studies such as analyses of classroom interaction and ethnographic studies of teachers' classroom expectations, teachers—what they do and how well they do it—have been a major research focus.

Thus educational researchers serve a surveillance function with the powerful, predominantly white and male researchers watching over the predominantly female, more ethnically diverse practitioners. The result is a lack of practitioners' trust of researchers and, by extension, of research, along with a distancing of practitioners from the research process and from decision making in research. This distancing limits what research is done as well as the degree to which research is used by practitioners. Campbell observes that this "model of a (male) expert coming in to collect data from and about the (female) practitioner and then to tell her what to do to improve practice follows a sexist practice used in so many aspects of our lives."[20] Some researchers who are concerned about these matters are attempting to do research with teachers, to work "in collaborative and reciprocal ways within unequal power relationships."[21]

Issues of power and gender are associated with what research is done in other ways as well. For many years, topics such as "math anxiety" and informal support networks were considered "women's issues" of little value and rarely examined. Even today when these topics are covered, it is frequently from a perspective based on limited ideas of the roles women and men should play.

The situation is especially bleak regarding research on both race and gender. Hull, Scott, and Smith conclude that an "intellectual void" exists among social science scholars concerning the life experiences of black women,[22] while Scott-Jones and Clark report that there are even fewer data about women and girls from other racial groups.[23]

A lack of interest in research on women can lead to such inappropriate research as a 1990 study of school spending and financial success that studied only men,[24] and to the exclusion of girls' experiences in the development of psychological categories such as "identity" and in the building of educational and psychological theory.[25] In addition, as recently as 1980, the editors of the *Handbook on Adolescent Psychology* announced that there was not enough research on adolescent women to warrant a chapter, even a short one.[26]

Even when research is done on white women and on women and men of color, it frequently focuses on them as deviant or as victims.

For example, researchers have asked: "Are women feminizing our schools?" but not "Are men masculinizing our schools?" And they have asked, "What are the negative effects of maternal employment on children's academic achievement?" instead of "What are the positive effects of increased family income and maternal intellectual stimulation on children's academic achievement?"[27]

Certainly the interests of sponsoring organizations have an impact on what research is done. The U.S. Department of Education, the largest funder of educational research, has no program devoted to research on women and girls. The only federal education program specifically related to women and girls, the Women's Educational Equity Act Program, was budgeted for fiscal year 1992 at $500,000, which is less than half the cost of a Patriot missile. Thus not only are most researchers white men, but most of the research funded, undertaken, and published is on topics of interest to white men.[28]

WHO IS STUDIED?

White men have traditionally been the population studied in research related to the development of social science and of educational theory and practice. From the results of these studies of white men, generalizations are made to "humanity" in all of its bi-gender, multicultural, and multiracial diversity. An analysis of samples in research published in education and social science journals found that 22 percent of the articles did not even give the sex of those studied; almost half of the articles that noted their subjects' sex reported studies of one sex, most frequently male.[29] While the number of single-sex studies has been reduced, they are still being done and the sex most likely to be studied is still male.[30] In addition, most longitudinal studies that began by collecting information on men and boys have not been updated to include women and girls.[31]

A somewhat different pattern appears for people of color. While there have been a number of studies of "minority issues," people of color are rarely included in studies of human behavior. Indeed, most of these studies do not even mention the racial breakdown of their subjects; however, we have found that the subjects in those studies are white.

Yet again the situation is worse when sex is considered together with race and ethnicity. For example, in their summary of the research on sex- and ethnic-related differences in mathematics for students in grades four to eight, Lockheed and others found thirty-one studies that addressed sex differences, sixteen that addressed ethnic differences, and only six that simultaneously examined differences related to sex and ethnicity.[32] Yet very often meaningful results can only be found when the interaction of gender and race/ethnicity is studied. For example, in the studies of suggestibility mentioned earlier the subjects were predominantly white. In studies that included black and white women and men, white women were found to be more suggestible than men while black women were less.[33]

Although most samples do not include girls and boys from a variety of racial or ethnic groups, researchers' conclusions sometimes include references to whole groups; for example, a conclusion might read "these data suggest for dyslexic children . . ." even though only boys were studied and no information about race was included.[34] One survey found that in over 90 percent of educational research studies the results were overgeneralized.[35]

One might question why researchers would use single-sex samples to study aspects of the human condition. In a 1974 study examining this issue, researchers gave three major reasons for working only with subjects of one sex: (1) scientific, (2) practical, and (3) extrascientific.[36] Scientific reasons given were that gender differences were known to exist in the phenomena and the investigator did not wish to explore them, or the theory being studied was restricted to one sex. The sex of those who were available to be studied and the need to keep the number of subjects "reasonable" were given as practical reasons. Extrascientific reasons were that the use of one sex reduced the variability of the data and that the experiment "favored" the use of one sex.

Nearly twenty years later researchers are still using the same excuses. In 1990, National Institute of Health researchers explained that the reason their major studies on heart attacks included men only was that it was too hard to find women with heart problems and that women would "complicate" the study.[37]

Broadening research communities to include both sexes and members of many ethnic and racial groups could stimulate the asking of different questions, encourage the study of more inclusive groups, and prevent the extrapolation to humankind of results gathered in studies of a few white males.

HOW IS RESEARCH DONE?

When research is done on women and girls, it is frequently not used in the design of other studies. Consider, for example, the following findings:

1. Boys have been found to exhibit more antisocial behaviors when an adult is present; girls' behavior does not change.[38] Studies of gender differences in behavior that ignore this information can lead to inaccurate conclusions and a reinforcing of stereotypes about boys' behavior.

2. Boys tend to perform better when someone is watching; girls tend to perform better in cooperative situations than in competitive ones, and both sexes tend to act more stereotypically in the presence of adults.[39] Studies with adult observers or studies using competitive testing that do not account for these findings will not be accurate. Not controlling for such findings, particularly in studies of gender differences, means that what is being studied is more apt to be some combination of the testing procedure and sex.

The decision as to which standardized test is used in research can also influence the results. Forty years ago it was found that differences in the intelligence test scores of bilingual students and Spanish-dominant students were much reduced when nonverbal IQ tests were substituted for verbal IQ tests.[40] Much more recently, we learned that gender differences in mathematics were significant if the Scholastic Aptitude Test: Math (SAT:M) was used but were minimal or nonexistent if the School and College Aptitude Test-Quantitative (SCAT—Q) was used.[41] Indeed, the New York State courts found that scores on the SAT:M were biased against women students and held that the New York State Department of Education would have to find another way to award state scholarships.[42]

Research suggests that girls do better on test items dealing with "stereotypically feminine" topics than on "stereotypically masculine" items covering the same skills. Tests, particularly achievement tests, have generally included more "stereotypically masculine" than "stereotypically feminine" topics, thus negatively influencing girls' scores.[43] Depending on such variables as the skill areas tested, the context in which test items are set (i.e., a birthday party or a football game), and the type of test item (i.e., a multiple-choice or an essay question), gender differences can be created or eliminated.[44]

Examples of biased testing include:

1. A test that measures "need to achieve" by asking subjects to make up stories about pictures shown to them. Girls' lower number of achievement-oriented stories about females is seen as evidence of girls' lower need to achieve, rather than as an awareness that girls and women as a group are not generally permitted to achieve in our society.[45]

2. Measures of children at play that do not take clothing into consideration. Otherwise studies of children at play might in reality be measuring differences in playing in dresses and playing in pants.[46]

3. Observations that can be affected by bias. Studies in which some observers were told they were observing a little boy and others were told the same child was a girl found the perceived sex of the child affected the observers' response.[47]

WHAT CONCLUSIONS ARE GENERATED?

Yet again we come back to the influence of researchers' beliefs and expectations. These can influence the interpretation of results, often to a greater degree than the data themselves. This is a problem that has been with us for hundreds of years. In the eighteenth century, Charles Babbage concluded that "if one hundred observations are made, the cook must be very unlucky if he [sic] cannot pick out fifteen or twenty which will do for serving up."[48] Two hundred years later, Lather's recommendation that "finding only what one is predisposed to look for in one's empirical work must be transcended" indicates that this problem too is still with us.[49]

This predisposition to search for data to support one's beliefs, holds for readers and reviewers of research as well as for researchers themselves. Broad and Wade reported that identical manuscripts suffered different fates based on the reviewers' agreement or disagreement with the results. When an error was introduced into the manuscripts, 25 percent of the reviewers who agreed with results found it versus 71 percent of the reviewers who disagreed with the results.[50] Gould reported that the urge to believe that with which one agrees is so strong that even in his own work exposing the "social embeddedness of science and the frequent grafting of expectation upon supposed objectivity," he reported an inconsistent error because it " 'felt' right and I never checked it."[51] Gould has a great deal more self-awareness than do most of us.

In their report of the impact of reviewer belief on the finding of research error, Broad and Wade uncritically used Rosenthal and Jacobson's work on expectation effects to support their results,[52] although the Rosenthal and Jacobson work has been heavily criticized by researchers who have not been able to replicate their results.[53] Even when one is studying bias, bias gets in the way.

Cultural myths and stereotypes set up and reinforce expectations that influence us as researchers as well as people. As Fausto-Sterling explains: "In analyzing male/female differences these scientists peer through the prism of everyday culture . . . to highlight their questions, design their experiments, and interpret their results."[54] And, of course, as Harding reminds us, the cultural beliefs and behaviors of researchers one might classify as "feminist" shape their research and the results of that research no less than do those of researchers considered "sexist."[55]

As a result, in research related to sex and to race, researchers have difficulty in acknowledging results that do not fit their preconceived stereotypes.[56] One often repeated technique is to compare black women to white women or to black men to show how well they are doing. Thus it is accurately reported that in 1988-89 black women earned 54 percent of all the doctorates earned by blacks.[57] However, the conclusions suggested by that statistic are very different from those generated from the equally accurate figures showing that in 1988-89 black women earned .016 percent of all doctorates awarded.

Other examples include researchers who were so sure of male superiority in areas such as mathematics and spatial skills that they concluded such a superiority existed even when no differences were found in the data.[58] One study of gender differences in mathematics concluded that girls were more apt than boys to make mistakes in mathematics even though a table on the same page showed no significant differences.[59] Similarly, Armstrong concluded "sex differences in achievement for the twelfth grade sample favored males on all four subtests, but the only statistically significant difference was in the problem-solving test."[60] Based on her results Armstrong could, and perhaps should, have said that no significant differences were found between females and males in tests of spatial visualization, algebra, and computation, and that only on the subtest on problem solving was there a significant difference favoring males. Similarly, a variety of researchers on reading have concluded that studies were flawed if sex differences favoring girls were not found.[61]

In their analysis of research on gender differences, Petersen, Crockett, and Tobin-Richards saw the lack of researcher objectivity as such a serious problem that they concluded "research attempting to prove one sex superior over the other or to prove there is no difference between males and females cannot be considered objective science."[62]

Difference-Based Research

Bias goes beyond the application of research methods to the methods themselves. Educational researchers tend to look at groups in terms of how they differ. Studies of the use of statistics in research reported in educational research journals consistently rank "difference-based" analysis of variance/covariance as the most frequently used statistic.[63] So mired in statistics of difference is our research, so committed are we to the notion that only studies that demonstrate differences are worthwhile, that statisticians and methodologists caution against desperate searches for differences in order to salvage a study.[64] It is not difficult to see how easily this observation applies to those who with equal desperation search for racial differences.

THE IMPACT OF THE NULL HYPOTHESIS

This emphasis on differences, desperate or not, grows out of the use of the null hypothesis (the hypothesis of no difference) as the basis for much of the statistical testing underlying quantitative educational research. In education and social science research we seek to "prove" our hypothesis that there are differences (or relationships) in some variables among some groups by positing a hypothesis of no difference and seeking to disprove it.

The null hypothesis is rejected when statistically significant differences are found. However, if no significant differences are found the null hypothesis fails to be rejected. Failing to reject the null hypothesis does not mean there are no differences between groups. It means that the probability that any differences found are due to error or to chance is too high to be acceptable. Thus, when you find significant differences you have something; if you don't find significant differences, you don't know what you have.

There are several flaws with this process. Indeed Ehrenberg calls it a game that researchers use to prove themselves scientific.[65] It is also a game that means that our best efforts are not used to test, challenge, or disprove our beliefs but are used to buttress or support our beliefs. Since Sir Frances Bacon, scientists have wanted to know not what proves your hypothesis but what disproves it. In the physical sciences it is generally believed that scientific knowledge advances only by disproof. In linguistics, too, a rule is proposed and then a search is made for counterexamples which are used to refine the rule.[66] In archeology "a hypothesis is said to be corroborated when it has survived serious attempts at falsification."[67] But in education and social science research, we don't try to disprove theories or hypotheses. Instead, we try to disprove null hypotheses, the opposite of what we believe, in order to prove that which we believe.

The use of the null hypothesis means that too often educational research becomes a search for differences and a search for reinforcement of our own beliefs. Research designs and statistical analyses are slanted toward the search for differences and so are researchers and reviewers. Because of the bias of social science and educational research, a finding of no differences is insignificant and is not to be taken seriously. Tresemer reports that there is a "great iceberg of studies unpublished because of their 'insignificant' findings."[68] Studies with significant differences are more likely to be submitted for publication and to be published.[69] As Spender explains, convention favors the publication of "successful" experiments, those in which differences are found.[70] Moreover, these "successful" studies are even more likely to be finished! Researchers whose preliminary work on a study reveals no significant differences are far more likely to give up their study than those who find significant differences early in their analyses of data.[71]

Studies of differences are appropriate when what is being studied is a particular treatment, where the issue is "what's better and what's worse?" They are inappropriate when we are exploring the similarities and differences between females and males or when we are studying people in their complexities.

DIFFERENCES AND GENDER DIFFERENCES

In studies of females and males, the dependence on differences is so great that the entire area of study is called "sex differences." The study of sex (or gender) differences has become a valid field of inquiry—research is done, books and articles are written, and conclusions are drawn, all based on differences.[72]

Sex, or gender, similarities are not studied; even the term sounds a little strange. Yet Tresemer feels that the major misleading assumption in research on females and males is "that differences between the sexes are more important than similarities, that the trait of masculinity-femininity is a bipolar, unidimensional, continuous, normally distributed variable that is highly important and consistently viewed."[73] As Spender concludes,

> [W]hile it is perfectly possible that many researchers are finding that there is NO DIFFERENCE between the sexes on many linguistic—or other—items (that is, that their performance can be construed as "equal"), knowledge of sex "differences" which frequently portrays women as deficient is still constructed and disseminated by some academic journals. . . . The

conceptualization of the sexes as different—rather than similar or the same—is reinforced and perpetuated through publication.[74]

The effects of these findings of differences are far from innocent. Differences are too often read as indicants of superiority and deficiency and it is most often the women who are believed to embody the deficiencies. Spender explains:

> Within . . . a framework of female deficiency . . . it becomes very difficult to have findings of "no difference" reported in the literature, because if the purpose of research is to find where females are deficient, and the deficiency cannot be located, then the experiment can be classified as a failure (rather than as a "breakthrough" to a reconceptualization of the problem). And it seems that few failures are reported in the literature, certainly in relation to the social sciences. It is *success* which is favored among the gatekeepers.[75]

There are political reasons for wanting, or not wanting, the inclusion of studies of no difference as well. A finding of no difference can be used to refute the argument that women are not as good as men in mathematics, administration, or whatever.

The overemphasis on differences, and the use of the concept of bipolarity of "female" and "male" characteristics, means that even small differences are reported and exaggerated. Tresemer feels that "this is the most dangerous use of statistics and leads to inappropriate generalizations such as 'men are instrumental, women are expressive'."[76]

The constant research reinforcement of the concept of females and males as opposite is made more egregious by the implication that female/male is a dichotomous notion. Let us look for a moment at the concept of aggression, a trait favored by researchers because it is supposed to be gender specific. The perception has been formed that all males are more aggressive than all females.

Even in an area of "large" gender differences, such as aggression, there is a large degree of overlap of female and male aggressiveness. Meta-analysis of studies of physical and verbal aggression found that there are many females who are more aggressive than many males. The differences within each sex are much greater than those between the sexes.[77] This is true in all affective and cognitive areas. Even in areas such as social behavior, meta-analysis found that gender accounted for only between 5 and 10 percent of the variance.[78]

The easy inevitability of research groupings by sex and/or race where questions of differences or superiority/inferiority are concerned reveals an interesting pattern. First, a difference is observed and described. (Females tend to be more skilled at small muscle manipulations than males.) Next, the post hoc fallacy comes into play and these correlational differences are seen as being caused by sex. (Females do better at small muscle manipulations *because* they are female.) Overgeneralization and the assumption of "oppositeness" follows. (All females are better in small muscle manipulation than all males.) Finally, this original observation becomes normative. (A female who is not better than males in small motor manipulation is abnormal.)

An overemphasis on differences causes much to be lost. While there are many ways human beings are different, there are even more ways in which we are alike. When research looks only at differences, the focus is on that which divides. The commonalities are not examined or even acknowledged. Thus we tend to ignore that which brings us together and focus instead on that which divides.

Critics of difference-based research suspect the basic intent of this body of work. They suggest that the desperate search for sex differences is desperate beyond the need to produce "significant research." Since females and males receive different treatment in the world, through some tortured logic the ability to prove differences between women and men is then seen as justification of this differential treatment.

Many researchers realize the limitations of using a difference-based research method when studying women and men. Petersen, Crockett, and Tobin-Richards acknowledge that "simply finding a difference between males and females . . . has no inherent value."[79] Fausto-Sterling believes that Maccoby and Jacklin, in their classic 1974 book, *The Psychology of Sex Differences*, "are perfectly aware that the frequent inability to find any differences (in male/female verbal skills) could be quite important."[80] Maccoby and Jacklin and Fausto-Sterling were aware of the limitations of the methodologies used and thus of the importance and ambiguities of repeated findings of no significant differences.

Tresemer went further by challenging the assumption that gender differences are more important than similarities.[81] He maintains that "attention to the relative size of an effect is necessary if we are to replace the either-or nature of current arguments about sex differences with a sense of proportion." Harding, taking that next step, concluded that "the orthodox methods of studying and interpreting sex differences were capable of delivering only mischievous and misleading trivia."[82]

DIFFERENCES AND SIMILARITIES

Greenberg agrees with Harding's conclusion. Analyzing studies of gender and race differences, Greenberg reminds us that "when we look for race or gender differences we clearly are not dealing with one large group that we can divide randomly into two or more groups. People are not randomly assigned to race and sex/gender. More importantly people believe that female and male are not similar, but are different, are 'opposite'."[83]

Insurance companies have always assumed an underlying difference rather than similarity in sex in terms of insurance tables. In their classic study, Broverman, Broverman, Clarkston, Rosencrantz, and Fogel found that people believe males and females are separate and different, not drawn from the same population.[84] Greenberg further points out that, in regard to females and males, it is the similarities not the differences that are startling.[85] In sports the big news was that runners such as Florence Griffen Joyner and Joan Benoit Samuelson were coming close to the men's records, not that the records were different.

Knowing this, Greenberg turns around the paradigm of difference-based research and asks "Of what use is the null hypothesis which requires the assumption of similarity at the beginning in order to give meaning to a difference produced at the end? If you begin with a belief in difference, similarities are what might be thought of as interesting."[86]

Why Is Change Occurring?

Analysis of the impact of sex bias on research and research methods and the new scholarship on women has generated awareness and has received a degree of acceptance from mainstream publications. For example, both the *Phi Delta Kappan* and the *Educational Researcher* have had special issues on the new scholarship on women.[87] However, comparable development, attention, and acceptance have not occurred in research focusing on minorities.

Why have researchers of women and of issues related to gender, unlike those working in other equity areas, gone on to form a new method of research? One answer to this queston can be found in numbers. As indicated earlier, 40 percent of educational researchers are women while 12 percent are women and men of color.[88] Absolute numbers can make a difference. While change is a process made first by individuals and then by institutions, a number of individuals must change before the institutions do. For example, it was not until a substantial number of women were active in the humanities and social sciences that the feminist perspective was felt and transformations in those disciplines occurred.[89]

Power is also an answer. In research communities, women appear to have greater political power than do minorities. Thirty-six percent of the white male educational researchers had positions at the highest levels (e.g., directors, principal investigators) compared to 16 percent of the white females and 3 percent of black researchers of either sex.[90] In the past ten years, there have been three white women presidents of the American Educational Research Association and no minority presidents of either sex.

Another aspect of power can be found in who is doing the research on women and on minorities. Those at higher salary levels have been found to be more apt to do research on issues related to gender than those with lower salaries. Researchers on issues related to gender regularly spent more time doing research than did others.[91] In addition, most researchers working on issues related to gender are women, but most researchers of minority issues are white.

Women are part of the mainstream power structure but at the same time are not of it. This contradiction of belonging and not belonging, of being immersed and yet estranged, develops a personal tension that informs critical dialogue.[92] The combination of being both on the inside and on the outside may help in terms of the development and, perhaps more importantly, the acceptance of new methodologies.

Recently there appears to be a greater willingness on the part of those in power to accept and acknowledge issues related to women and to sex. The American Educational Research Association has adopted guidelines to reduce sex and race bias in research; however, other social science organizations have addressed only issues of sex bias in research in their guidelines.[93]

A variety of private and public agencies are funding efforts to integrate the results of the new scholarship on women in such diverse colleges and universities as the University of Arizona, Colgate, Duke, Memphis State, Spelman, and Wheaton. The relationship between gender roles and science are being explored at over forty universities. Even at Yale, long a bastion of male supremacy, over 750 students take women's studies courses.[94]

This willingness to accept the new scholarship on women may also be related to its perceived support of gender role stereotypes.

While our society has grown impatient with the notion of racial differences, the notion of "opposite sex" continues to permeate discussions of women and men. Since the mid-1970s two separate strands of scholarship on women have developed. One has the goal of "de-emphasizing differences by sorting out genuine male-female differences from stereotypes" while the other "takes as its goal the reaffirmation of gender differences."[95] Gilligan's work on moral development, which asserts differences between male and female approaches to moral issues, is an example of the second orientation.[96] While some feminists see this as listening to the previously silenced voices of women, other feminists see it as both reinforcing stereotypes and once again presenting women as monolithic. And as Unger questions, can any human group "be said to speak in a different voice?"[97]

Infusing Equity in Research

We suggest here a number of things researchers can do to make their research more equitable, whether they use methods developed from the new scholarship on women or more traditional methodologies. We then also offer suggestions for readers of research to call their attention to possibilities of bias.

SUGGESTIONS FOR RESEARCHERS

1. *Acknowledge your biases.* Researchers should follow the advice of Fausto-Sterling to "articulate, both to themselves and publicly, exactly where they stand, what they think and most importantly, what they feel deep down in their guts about the complex of personal and social issues that relate to their area of research."[98]

2. *Account for possible confounding variables in the research design.* The research design should account for confounding variables related to the gender of the subjects as well as to other demographic variables such as age, race/ethnicity, or socioeconomic status. Independent variables that define one group in terms of another, such as basing a woman's socioeconomic status on that of her husband or father, should not be used.

3. *When researching issues of gender using quantitative methods, use statistics that compute the amount of variance accounted for by gender rather than just computing differences.* Based on the statistics used, the results can be quite different, even when the statistics are used on the same data. For example, when analysis of variance was done on scores of 10,000 students on a test of reading achievement, a difference favoring

males over females, significant at the .001 level, was found. When regression was used on the same data to determine the relationship between subjects' sex and scores on the test, it was found that the sex of the subjects accounted for less than 1 percent of the variance in reading achievement scores.[99] The first results found a difference between the sexes, while the second provided an idea of the relative importance of that difference.

4. *Search for similarities as well as differences.* For researchers using quantitative research methods, ways of computing similarities include: (a) "counting" the number of scores in common and computing a percentage; (b) computing the percentage of overlap within plus or minus two pooled standard deviations from the pooled mean; and (c) using calculus to compute the common area under the two distributions.

5. *Include females and males from different ethnic groups in samples unless there is a demonstrable rationale for not doing so.* Researchers should include white women and women of color in the development and testing of models rather than using them, post hoc, to investigate how well they fit existing models devised from white male samples. If samples are not multiracial or do not include females and males, then a justification for the makeup of the sample should be made and the results should *not* be generalized to groups not represented in the sample. A sample's demographic characteristics, including gender and race/ethnicity, should always be described in any report of the research.

6. *Use tests and measures that are as unbiased as possible.* Researchers should check for bias in any measures used including tests, questionnaires, observation schedules, and interviews. In developing or selecting measures for research, researchers should avoid measures that (a) use exclusionary language or other offensive language or questions; (b) do not include materials relevant to females of different races or ethnicity; and (c) give no evidence of validity for the individual groups being tested.

7. *Reference the conclusions directly to the results of the study.* In quantitative research, nonsignificant differences should not be reported as differences. When significant differences are found, all possible explanations for the differences should be considered.

SUGGESTIONS FOR READERS OF RESEARCH

Readers of research should evaluate studies for bias. At a very basic level, the following questions can be asked about research:

1. Can you discern the author's opinions or biases? For example, a study to determine the *negative* influence of mothers' employment on children's achievement clearly suggests the author's bias.

2. Do authors use different words depending on the sex and race of those being studied? For example, if studies of father absence are labeled "father absence" while studies of mother absence are labeled "maternal deprivation," bias is present.

3. Are the tests used "fair"? Does the study indicate whether the tests were developed and tested over females and males from a variety of racial and ethnic backgrounds?

4. Does the study describe the sex and race/ethnicity of those being studied?

5. Are the results of the study applied only to people like those being studied or are they overgeneralized to include others?

6. In studies comparing groups, are similarities as well as differences reported?

7. Are the conclusions based on the author's results or on the author's expectations?

Biased research has provided ammunition denying women access to higher education in the nineteenth century and equal access to scholarships in the twentieth century.[100] However, nonbiased research has had an influence on policy and practice as well, fueling efforts to change curriculum,[101] encourage girls in mathematics and science,[102] and increase the numbers and roles of women in educational administration.[103]

Educational research and related equity issues are at a turning point. While the influence of gender, or people's expectations of gender, affects every aspect of research, we can increase awareness of that influence and balance its negative effects.

Notes

1. Catherine Stimpson, "The New Scholarship about Women: The State of the Art," *Annals of Scholarship* 2 (1980): 5.

2. Sari Biklen, "I Have Always Worked: Elementary School Teaching as a Career," *Phi Delta Kappan* 67, no. 7 (1986): 504-508.

3. Carol Gilligan, *In a Different Voice* (Cambridge, MA: Harvard University Press, 1980).

4. Rachel Hare-Mustin and Jeanne Marecek, "Gender and the Meaning of Difference: Postmodernism and Psychology," in *Making a Difference*, edited by Rachel Hare-Mustin and Jeanne Marecek (New Haven: Yale University Press, 1990), p. 56.

5. Isaac W. Watts, *Improvement of the Mind* (Groton, MA: Helfant Publishing Company, 1741). Reprinted in 1987.

6. Maurice Tatsuoka, "Statistical Methods," in *Encyclopedia of Educational Research*, edited by Harold Mitzel (New York: Macmillan, 1982), p. 1782.

7. Alice Eagly and Linda L. Carli, "Sex of Researchers and Sex-typed Communications as Determinants of Sex Differences in Influenceability: A Meta-analysis of Social Influence Studies," *Psychological Bulletin* 90 (1981): 1-20.

8. Patricia B. Campbell and Mary V. Brown, *Surveying the Status of Educational Researchers* (Washington, DC: National Institute of Education, 1982).

9. Ibid.

10. Florence L. Geis et al., *Women's Educational Equity Act Program* (Newark, NJ: Office of Women's Affairs, 1982), p. 2.

11. Campbell and Brown, *Surveying the Status of Educational Researchers.*

12. American Educational Research Association, "Annual Report, 1988-1989," *Educational Researcher* 18, no. 6 (1989), table 1, p. 20.

13. National Center for Education Statistics, *Digest of Education Statistics, 1990* (Washington, DC: National Center for Education Statistics, 1991), table 250, p. 271.

14. Ibid., table 274, p. 285.

15. Dwight G. Dean, "Structural Constraints and the Publication Dilemma: A Review and Some Proposals," *American Sociologist* 20 (1989): 181-187.

16. American Educational Research Association, "Annual Report," table 2, p. 31.

17. Ibid.

18. Ibid.

19. Lee K. Nicoloff and Linda Forrest, "Gender Issues in Research and Publication," *Journal of College Student Development* 29 (1988): 521-528; Caroline Persell, "Gender, Rewards, and Research in Education," *Psychology of Women Quarterly* 8 (1983); 33-47.

20. Patricia B. Campbell, "Researchers and Practitioners Talk to Each Other about K-12 Education: Applied Research" (Paper presented at the annual meeting of the AERA Special Interest Group: Research on Women in Education, Hempstead, NY, 1989), p. 1.

21. Janet L. Miller, "Breaking Forms and Authority in Academic and Feminist Discourse" (Paper presented at the annual conference on Curriculum Theorizing, Bergamo, Ohio, 1990), p. 2.

22. Gloria Hull, Patricia B. Scott, and Barbara Smith, *But Some of Us Are Brave* (New York: Harper and Row, 1982).

23. Diane Scott-Jones and Maxine Clark, "The School Experiences of Black Girls: The Interaction of Gender, Race, and Socioeconomic Status," *Phi Delta Kappan* 67 (1986): 520-526.

24. David E. Card and Allan B. Kruger, *Does School Quality Matter? Returns to Education and the Characteristics of Public Schools in the United States* (Cambridge, MA: National Bureau of Economic Research, 1990).

25. Nora Lyons, "Listening to the Voices We Have Not Heard," in *Making Connections: The Relational Worlds of Adolescent Girls at Emma Willard School*, edited by Carol Gilligan, Nora Lyons and T. Hanmer (Troy, NY: Emma Willard School, 1989), pp. 30-72.

26. Carol Gilligan, "Changing the Questions: Women's Studies and Psychological Development" (Inaugural speech of the Edith Blanche and Irving Laurie New Jersey Chair in Women's Studies, Douglass College, Rutgers University, New Brunswick, NJ, 1986).

27. Patricia B. Campbell, *The Hidden Discriminator*, Monograph and Pamphlet Series (Newton, MA: WEEAP Publishing Center, Education Development Center, 1989), p. 8.

28. Patricia B. Campbell, "Educational Equity and Research Paradigms," in *Equity in Education*, edited by Walter Secada (London: Falmer Press, 1989), pp. 26-42.

29. Patricia B. Campbell, *The Impact of Societal Biases on Research* (Washington, DC: National Institute of Education, 1981).

30. Kathryn Ward and Linda Grant, "The Feminist Critique and a Decade of Published Research in Sociology Journals," *Sociological Quarterly* 26 (1986): 139-158.

31. Campbell, *The Hidden Discriminator.*

32. Marlaine Lockheed, Margaret Thorpe, Jeanne Brooks-Gunn, and Ann McAloon, *Understanding Sex/Ethnic Related Differences in Mathematics, Science, and Computer Science for Students in Grades Four to Eight* (Princeton, NJ: Educational Testing Service, 1985).

33. Bernice Lott, "Dual Nature or Learned Behavior: The Challenge to Feminist Psychology," in *Making a Difference*, edited by Rachel Hare-Mustin and Jeanne Marecek (New Haven: Yale University Press, 1990), pp. 65-101.

34. John G. Frauenheim, "Academic Achievement Characteristics of Adult Males Who Were Diagnosed as Dyslexic in Childhood," *Journal of Learning Disabilities* 11 (1978): 21-28.

35. Campbell, *The Impact of Societal Biases on Research.*

36. Suzanne Prescott and Kathleen Foster, "Why Researchers Don't Study Women: The Response of 67 Researchers" (Paper presented at the Annual Meeting of the American Psychological Association, New Orleans, 1974).

37. Andrew Purvis, "A Perilous Gap," *Time Magazine*, Special Issue on "Women: The Road Ahead," Fall 1990, p. 67.

38. Paula Caplan, "Sex Differences in Antisocial Behavior: Does Research Methodology Produce or Abolish Them?" *Human Development* 18 (1975): 444-460.

39. Eleanor Maccoby and Carol Jacklin, *The Psychology of Sex Differences* (Stanford, CA: Stanford University Press, 1974); Gilligan, *In a Different Voice.*

40. Anne Anastasi and Fernando A. Cordova, "Some Effects of Bilingualism upon the Intelligence Test Performance of Puerto Rican Children in New York City," *Journal of Educational Psychology* 45 (1953): 1-17.

41. Camilla Benbow and Julian Stanley, "Differential Course-taking Hypotheses Revisited," *American Educational Research Journal* 20 (1983): 469-473.

42. William Glaberson, "U. S. Court Says Awards Based on S.A.T.s Are Unfair to Girls," *New York Times*, 4 February 1989, pp. 1, 50.

43. Paula Selkow, *Assessing Sex Bias in Testing* (New York: Greenwood Press, 1984); Phyllis Rosser, *The SAT Gender Gap* (Washington, DC: Center for Women's Policy Studies, 1989).

44. Marcia Linn and Jane Hyde, "Gender, Mathematics, and Science" (Unpublished paper, December, 1988); C. L. W. Wendler and S. T. Carlton, "An Examination of SAT Verbal Items for Differential Performance by Women and Men: An Exploratory Study" (Paper presented at the Annual Meeting of the American Educational Research Association, Washington, DC, 1987).

45. Debra R. Kaufman and Barbara Richardson, *Achievement and Women* (New York: Free Press, 1982).

46. Campbell, *The Impact of Societal Biases in Research.*

47. Sharon B. Gurwitz and Kenneth A. Dodge, "Adults' Evaluation of a Child as a Function of the Sex of the Adult and the Sex of the Child," *Journal of Personality and Social Psychology* 32 (1975): 822-828.

48. Quoted in William Broad and Nicholas Wade, *Betrayers of the Truth: Fraud and Deceit in the Halls of Science* (New York: Simon and Schuster, 1982), p. 30.

49. Patti Lather, "Issues of Data Trustworthiness in Openly Ideological Research" (Paper presented at the Annual Meeting of the American Educational Research Association, San Francisco, 1986), p. 1.

50. Broad and Wade, *Betrayers of the Truth*, p. 103.

51. Stephen J. Gould, *The Mismeasure of Man* (New York: W. W. Norton, 1981), p. 660.

52. Broad and Wade, *Betrayers of the Truth.*

53. Robert Rosenthal and Lenore Jacobson, *Pygmalion in the Classroom: Teacher Expectation and Pupils' Intellectual Development* (New York: Holt, Rinehart and Winston, 1968). For critical assessments of *Pygmalion in the Classroom*, see Janet D. Elashoff and Richard E. Snow, *Pygmalion Reconsidered* (Worthington, Ohio: Charles A. Jones Publishing Co., 1971).

54. Anne Fausto-Sterling, *Myths of Gender* (New York: Basic Books, 1985), p. 9.

55. Sandra Harding, *Feminism and Methodology* (Bloomington, IN: Indiana University Press, 1987).

56. Campbell, "Educational Equity and Research Paradigms."

57. National Center for Education Statistics, *Digest of Education Statistics, 1991*, tables 249 and 250, pp. 270, 271.

58. Campbell, "Educational Equity and Research Paradigms."

59. Paula J. Caplan, Gael M. MacPherson, and Patricia Tobin, "Do Sex-related Differences in Spatial Abilities Exist? A Multilevel Critique with New Data," *American Psychologist* 40 (1985): 786-799.

60. Jane Armstrong, "A National Assessment of Participation and Achievement of Women in Mathematics," in *Women and Mathematics: Balancing the Equation*, edited by Susan Chipman, Lorelei Brush, and Donna Wilson (Hillsdale, NJ: Erlbaum, 1985), p. 69.

61. See Campbell, *The Hidden Discriminator*; Fausto-Sterling, *Myths of Gender.*

62. Anne C. Petersen, Lisa Crockett, and Maryse H. Tobin-Richards, "Sex Differences," in *Encyclopedia of Educational Research*, edited by Harold Mitzel (New York: Macmillan, 1982), pp. 1696-1709.

63. Patricia B. Elmore and Paula L. Woehlke, "Statistical Methods Employed in *American Educational Research Journal*, *Educational Researcher*, and *Review of Educational Research* from 1978 to 1987," *Educational Researcher* 17, no. 9 (1988): 19-20.

64. Tatsuoka, "Statistical Methods."

65. A. S. C. Ehrenberg, *Data Reduction* (New York: Wiley, 1975).

66. Noam Chomsky, *Language and Mind* (New York: Harcourt Brace Jovanovich, 1968).

67. Marion H. Salmon, *Philosophy and Archaeology* (New York: Academic Press, 1982), p. 35.

68. David Tresemer, "Assumptions Made about Gender Roles," in *Another Voice*, edited by Marcia Millman and Rosabeth M. Kantor (Garden City, NY: Anchor Press, 1975), p. 313.

69. Anthony Greenwald, "Consequences of Prejudice against the Null Hypothesis," *Psychological Bulletin* 82 (1975): 1-20.

70. Dale Spender, "The Gatekeepers," in *Doing Feminist Research*, edited by Helen Roberts (London: Routledge and Kegan Paul, 1981), p. 192.

71. Mary Lee Smith, "Publication Bias and Meta-analysis," *Evaluation in Education* 4 (1980): 22-24; Greenwald, "Consequences of Prejudice against the Null Hypothesis."

72. Petersen, Crockett, and Tobin-Richards, "Sex Differences."

73. Tresemer, "Assumptions Made about Gender Roles," p. 308.

74. Spender, "The Gatekeepers," p. 193.

75. Ibid., p. 192.

76. Tresemer, "Assumptions Made about Gender Roles," p. 315.

77. Janet Hyde and Marcia Linn, *The Psychology of Gender: Advances through Meta-Analysis* (Baltimore, MD: Johns Hopkins University Press, 1986).

78. Alice Eagly, *Sex Differences in Social Behavior: Social Role Interpretation* (Hillsdale, NJ: Lawrence Erlbaum, 1987).

79. Petersen, Crockett, and Tobin-Richards, "Sex Differences," p. 1696.

80. Fausto-Sterling, *Myths of Gender*, p. 29.

81. Tresemer, "Assumptions Made about Gender Roles," p. 313.

82. Harding, *Feminism and Methodology*, p. 39.

83. Selma Greenberg, "Race and Gender: Effects of a Difference-based Model" (Paper presented at the Annual Meeting of the American Educational Research Association, Boston, 1990), p. 5.

84. Inge K. Broverman, Donald M. Broverman, Frank E. Clarkston, Paul S. Rosencrantz, and Susan R. Fogel, "Sex Role Stereotypes and Clinical Judgments on Mental Health," *Journal of Consulting and Clinical Psychology* 34 (1970): 1-7.

85. Greenberg, "Race and Gender."

86. Ibid., p. 5.

87. Charol Shakeshaft, ed., "Women in Education," *Phi Delta Kappan* 67, no. 7 (1986): 499-526; Sari Biklen and Carol Dwyer, eds., "The New Scholarship on Women in Education," *Educational Researcher* (Special Issue) 15, no. 6 (1986): 6-23.

88. Campbell and Brown, *Surveying the Status of Educational Researchers.*

89. Margaret MacIntosh, "Interactive Phases of Curricular Re-vision: A Feminist Perspective," Working Paper No. 124 (Wellesley, MA: Wellesley College, Center for Research on Women, 1983).

90. Campbell and Brown, *Surveying the Status of Educational Researchers.*

91. Ibid.

92. Marcia Weskott, "Feminist Criticism of Social Science," *Harvard Educational Review* 49, no. 4 (1979): 422-430.

93. Charol Shakeshaft, Gwendolyn Baker, Patricia Campbell, Carol Anne Dwyer, Tito Guerrero, and Robert Murphy, "AERA Guidelines for Eliminating Race and Sex Bias in Educational Research and Evaluation," *Educational Researcher* 14, no. 6 (1985): 16-17.

94. Liane V. Davis, "A Feminist Approach to Social Work Research," *Affila* 1, no. 1 (1986): 32-46.

95. Hare-Mustin and Marecek, "Gender and the Meaning of Difference," p. 22-23.

96. Gilligan, *In a Different Voice.*

97. Rhoda Unger, "Imperfect Reflections of Reality: Psychology Constructs Gender," p. 132.

98. Fausto-Sterling, *Myths of Gender*, p. 10.

99. Mark C. Hogrebe, Sherrie L. Nist, and Isadore Newman, "Are There Gender Differences in Reading Achievement? An Investigation Using the High School and Beyond Data," *Journal of Educational Psychology* 77, no. 6 (1985): 716-724.

100. Edward H. Clarke, *Sex in Education or a Fair Chance for Girls* (Boston: James R. Osgood, 1873; reprinted by Arno Press, 1972); Rosser, *The SAT Gender Gap.*

101. MacIntosh, "Interactive Phases of Curricular Re-vision: A Feminist Perspective."

102. Campbell, "Educational Equity and Research Paradigms"; Elizabeth Fennema, Penelope L. Peterson, Thomas P. Carpenter, and C. Lubinski, "Teacher Attributes and Beliefs about Girls, Boys, and Mathematics," *Educational Studies in Mathematics* 21 (1990): 55-69.

103. Shakeshaft, "Women in Education."

CHAPTER VI

Gender and Achievement

DIANE S. POLLARD

Academic achievement is the cornerstone of the educational enterprise. It is most often used as the basis for judging individual and systemic educational outcomes. This construct has also been used to refer to the methods by which students process information as well as to the knowledge they are required to learn.

Because of the pervasiveness of this construct, academic achievement is an extremely important variable to educators, the society at large, parents, and students. For many, academic achievement assumes almost mythical importance in judging both student and institutional fitness. Individual students are categorized, their educational futures are predicted, and they are often placed in specific school environments based on measures of their academic achievement. Furthermore, schools and school districts are judged and oftentimes rewarded or punished on the basis of their students' academic achievement, most often measured by grades and test scores.

Concern with academic achievement is not limited to the school setting however. Real estate agents often use the reputation of schools for academic achievement in particular residential areas as selling points in their negotiations with clients. Similarly, the spate of reports in the 1980s on the nation's educational situation, exemplified by *A Nation at Risk* in 1983,[1] used academic achievement as a reference point not only for this country's educational system, but also for its political, economic, and moral standing in the international setting.

Emphasis on the importance of academic achievement extends to individual families and students as well. Many parents begin to stress this type of achievement to their children well before they enter school. In addition, the most common feedback parents receive from schools revolves around how their children compare to others on some measure of achievement. Not surprisingly, children learn early

Diane Pollard is an Associate Professor in the Department of Educational Psychology in the School of Education at the University of Wisconsin—Milwaukee.

in their school careers that academic achievement is an important aspect of the judgments others make about them, and subsequently of their own judgments of their self-worth, as well as a major factor in determining their future prospects in society.

Given the importance of academic achievement to individuals, institutions, and the society at large, it is not surprising that group differences on this variable frequently attract attention. For many years, achievement differences between women and men and between whites and people of color have been the focus of considerable discussion. Very often these discussions use a deficit-oriented model, that is, they focus on describing actual and perceived lower levels of achievement among men of color and among women when these groups are compared with white men. In addition, questions about group differences in achievement have been raised in connection with quite dissimilar underlying agendas. In some cases the racial, ethnic, and gendered differences in achievement have been used to rationalize discriminatory practices and policies that preserve the positions of those with power and privilege, i.e., white males. In other cases, however, the differences have been explored in connection with efforts to identify and implement policies and practices that could lead to more equitable school and societal arrangements and encourage higher levels of achievement among women and among men of color.

Increasingly, educators are seeking ways to improve academic achievement among women and among men of color. This interest is sparked by several interrelated issues. First, this society is becoming inevitably more pluralistic. Second, women as well as men of color have become more insistent in their demands for equitable access and status in schools and in the society at large. Third, many groups in this society, including educators, business people, and politicians, are recognizing that white women and women and men of color will be large components of the future work force. Therefore, their educational achievement may begin to be seen as necessary to societal self-interest.

This chapter is divided into two sections. In the first, I will discuss the evidence concerning the extent of gender differences in academic achievement. In the second section, I will review two perspectives on enhancing academic achievement among women. Many writers have considered separately the relationships between achievement and race, achievement and ethnicity, achievement and social class, and achievement and gender. Such formulations tend to emphasize one sociodemographic characteristic at the expense of others. While I will focus here on relationships between achievement and gender, I recognize that in reality gender, race, ethnicity, social class, and other sociodemographic characteristics all intersect to help shape our lives. Therefore, when possible, I make note of these relationships.

Gender Differences in Academic Achievement

Quite frequently, discussions concerning gender and academic achievement begin with explicit or implicit assumptions that men consistently outperform women. Much of the evidence gathered a decade or so ago seemed to support this assumption. Men, specifically white men, scored higher than women on standardized tests, did better in mathematics and science courses, and generally were more likely than females to obtain advanced academic degrees.

Given the apparent consistency of these differences, many writers then turned their attention to identifying the reasons for these sex differences. Some writers attributed the presumed lower levels of achievement among females to sex-based biological characteristics. This view argued that men were somehow genetically more capable academically than women, particularly in subjects such as mathematics and science. In spite of this view which, unfortunately, has been accepted by many, including some women, Campbell has noted that no evidence of a "mathgene" exists.[2] Furthermore, Linn and Petersen argued that there is no clear-cut evidence of how genetic factors might function in such a way as to lead to differences in academic performance.[3]

Others explained sex differences in achievement in terms of sociocultural factors in the environment. Some of these included socialization experiences in the family and school, school practices that discriminate against girls, and societal expectations that girls and women were not "supposed" to be high achievers, at least on these measures. Through combinations of these factors, it was believed, significant others did not expect or prepare females to achieve at high levels in school. An example of the power of others' expectations is reported by Ware and Lee in their analysis of data from the High School and Beyond longitudinal study.[4] Both women and men indicated that high school teachers and counselors were major influences in their decisions regarding educational planning. However, women who reported this were *less* likely to take mathematics and science courses than women who reported they had not been helped by these school staff members. Furthermore, men reported that they received help in making decisions about college from teachers and counselors more often than women reported receiving such help.

While much of the discussion of the effect of environment on sex differences in achievement focused on the direct actions of school staff, another perspective pointed to differences in psychological characteristics of men and women. Linn and Petersen identified several such characteristics which have been hypothesized to underlie differences in achievement between males and females.[5] These include: lower self-confidence and self-esteem among women (two factors which have been associated with higher achievement), and higher levels of anxiety, conformity, and dependence in women (variables which are thought to be associated with lower achievement). In addition, aggression among males has been hypothesized to be associated with higher achievement. However, Linn and Petersen noted that while the findings of sex differences in aggression are fairly strong, the evidence of differences in the other factors is considerably weaker and less consistent across studies.

Furthermore, there is strong overlap between these psychological characteristics and experiential factors such as those described by Ware and Lee. It seems quite logical to expect that many of the socialization experiences young girls have as well as the social expectations they are confronted with in family and school settings lead to greater anxiety, conformity, and dependence, especially if achievement is devalued for them.

During the past several years, some writers have begun to raise questions about the basic assumptions that females' school achievement is consistently lower than males. For example, Mickelson reported that women achieve as well as men.[6] Similarly, Adelman analyzed data from the National Longitudinal Study (NLS) of the high school graduating class of 1972 and found that "women's performance in high school was far stronger than that of men."[7] This was true for grades in mathematics and science courses, for scores on the Scholastic Aptitude Test, and for grades in postsecondary classes. Yet, Adelman noted, women's educational aspirations and plans were lower than those of men. Furthermore, in an extensive review of literature on sex differences in achievement, Eccles found few consistent differences.[8]

This and other information clearly indicate that the relationships between gender and achievement are not as simple and straightforward as commonly held assumptions suggest. Rather they are complex and multifaceted. I believe that three factors contribute to this complexity: (1) inconsistencies and misinterpretations of data on sex differences in achievement, (2) limitations of discussions on gender and achievement to white and middle-class people, and (3) inadequate attention given to the relationships between achievement in the school and in work settings.

INCONSISTENCIES AND MISINTERPRETATIONS IN THE RESEARCH

Linn and Petersen also reviewed a number of studies of academic achievement differences between males and females and, like Eccles, reported many inconsistencies in the results.[9] Similarly, Becker reanalyzed two meta-analyses of gender differences in science achievement and found mixed results: while males achieved at higher levels in some areas of science, females showed greater achievement in other areas.[10] One issue is whether differences noted are related to sex per se or to some other characteristic. For example, Burke investigated the grade point averages of a large sample of seventh and eighth graders and found that gender role identity influenced these measures of achievement more than biological sex.[11]

Another problem with this research may be that sex differences which are reported as "well established" might actually be rather small. Linn and Petersen note that "well established" is often interpreted as "large."[12] They also point out that even though some sex differences in achievement are statistically small, they may be quite important. Finally, some writers have suggested that the research on differences between males and females in achievement may be biased through the ways that questions are asked and research designs are established. These procedures may actually overemphasize any differences that exist.

INADEQUATE ATTENTION TO DIVERSITY AMONG WOMEN

Most research on women in general, as well as on women and achievement, has focused on white, and to a large extent, on middle-class people. Furthermore, writers have tended to generalize findings on these samples to all women. These types of generalizations are not always warranted because they tend to overlook racial, ethnic, and socioeconomic differences in achievement. More important, these generalizations ignore the intersections of gender, race, ethnicity, and social class. The nearly exclusive focus on white women's behavior in this arena also overlooks important historical and cultural differences in gendered patterns of academic involvement and achievement.

An understanding of the forces influencing gender and achievement among African Americans provides an example of the role that history and culture play in gendered achievement patterns. In her historical analysis of African-American women in the United States, Jacqueline Jones describes the importance of schooling for African-American girls.[13] According to Jones, from the period shortly after slavery into the early twentieth century, African-American families tended to encourage education more for their female than their male children. There were a number of complex reasons for this: most African-American families were small subsistence farmers during this period and males were desperately needed to work for the economic survival of the unit. In addition, there was little economic reward to be obtained from education for African-American males who were systematically barred from all but the most menial jobs off the farms. For African-American females, who were largely required to work outside the home to help maintain their families, occupational choices consisted of low-paid domestic work with its concomitant hazards of physical, social, and sexual abuse or the professions of teaching and, to a lesser extent, social work, both of which required a degree of educational attainment.

Contemporary studies suggest that African-American females continue to be encouraged to achieve more than African-American males. Linda Grant observed a variety of first grade classrooms and found that teachers rated the academic performances of black females higher than that of black males but lower than that of white females.[14] From the evidence that teachers' expectations influence performance, it would follow that African-American girls might actually achieve at a higher level than African-American boys. However, Grant also observed that teachers placed African-American girls at a disadvantage relative to white girls. Specifically, Grant noted that while white girls were encouraged to pursue academic activities, African-American girls were encouraged to develop certain social skills. Indeed, Grant argued, these first-grade teachers encouraged both African-American females and African-American males to take on behaviors consistent with stereotypes held of them in this society. Grant's findings are corroborated by the recent report of the American Association of University Women which reviewed research on the educational experiences of girls in kindergarten through the twelfth grade.[15] The report concluded that African-American girls are treated less positively than white girls in the classroom.

These studies suggest that work on the relationships between gender and achievement must consider race, ethnicity, and social class factors. The limited research that has been done on African Americans suggests that gender differences in this community have been shaped partially by patterns of resistance developed to counteract racist and discriminatory practices. More work is needed on African Americans and other people of color. Little is written about the forces underlying gender-related patterns of achievement among American Indians or the various ethnic Asian and Hispanic groups. Additional work in this area must be aimed not only at documenting these cultural influences but also at recognizing that differences in cultural conceptualizations of various gender roles are legitimate.

INADEQUATE ATTENTION TO RELATIONSHIPS BETWEEN ACHIEVEMENT IN SCHOOL AND IN THE WORKPLACE

In the United States, achievement in school is purportedly related to achievement in the workplace. Conventional wisdom holds that high scholastic achievement will be rewarded with high occupational achievement. However, this assumption has been questioned with respect both to women and to men of color. A particularly vivid example of the fallacy of this assumption is demonstrated in Clifford Adelman's publication *Women at Thirtysomething: Paradoxes of Attainment* (1991).[16] Adelman found not only that women achieved academically at higher levels than men in high school and college, but that they also seemed to value education more. Women also reported more satisfaction with their educational experiences than was reported by men. However, their educational aspirations and plans were lower than those of men.

Unfortunately, in the work arena, women neither achieved to the same degree as men nor to the extent predicted by their school achievement. In fact, Adelman found that women between the ages of twenty-five and thirty-two who earned bachelor's degrees were more likely to be unemployed (but looking for work) than men, and when employed, were more likely to be in lower-paying jobs than men. Furthermore, when women held jobs similar to those men held, they earned less.

Adelman did report some racial and ethnic differences in women's earning patterns. Specifically, he found that African-American and Hispanic women who had bachelor's degrees earned more than white women with those degrees. However, among those who earned graduate degrees, Hispanic women and African-American men earned more than white women and there were no differences between the earnings of African-American and white women. In this study, Adelman did not analyze these findings in terms of major fields. These findings indicate once more the need to obtain a better understanding of the intricacies of race, ethnic, and social class interrelationships.

Some may find it puzzling that considerable numbers of women continue to strive for high academic achievement even though it does not pay off consistently with respect to occupational outcomes. However, others have argued that women achieve for different reasons than men do. For example, Mickelson suggests that women are less concerned than men with making direct links between academic and occupational achievement because women's lives are less dichotomized between public and private spheres than men's lives are.[17]

Other writers have suggested similar themes. Eccles found that high school males and females gave different reasons for choosing to take the same mathematics and English courses.[18] The males focused on performance aspects of the work while the females were more concerned with what they saw as the value of the course. She suggested that more attention needs to be paid to the choices people make with respect to achievement. Noting that girls still tend to be socialized in different ways than boys, Huston suggests that women may view achievement as a manifestation of their social skills rather than skills in other domains.[19] She also suggests that this perspective on achievement accounts for girls' higher grades in school. They use their social skills to negotiate the classroom more effectively than boys do.

In summary, the numerous investigations of gender differences in academic achievement reveal two major issues. First, these relationships are truly multifaceted. One simply cannot predict differences in academic performance on the basis of sex alone. Other factors must be taken into account, such as sociocultural background, previous socialization experiences, and the student's interpretations and expectations of the specific situation. Second, although evidence of successful academic achievement among girls and women exists, this does not mean that equity has truly been obtained in this arena. Many women are still discouraged from achieving in certain areas, such as engineering; others do not exert themselves in school because of lingering perceptions that academic achievement is not feminine. Gains in achievement for women are uneven across racial, ethnic, and socioeconomic groups: poor women and women of color still lag behind both white middle-class women and white men. Finally, even when they do achieve in school, women receive fewer rewards in the workplace. As Adelman suggests, this fact sends a message to women that their achievement does not matter and could ultimately discourage them from continuing to strive. Although several writers have suggested that the factors underlying women's achievement differ from those underlying the achievement of men, one might ask how long these differences will continue to be viable if women's achievement remains devalued in the larger society. As a result, educators still need to be concerned about implementing initiatives aimed at enhancing achievement among all women, and indeed among all students.

Models for Enhancing Achievement among Women

I turn now to two approaches educators have taken to enhance academic achievement among women. The first approach argues that women's academic performance will be improved when they are provided with the same resources, training, and opportunities that privileged white men have. The second approach contends that effective procedures for enhancing women's academic achievement require building upon the particular perspectives women hold. This approach advocates a focus on sociocultural differences in ways that groups process information as well as building curriculum on the specific historical and contemporary cultural experiences of these groups.

THE "EQUAL OPPORTUNITIES" APPROACH

For many years, the most common approach to enhancing academic achievement among women has focused on providing them with access to experiences similar to those privileged white men are presumed to have. One major thrust in this direction has been to encourage girls and women to enroll in the same courses that men take with the expectation that they will then learn the same skills men learn. For example, for at least the last decade, there have been deliberate and systematic efforts to influence girls and women to enroll in courses in mathematics, science, and computer utilization. A second thrust has involved providing female students with interpersonal support for their achievement through mentors and "role models."

The results of these types of interventions are mixed. Clearly, some women have gained from them. For example, more women are participating in mathematics, science, and engineering.[20] However, these gains are more evident among economically privileged white girls who score high on standardized tests. Girls and women from other cultural and socioeconomic groups are still not receiving the same access to these experiences.[21] Similarly, the impact of exposure to role models has yet to be systematically assessed, and it is not clear what types of mentoring processes are most effective.

In addition, there is evidence that many adults, particularly parents and teachers, still view girls and women as unable to achieve at the same level as boys and men and they communicate this message to students of various ages and cultures.[22] These adults, as well as some girls, have to be resocialized to accept the idea that academic achievement is a legitimate pursuit for all people.

I would argue that one problem with this model is that it implies a continuation of the deficit approach to group differences in achievement. Those who are viewed as performing at lesser levels need to be changed to be more like the "standard bearers." This is not to suggest that women be denied access to opportunities available to privileged men; in fact, I would contend that interventions in this direction need to be expanded. However, this approach, while necessary, may not be sufficient for all women in all situations.

THE "SOCIOCULTURAL DIFFERENCES" APPROACH

There are alternative ways of conceptualizing academic achievement with respect to women and possibly with respect to men as well. Two such perspectives are seen in a "sociocultural differences" approach, which focuses on the processes of knowing and on the nature of the knowledge to be attained. These would seem to be useful starting points for obtaining a clearer picture of the relationships between gender and achievement.

Differences in learning style. It has been suggested by Eccles, by Huston, and by Mickelson that differences in achievement outcomes are caused by, or at least related to, differences in the ways in which women perceive and process information.[23] The idea that different groups may exhibit different learning or knowing styles is not new. Much of the work in this area has focused on African Americans and other people of color.[24] These studies, conducted primarily with elementary and secondary level students, provided some evidence that these groups brought certain cultural characteristics into the school setting which involved particular ways of perceiving and interpreting the environment and which were hypothesized to have an impact on the students' school achievement.

Recently, the research of Belenky and others, compiled in *Women's Ways of Knowing*,[25] suggested that there are gender-related styles of perceiving, interpreting, and processing information from the environment. These researchers suggested that there are different categories of knowing that are useful in describing how women deal with knowledge. For example, some women believe that all knowledge comes from outside the self, primarily from recognizable authorities and experts. These women look to others for all information and expect that it will be valid if it comes from the "correct" sources. Other women focus on subjective knowledge, believing that "true" knowledge comes only from within. Unlike those in the first category, these women would ignore the "experts." Still others see knowledge in terms of acquiring specific procedures and skills and using them in a reasoned manner.

Belenky and her colleagues describe other categories of knowing. It is important to note that these categories should not be construed as "stages" of development in knowing, nor are they necessarily mutually exclusive. However, they do suggest that how one processes information will affect what one knows. It is possible, for example, that a subjective knower might just never get around to "learning" the material assigned by teachers because she does not consider it to be important. As a result, when asked to demonstrate what she has "learned," she will not be able to do so in traditional academic ways.

In general, studies of differences in learning styles or ways of knowing have received relatively short shrift in analyses of academic achievement. Part of the reason for this is that most tools available to assess achievement can only measure restricted types of knowledge outcomes. Furthermore, much of the work on achievement has been done from a masculinist perspective, which often seems to assume there is only one way of knowing and it is embodied in the processes thought to be utilized by white middle-class men. Given the national focus on achievement defined in terms of standardized test scores, it is not surprising that school administrators would be reluctant to shift to evaluations where the emphasis is on describing and understanding different processes of knowing.

Yet, there is some evidence that understanding and attending to differences in learning styles can, in fact, have a positive impact on achievement outcomes. Working with African-American elementary students, Bell and McGraw-Burrell conducted an experiment in which tasks were presented in a format consistent with these children's learning styles.[26] They used a great deal of variation in the presentation of stimulus materials and focused on interpersonal interaction. These researchers found improved achievement outcomes with these methods. Similarly, Shade found that African-American ninth graders employed a more spontaneous, flexible, and less structured learning style than whites did.[27]

A few accounts suggest parallels for women. Adelman suggests that for the women in the NLS sample educational attainment is linked to a particular way of knowing described by Belenky and others as the discovery of "personal authority."[28] In a recent conference presentation, Curran described how she encouraged achievement among working-class college women through a relational, exploratory style of teaching, which, she argued, was linked to her students' preferred style of knowing.[29]

The emerging information on differences in styles of learning and knowing and their relationships to achievement outcomes suggests an additional intervention for encouraging academic achievement among women. The traditional approach, which emphasized sex differences in performance levels, assumed that women's achievement levels could be enhanced primarily by focusing on creating change within the women so that they could acquire the same skills and share the same experiences as males. However, the perspective on learning and knowing styles suggests that educators also need to be aware of women's diverse learning styles and must adjust their instructional strategies accordingly.

Some questions need to be answered regarding differences in learning styles. First, as indicated earlier, this work has not sufficiently taken into account intersections of race, gender and class. Are the "women's ways of knowing" described by Belenky characteristic primarily of white women? Are the cultural differences in learning styles described by Shade and by Willis[30] as characteristic of African Americans equally evident in African-American males and African-American females? Where does social class fit in? To what extent are differences in learning styles shared across cultural groups? How are these learning styles developed? More research in this area will be useful to educators as they work to accommodate their diverse student populations.

Curriculum content and academic achievement. In addition to a concern for differences in learning styles there has been some concern with the impact of curriculum content on academic achievement. Schools codify and transmit the knowledge judged as important; therefore, achievement is often operationally defined as the degree to which an individual can demonstrate the knowledge deemed important by those in power in society. Yet, Eccles indicates that achievement is operationalized in a wide variety of ways, not only in academic settings but also in real life.[31] In highly homogeneous and consensual societies, it may be possible to identify what is important knowledge for everyone. In pluralistic societies, however, there are frequently tensions between those who have the power to dictate what knowledge is important and those who have alternative ideas about what should be known but do not have the status and authority to have their ideas accepted as valid cultural knowledge.

This tension has been evident for many years in the knowledge by and about African Americans that is perpetuated in schools. Not too long ago, the only information that was considered "important" to know about African Americans was that they were "happy slaves" and the only people who provided this knowledge were whites. Major changes have occurred not only in what is known about this group, but also in who develops and presents this information. African-American Studies are widespread in colleges. However, many advances in this area are contested by those power and privilege holders who see that control of knowledge is a means of maintaining the status quo.

Women's studies developed with some of the same goals as ethnic studies: to provide access to knowledge that had been deemed unimportant or useless by those in power, to allow for alternative explanations of reality, and to offer information that students might find particularly interesting and useful in relation to their own experiences. And, just as some react negatively to providing knowledge about racial and ethnic groups, so do many in this society continue to disparage knowledge about women.

It can be argued that one way to encourage achievement is by allowing students to learn information they can see as having some relationship to their own lives. Ironically, much of the nineteenth century education for women, particularly affluent women of this society, was designed to do just that—focus on their own lives. Therefore, these women were educated to participate in the "cult of true womanhood," as Perkins writes. This type of education emphasized "modesty, piety, purity, submissiveness and domesticity."[32]

During this same time, according to Perkins, the education of African-American women was geared toward helping in racial uplift, that is, toward improving the conditions of all African Americans. However, as African Americans began to accept the dominant attitude toward appropriate gender role behavior, some of the ideas from the "cult of true womanhood" began to find their way into the education of African-American women also. As a result, although racial uplift remained the overriding focus of African-American education in general, African-American women were less likely to be educated for leadership roles.[33]

Eventually, the roles of white women in society, like the roles of people of color, seemed to disappear from the curricula presented to elementary, secondary, and postsecondary students. In these curricular materials white middle-class males often predominated in all kinds of settings and roles and if any women or men of color were discussed at all, the discussion was in very restricted and stereotypical terms.

Since the 1970s, in response to demands from white women and both women and men of color, knowledge by and about these groups is slowly becoming incorporated into the curriculum. At this time, the impact of these relatively recent curricular changes on the achievement of women and men of color cannot be assessed. However, some anecdotal accounts suggest that access to this type of information can have a positive effect. For example, Pennington, an African-American woman, has written about how knowledge incorporating an African worldview as well as African-American religious perspectives helped African-American women develop strategies for achievement.[34] Similarly, Springer discussed how knowledge about how women have dealt with, and continue to deal with, power can be helpful to women in higher education administration.[35]

In summary, this model suggests that the assessment of academic achievement has to expand to include both variations in processes of knowing and in what is known. Furthermore, interventions to enhance achievement among white women as well as among women and men of different racial and ethnic groups will have to include changes in instruction and curriculum as well as the provision of equal resources and training.

Summary: Gender and Achievement—A Multifaceted Inquiry

During the past several years, educational policymakers and business people in this society have noted that in the coming years white women and women and men of color will form a major portion of the work force of the nation. While some have seen this demographic projection as a source of alarm and have reacted by circling their wagons, others have tried to intervene to ensure that all of these groups will be well educated and able to function adequately to serve both themselves and the society at large. This has led to increased scrutiny of the academic achievement of women and of men of color. With respect to women, most of the work in this area has been concerned with sex differences in achievement outcomes. Three questions have been asked. First, are there differences between females and males in achievement outcomes? The answer seems to be yes or no depending on a variety of conditions. Second, what are the sources of these differences? The answer seems to be that there are many sources, depending again on a variety of conditions. Third, what kinds of intervention are likely to help females achieve at the same levels as males? The answer seems to be that several types of intervention can be effective.

It certainly seems clear that when women are provided with certain important resources and with opportunities to learn and practice specific skills, their academic achievement improves. However, this is not necessarily the case for all women or in all circumstances. In addition, evidence suggests that the advances in academic achievement that some women have made still have not resulted in concomitant advances in other types of achievement, as Adelman and Mickelson have noted.[36]

This approach is but one consideration necessary to understanding relationships between gender and achievement and enhancing achievement among women and girls. We also need to acquire a better understanding of how women perceive and interpret information and to recognize that the achievements of women are an important part of the knowledge deemed worth knowing by all members of this society.

That educators are faced with providing instruction to an increasingly pluralistic body of students has almost become a cliché. However, the dominant belief still seems to be that academic achievement and its consequent rewards are restricted to those groups of students who conform to one mode of learning and knowing. These are the people who will succeed in school and in society. An alternative view is that achievement must be encouraged for all groups in the society. This will require serious attempts to understand the conditions under which various groups succeed, recognition of differing modes of learning and knowing, and support for instruction that will build on these differences so as to enhance access to achievement for all students and expand this society's perspective of what academic achievement means.

Notes

1. National Commission on Excellence in Education, *A Nation at Risk: The Imperative for Educational Reform* (Washington, DC: U. S. Government Printing Office, 1983).

2. Patricia B. Campbell, *Girls and Math: Enough Is Known for Action* (Newton, MA: Women's Educational Equity Act Publishing Center, Education Development Center, 1991).

3. Marcia C. Linn and Anne C. Petersen. "Facts and Assumptions about the Nature of Sex Differences," in *Handbook for Achieving Sex Equity through Education*, edited by Susan S. Klein (Baltimore, MD: Johns Hopkins University Press, 1985), pp. 53-77.

4. Norma C. Ware and Valerie E. Lee. "Sex Differences in Choice of College Science Majors," *American Educational Research Journal* 25, no. 4 (1988): 593-614.

5. Linn and Petersen, "Facts and Assumptions about the Nature of Sex Differences."

6. Roslyn Arlin Mickelson, "Why Does Jane Read and Write So Well? The Anomaly of Women's Achievement," *Sociology of Education* 62 (1989): 47-63.

7. Clifford Adelman, *Women at Thirtysomething: Paradoxes of Attainment* (Washington, DC: Office of Eduational Research and Improvement, U. S. Department of Education, 1991), p. v.

8. Jacquelynne Eccles, "Sex Differences in Achievement Patterns," in *Psychology and Gender: Nebraska Symposium on Motivation 1984*, vol. 32, edited by Theo B. Sonderegger (Lincoln: University of Nebraska Press, 1984), pp. 97-132.

9. Linn and Petersen, "Facts and Assumptions about the Nature of Sex Differences."

10. Betsy J. Becker, "Gender and Science Achievement: A Reanalysis of Studies from Two Meta-Analyses," *Journal of Research in Science Teaching* 26, no. 2 (1989): 141-169.

11. Peter J. Burke, "Gender Identity, Sex, and School Performance," *Social Psychology Quarterly* 52, no. 2 (1989): 159-169.

12. Linn and Peterson, "Facts and Assumptions about the Nature of Sex Differences."

13. Jacqueline Jones, *Labor of Love, Labor of Sorrow: Black Women, Work, and the Family from Slavery to the Present* (New York: Basic Books, 1985).

14. Linda Grant, "Black Females' 'Place' in Desegregated Classrooms," *Sociology of Education* 57 (1984): 98-111.

15. American Association of University Women, *How Schools Shortchange Girls: Executive Summary* (Washington, DC: American Association of University Women Educational Foundation, 1992).

16. Adelman, *Women at Thirtysomething.*

17. Mickelson, "Why Does Jane Read and Write So Well?"

18. Eccles, "Sex Differences in Achievement Patterns."

19. Aletha C. Huston, "Gender, Socialization and the Transmission of Culture," in *Seeing Female: Social Roles and Personal Lives*, edited by Sharon S. Brehm (New York: Greenwood Press, 1988), pp. 7-19.

20. Peggy J. Blackwell and Lillian N. Russo, "Sex Equity Strategies in the Content Areas," in *Handbook for Achieving Sex Equity through Education*, edited by Susan S. Klein (Baltimore, MD: Johns Hopkins University Press, 1985), pp. 53-57.

21. Campbell, *Girls and Math.*

22. Shoshanna Ben Tsvi-Mayer, Rachael Hertz-Lazarowitz, and Marilyn P. Safir, "Teachers' Selections of Boys and Girls as Prominent Pupils," *Sex Roles* 21, nos. 3-4 (1989): 231-246; Brett Silverstein, Lauren Perdue, Cordulla Wolf, and Cecilia Pizzolo, "Bingeing, Purging, and Estimates of Parental Attitudes Regarding Female Achievement," *Sex Roles* 19, nos. 11-12 (1988): 723-733; Nelly P. Stromquist, "Determinants of Educational Participation and Achievement of Women in the Third World: A Review and Evaluation of the Evidence and a Theoretical Critique," *Review of Educational Research* 59, no. 2 (1989): 143-183.

23. See, for example, Eccles, "Sex Differences in Achievement Patterns"; Huston, "Gender, Socialization, and the Transmission of Culture"; and Mickelson, "Why Does Jane Read and Write So Well?"

24. Barbara J. Shade, "Is There an Afro-American Cultural Style? An Exploratory Study," *Journal of Black Psychology* 13, no. 1 (1986): 629-634; Madge Gill Willis, "Learning Styles of African-American Children: A Review of Literature and Interventions," *Journal of Black Psychology* 16, no. 1 (1989): 47-65.

25. Mary Field Belenky, Blythe McVicker Clinchy, Nancy Ruls Goldberger, and Jill Mattuck Tarule, *Women's Ways of Knowing* (New York: Basic Books, 1986).

26. Y. R. Bell and F. McGraw-Burrell, "Culturally Sensitive and Traditional Methods of Task Presentation and Learning Performance in Black Children," *Western Journal of Black Studies* 12 (1988): 187-193.

27. Shade, "Is There an Afro-American Cultural Style?"

28. Adelman, *Women at Thirtysomething*, p. 17.

29. Jeanne Curran, Susan Takata, and Faye Arnold, "Women Producing Knowledge in Working Class Institutions of Higher Education: Valuing Our Differences" (Paper presented at the 17th Annual Conference of the Special Interest Group: Research on Women and Education, San Jose, CA, November 1991).

30. Shade, "Is There an Afro-American Cultural Style?"; Willis, "Learning Styles of African-American Children."

31. Eccles, "Sex Differences in Achievement Patterns."

32. Linda M. Perkins, "The Impact of the 'Cult of True Womanhood' on the Education of Black Women," *Journal of Social Issues* 39, no. 3 (1983): 15.

33. Ibid., pp. 17-28.

34. Dorothy L. Pennington, "Afro-American Women: Achievement through Reconciliation of Messages and Images," in *Seeing Female: Social Roles and Personal Lives*, edited by Sharon S. Brehm (New York: Greenwood Press, 1988), pp. 33-41.

35. Marlene Springer, "Women and Power in Higher Education: Saving the Libra in a Scorpio World," in *Seeing Female: Social Roles and Personal Lives*, edited by Sharon S. Brehm (New York: Greenwood Press, 1988).

36. Adelman, *Women at Thirtysomething*; Mickelson, "Why Does Jane Read and Write So Well?"

CHAPTER VII

"Who Benefits and Who Suffers": Gender and Education at the Dawn of the Age of Information Technology

JOAN N. BURSTYN

Technology and the Distribution of Power

Today many people believe that information technology is revolutionizing the way we structure and communicate knowledge. We handle more data than ever before; we have created new information networks; and we are learning new kinds of knowledge. "None of this implies that the data are correct; information, true; and knowledge, wise. But it does imply vast changes in the way we see the world, create wealth, and exercise power."[1] In this chapter I consider gender, technology, and education within a broad context because "social, political, and economic factors, in conjunction with currents within the scientific and technical fields themselves, all combine to create the technologies of a particular era."[2] I will examine the way women and men have acted in the past in relation to technology, and how the distribution of power between them is likely to change with new technologies. "Technology has everything to do with who benefits and who suffers, whose opportunities increase and whose decrease, who creates and who accommodates."[3]

An example of how unmindful people are of the equity issues involved with new technologies is found in our obsession with computers. Many leaders in American business and industry, believing that computers offer a panacea for the problems of American education, urge a national commitment to equip electronic schools across America. "This commitment must have the urgency of the Marshall Plan, the single-mindedness of the Manhattan Project, and the vision of the Apollo moon landing."[4] Not everyone agrees, however, that the problems of American education will be solved by

---

Joan N. Burstyn is Professor of Cultural Foundations of Education and of History at Syracuse University.

electronic schools. Some educators claim that the decision to equip schools with computers is value-laden; proponents ignore the ways that technology may affect children differentially according to their socioeconomic status, race, or gender. We need to address the ways society discriminates against people by socioeconomic status, race, and gender and initiate procedures to counter such discrimination in order to overcome the problems plaguing American education.

In relation to gender discrimination, studies of the use of computers by girls and boys in the United States suggest that less frequent use of them by girls may be linked to gender socialization. The fact that girls and boys are likely to be differentially impacted by the introduction of computer technology was pointed out by scholars several years ago.[5] Socialization is one of several influences that affect the impact on girls and boys not only of computers but of other technologies as well. In this chapter, I will discuss the implications of changes over the last fifty years brought about by several technologies.

Communication Technologies and Education

As well as being affected by computers, communication has been affected by changes in transportation through a vast extension of jet air travel; in telecommunications through cellular telephones and FAX machines; in space shuttles and satellite transmission of visual images and sound; in the extension of television through satellite transmission and through more sophisticated use of the medium; in the development of new uses of photographic technology to develop film instantaneously, to speed up, slow down, and splice film footage, and in the linking of the camera to the computer.

Each of these technologies has the potential to affect teaching and learning. By the time a person graduates from high school, for instance, he or she will, on the average, have spent at least as many hours watching television as studying. As well as enjoyment, commercial television provides education. Viewers absorb facts, ideas, and attitudes from what they see and hear. Only a small proportion of those facts, ideas, and attitudes come from watching television in a classroom; the rest are acquired at home. And, whether they are discussed or not, they make up a large part of the educational background, the world view, that children bring into the classroom. Recently owners of commercial television products have moved more aggressively to introduce their products into the classroom using Channel One. At the same time, state and federal governments have encouraged the use of distance education where a few students in one school district are provided the opportunity to participate in a group learning process, linking them via phone line, cable, and/or satellite through television and/or computer with students in other districts.

At first glance, it may seem surprising that television, which has had a profound impact on society as a whole, has had comparatively little impact on schooling. There are several reasons for this. One is that television challenges some basic tenets of schooling. Schools have traditionally constructed their curricula around the spoken and written word. Using words, schools emphasize the development of rationality. Words both describe what we experience and allow us to distance ourselves from the experience itself. At the same time, words, one's own or others', provide each person with a means to create an inner imagined reality. As I describe in more detail below, any new technology, as well as providing people with added powers, transfers to a machine (or to an expert or neural network system[6]) some skills that previously inhered in individual human beings.

The technology of television, which depends upon the earlier technologies of camera, film, and radio, has transferred to a machine the power to make visible events and ideas that people previously created with their imaginations. Where words provide descriptions that each person translates into mental pictures of his or her own, television provides the same pictures for all to share. Thus each viewer sees what the person directing the camera (or editing the film) decides is important as he or she scans the site of a plane crash, watches an insect transform from caterpillar to monarch butterfly, or portrays the reconciliation of the hero and heroine in a play.

Some educators deplore video technology because children no longer need their imagination to visualize an event. Some fear that children who watch two-dimensional images on a screen are deprived of sensory knowledge because they cannot touch, smell, or taste them, or experience them in three dimensions. They fear such children will grow up with a damaged ability to interact with others, aware only of their own responses to situations, and not knowing how to take into account the responses of other people to their actions.[7] Others fear that emotion replaces rationality as people respond to what they see on television. These educators see traditional approaches to learning as more necessary than ever because they offer a proven way to develop the skills of rational thought.

Only in the last few decades has there developed a genre of film and television criticism that can serve as a model for schoolteachers.[8]

Even so, some people are uneasy in their attempts to unite emotion and reason in their discussions. Some years ago, the School Without Walls in Philadelphia used the scripts of soap operas to develop among students the ability to analyze and critique what they watched on television. Other schools have since followed suit, but the larger implications of visual imagery and the changes that film and television have made in people's ways of knowing have been evaded by educators.

Television impacts not only the rational but also the emotional understandings of those who watch it. Our schools are adept at developing rational responses, those that can be labeled "intellectual"; they are less adept with emotional responses. Schools place less value on emotional than on rational responses, in part because the construction of knowledge is itself genderized. Knowledge considered masculine is prized; knowledge considered feminine is not. And, in the Western tradition, knowledge linked to reason has been considered masculine, while knowledge linked to emotion has been considered feminine. Such dichotomies in the way we perceive knowledge to be constructed through reason and emotion, and the way we associate the one with men and the other with women, now serve us ill. The visual images created by camera, film, and video provide knowledge that is based upon both emotion and reason. Visual images elicit emotional responses and, at the same time, they are the source of rational stimulation. Both become sources of learning for girls and boys, women and men. Nevertheless, few traditionally educated teachers are skilled enough to guide students to a sophisticated analysis of their emotional and reasoned responses to visual and oral material. New skills need to be learned by teachers and students in order for them to use television effectively as a vehicle for learning

Another reason why film and television have not yet impacted the schools as much as they have society at large is that schoolteachers are not prepared to discuss many of the issues raised in those media, often metaphorically, as in Space Age mythology. "If mythology is a symbolic expression of relationships between human beings and their environment, then of course, if the environment changes in a fundamental way, the mythology must change," writes Sylvia Engdahl.[9] She explains how Space Age mythology is evolving from the imagery of works such as "Star Trek," "Star Wars," and "ET":

> Mythological space fiction portrays our feelings about the universe we live in. It does not accurately explain the universe, because by definition, myth deals metaphorically with things of which we have no literal understanding. Space

> stories that deal with something we really know about (for instance, travel to the moon within our era) are no longer part of our culture's mythology; they're simply fiction, no matter what label is put on them. There are no metaphors involved, at least not apart from those concerned with individual psychology. Metaphors are needed only for things whose reality is likely to be quite different from our current conception.[10]

Space Age mythology, then, explores "the larger questions of our place in the cosmos, of which Earth is no more the spiritual center than it is the physical one,"[11] a concept that might cause some parents, and some teachers also, to object to its being discussed in school. Without discussion, however, all presuppositions remain hidden even though these myths have been created by our peers who, like ourselves, may carry with them unexamined prejudices. Without discussion, the metaphors presented in the media to help us cope with our environment remain unexamined; neither adults nor children develop the skills to critique them.

Why New Technologies Challenge Educators

Before considering the impact of other technologies on education and gender relations, I expand here upon some issues raised above. A technology is a tool that enhances a person's capacity to act. This definition might lead one to believe that a new technology makes individuals feel more powerful than before. In seeming contradiction, however, the individual often experiences a loss of power and a feeling of vulnerability when a new tool is introduced, because, as Marshall McLuhan pointed out in *Understanding Media* (1964), skills that were until that moment resident in the individual are now transferred to the tool.[12] For example, as a result of the introduction of cash registers and personal calculators, children no longer have to learn "mental arithmetic," and few of us have the skill to calculate quickly in our heads the way our grandparents could. That ability has been transferred to the cash register or calculator, leaving each of us the less skilled. Many who were taught mental arithmetic, however, worry that children may become less capable adults by not having that skill.

New technologies, therefore, present educators with a dilemma. If a new technology provides machines to calculate change, or to check the spelling of written words, should children and adults spend their time learning how to do those tasks? Some argue that they should, because when machines break down people who do not know how to calculate in their head or spell correctly cannot function. Hence, they argue, even though there are now calculators and software for checking spelling, none of the traditional subjects taught to children should be dropped. Other people who developed specific skills when they were children do not realize that new technologies have made some of those skills obsolete. They perceive only that children can no longer do mental arithmetic or spell, and they then assume schools are not doing their job properly. They therefore demand a return to "basics." Still others understand that young people need additional skills to benefit from a new technology but have no idea what those skills should be; they may even latch on to bogus solutions that offer a "quick fix."

The dilemma for educators becomes more acute if we add McLuhan's insight:

> [M]edia as extensions of our senses institute new ratios, not only among our private senses, but among themselves, when they interact among themselves. Radio changed the form of the news story as much as it altered the film image in the talkies. TV caused drastic changes in radio programming, and in the form of the *thing* or documentary novel.[13]

How are educators to respond to changing ratios among several media and to changing ratios among "our private senses"?[14] Perhaps learners need to develop new styles of learning to deal with the new ratios; perhaps they need to emphasize one way of knowing over another. But before teachers and learners abandon *any* approach to knowledge, they will have to see that the change is both necessary and beneficial.

On the issue of what should be taught and learned, educators have to decide whether they will be merely responsive to societal changes, or whether they will themselves influence those changes. If they decide to influence the changes, how can they determine in advance the changes likely to take place, for instance, in the ratios "among our private senses" and among the media as a result of new technologies? Without understanding possible futures and without the political motivation to prevent the futures they oppose from happening, educators can only react to change that has already taken place.

Technology and Gender

Any new technology is introduced into a preexisting social and economic environment. We therefore have to consider which of our social mores may influence the uses for a new technology and the decisions about who may use it. I concentrate here on the influence of gender roles, but they are only one of the many social, political, and economic influences that shape the use of a new technology. Gender is significant as a category of analysis because it provides an opportunity to examine presuppositions that otherwise remain hidden and are thus taken for granted. "Rather than just filling in gaps or recounting the barriers experienced by women in scientific and technological fields, the [gender] framework would provide the context and the tools for understanding why the situation occurred and how change needs to take place."[15]

All societies divide some activities according to the gender of the person undertaking them. However, the specific activities accorded to one gender or the other vary across cultures, and the percentage of activities divided by gender may vary between cultures and within a given culture at different periods in its history.[16] For example, the number of jobs in Europe and the United States segmented by gender increased with industrialization. In many cases, men and women became segregated in different occupations. Some occupations were not segregated, however. Nevertheless, in these occupations, employers tended to establish horizontal segregation by job category, with men in the higher-paying and women in the lower-paying jobs. In the United States, as in other countries, occupational and job segregation still exist, even though during the later nineteenth and early twentieth centuries women fought to obtain access to higher-paying managerial positions in industry and in newly created social institutions, such as school systems, libraries, and social service organizations, and even though more recently our society has begun to criticize both job classification and job stratification by gender. As a result of this criticism, we have removed gender-specific entry requirements from several occupations, including ones in the military, and we have passed laws to eliminate gender discrimination in hiring. Nevertheless, gender segregation still exists in some occupations and some job categories.

Gender segregation should be a source of great concern to all citizens, but especially to educators. It indicates that, while we may claim to be a society committed to equal opportunity and to eliminating gender (as well as racial and other) inequities, we hold to an ideology that runs counter to this claim. We are not willing to eliminate sources of unequal opportunity. Research in the United States has shown that differences between men and women on the performance of tasks and on their assessment of success in accomplishing tasks appear most frequently when the tasks are considered masculine. In these settings, women perform less well and feel less empowered and less successful than men.[17]

Another reason to be concerned about gender inequities is that our society rewards those who develop skills related to technology. So long as women are not expected to work at or accept jobs involving the use of sophisticated technology, they will be denied access to the economic and social power the jobs provide. For a variety of reasons, including the rigorous training needed to become a successful scientist or engineer, fewer people than we need complete a bachelor's degree in science and engineering. Fewer still complete a doctorate. According to a 1989 report, the proportion of women, minority and white, in the sciences and engineering is still low.[18] Because of our ideology of gender discrimination, we deprive society of the talent of women in science and engineering. Among other items (including actions to be taken by federal and state governments, and universities and colleges), the report recommended that school boards "ensure that the maximum number of students—especially minority, women, and the disabled—take college preparatory mathematics and science. . . . [Boards should] expand innovations which produce better educated students, especially women, minorities, and the disabled. Where necessary [boards should] restructure schools, curricula, teaching practices, and educational experiences."[19]

In considering the influence of technology and gender in education, therefore, we have to take into account the ideology that shapes gender roles, and the ways that ideology influences the long-term career aspirations of women and men. "Technology is not an independent force; the way in which it affects the nature of work is conditioned by existing relationships."[20] In this context, educators have to inquire whether women and men expect to use any given technology. If both expect to use it, do they expect to use it for similar or different purposes? If women expect to use a technology for purposes different from those of men, or if they do not expect to use a particular technology at all, how have their different expectations arisen and why? Are the assumptions of either gender serving as barriers to their occupational mobility?

Ideology has other, less direct effects. Studies of the way people assess their own capabilities suggest that women more than men pay attention to external measures of their ability. A survey of courses chosen by college students over a twenty-year period indicated that "without high mathematics ability, women tended to avoid the technical disciplines almost completely. The same trends were noted for men, but they seemed less dependent upon confirmation of mathematics ability in making these choices."[21] Irene T. Miura suggests that a woman's feelings of self-efficacy in taking computer courses in college may increase as she is encouraged to take more of them.[22] Miura does not take into account, however, the barriers to women receiving such encouragement from male faculty socialized to accepting male superiority in mathematics and science and the dominance of men in the professions. In order to overcome such barriers, ways must be found to overcome the opposition of male professionals to women colleagues.[23]

COMPUTERS AND GENDER SEGREGATION: JOBS

Recent studies suggest that in the United States and other countries where computers are manufactured, the job market relating to computers has already become segmented by gender. In California's Silicon Valley, for instance, "the primary sector comprises the elite technicians, managers, and sales personnel. In the secondary sector are the women and minorities for whom high-tech industry means low-wage, dead-end jobs, unskilled, tedious work, and exposure to some of the most dangerous occupational health hazards in all of American industry."[24] This division has also been substantiated by the 1985 Kirby Report, which comments on a "high degree of market segregation on the basis of gender."[25] Several studies conclude that increased technology has intensified male/female job stratification.[26] Ruth Perry and Lisa Greber comment that computers

> support the power of capital by moving information and skills from workers to managers; they reinforce the power patriarchy by pushing women, particularly women of color, into low-skilled, low-paying, and highly controlled jobs. These effects are certainly not inherent in the technology: to program a user-monitoring dimension into word-processing software is a sociopolitical choice, not a technological necessity.[27]

Other writers suggest that computers will de-skill the occupation of teaching itself if they are accepted uncritically into the classroom, and that the de-skilling may affect women teachers more than men teachers. As Michael Apple points out,

> Because of the large amount of time it takes to become a "computer expert and because of the patriarchal relations that still dominate many families, *men*

teachers will often be able to use "computer literacy" to advance their own careers while women teachers will tend to remain the recipients of prepackaged units on computers or "canned" programs over which they have little control.[28]

COMPUTERS AND GENDER SEGREGATION: SOCIALIZATION AND LEARNING

Girls and boys become socialized to gender differentiation not only because jobs are segmented by gender, but also because certain knowledge is perceived to appeal more to men than women. As Lockheed and others have pointed out, computer games are often played in arcades where more boys than girls tend to congregate. These games are also sold widely for use in the home, where their use may not be gender specific. However, many of these games are associated with battle and appeal more to boys than to girls; they also are purchased by parents more often for boys than for girls. As insidious, but less obvious, is the fact that computer games are often designed with women as victims. In a study of forty-seven Nintendo games highly rated by groups of players, dealers, and Nintendo employees, "30 percent of the games contained scenarios in which women were kidnapped or had to be rescued as part of the game." Another examination of the covers used to market the same forty-seven games revealed the portrayal of 115 male but only nine female characters.[29] Even in informal settings, therefore, computers are associated in people's minds more with men than women, and more with boys than girls.

Children associate computers with science and mathematics, both subjects appealing more to males than females. Boys in the United States do better than girls and are more interested than girls in mathematics and science. Hence, if computers are linked in people's minds with mathematics and science, it follows that boys are likely to "do better with computers" than girls. Recent studies have explored the reasons why boys are better at and more interested in mathematics and science than girls.[30] A cross-cultural study supports the notion that socialization rather than innate ability in mathematics and science contributes to gender differences in performance.[31] The directors of this study used Raven's test of analogical reasoning as a computer-based test of the ability of Japanese and American girls and boys to deal with solutions to figural matrices. They found no differences among Japanese girls and boys but did find gender differences among American children, with boys outperforming girls. In this instance, the Japanese children had little computer experience, while all the American children had a computer at home. The authors found, however, that it was "the boys, not the girls, who were playing with them alongside of their fathers."[32] Other research suggests that socioeconomic status may play a greater role than gender in influencing the differences among middle-school American students in such areas as interest in computers and willingness to think of a computer-related career. In a study conducted in California, girls of low socioeconomic status evinced a more positive response on these issues than did girls of high socioeconomic status.[33] The author suggests that the life-style of the high socioeconomic group was more traditional than that of the low socioeconomic group. Few children in the former group had mothers who worked in paid employment, while most of the mothers of the latter group were wage-earners, "in some cases working in the computer-related industries of Silicon Valley."[34]

Research on mathematics achievement in the United States reveals gender-related differences, not only in areas relating to societal expectations such as in perceptions of mathematics as an appropriate field for women and self-confidence in relation to mathematics, but also in student behavior in relation to their peers[35] and in student-teacher interactions.[36] A study of 160 high school girls taking advanced placement courses in mathematics and physics reported that 40 percent "played down good grades in mathematics in front of classmates and peers, especially male classmates and peers."[37] Several studies by Fennema and Peterson suggest that differences in the cognitive responses of girls and boys in mathematics classes could result from differences in student-teacher interactions that involve girls. The authors say that boys are more likely than girls to be taught autonomous learning behavior, which enables the student to take responsibility for his or her own learning without the intervention of a teacher or even a facilitator.[38] Ways to change teacher behaviors so that they encourage girls as well as boys to become autonomous learners have been suggested, but they are unlikely to be taken up nationwide without encouragement. Work with mixed-sex instructional groups demonstrates that it is possible to encourage gender integration and decrease sex-role stereotyping among fourth and fifth graders.[39] However, we need a national effort to educate the public at large and particularly teachers, parents, and software manufacturers about why they should change their behaviors. In order to eliminate gender discrimination in jobs as well as in learning, they have to appreciate the link computers have to all subjects in the school curriculum, not merely to mathematics and science. Once teachers, parents, and software manufacturers change their behaviors in relation to computers, girls and boys in our society need no longer be socialized into thinking that the computer is a "masculine" technology, but one that belongs equally to both genders.

ALTERNATIVES TO PERCEIVING THE COMPUTER AS A "MASCULINE" TECHNOLOGY

One way to counter this perception is to encourage the use of computers to enhance the whole school curriculum. In this context, experiments with writing to "pen pals" in other schools, some as far away as Europe, enable girls as well as boys to experience the computer as user friendly. There have been pilot projects, supported by AT&T, linking students in specific schools around the world by computer to undertake a unit of study. Each project culminates in a document, with different parts written by students in each school and published with desktop publishing technology at each node.[40]

It has been suggested that the very field of educational technology has been designed on a male model of hierarchy and scientific objectivity. An "unthinking" of educational technology "might begin with the examination of both the purported benefits of the technology for the user and the changes which the technology imposes on the users with respect to standards, schedules, social structures, and social credit."[41] Such a process of deconstruction would provide both teachers and students with skills to decide how each might benefit most from projects using a technology such as the computer, as well as enabling them to decide when the use of a particular technology may not be appropriate.

Interactive media, which combine computers, visual images, and sound, provide another avenue to link computers to social studies, art, and the rest of the curriculum. This variety in the use of computers also affects ways of programming. A recent article describes ways to hook people, particularly girls, into programming: introduce graphics as soon as possible, give "as much time to words as to numbers" and some time to music, provide "a context in which students need to know a command or concept to make their lives easier or to make new things possible," accept both top-down and bottom-up programming styles, encourage cooperation on projects, and allow room for individuals to elaborate on initial frameworks, and to share final products.[42]

Sherry Turkle and Seymour Papert have recently suggested an even more dramatic shift in thinking about computers. They propose a theoretical challenge to both Piaget's hierarchy of stages in an individual's approach to knowledge and to the notion that there is a conceptual bond between computers and mathematics and science and not between computers and other areas of knowledge or ways of knowing.[43] The conclusions reported below are based on extensive work, especially by Turkle, on the implications of gender differences in computer use.[44] Turkle and Papert's report of their research into the programming styles of grade school children and of college students taking a first programming course suggests that Piaget's interpretation may not be the only, or even the most useful, interpretation of the differences in forms of knowledge that he saw. "Where he saw diverse forms of knowledge in terms of stages to a finite end point of formal reason, we see different approaches to knowledge as styles, each equally valid on its own terms."[45] They draw on Claude Lévi-Strauss's "bricolage" (a "science of the concrete") and the people who practice it (his "bricoleurs") to describe people who use a concrete rather than a formal approach to programming. Unlike those who provide access to programming through formal operations in mathematics, Turkle and Papert claim that "the computer, with its graphics, its sounds, its text, and its animation, can provide a port of entry for people whose chief ways of relating to the world are through movement, intuition, and visual impression."[46]

According to Turkle and Papert, structured programmers develop a plan in abstract terms, using a rule-driven system, before they begin programming; bricoleurs do not. They allow the material to interact with them, and, through a process of negotiation, they arrive at a product. Bricoleurs "are not drawn to structured programming; their work at the computer is marked by a desire to play with the elements of the program, to move them around almost as though they were material elements—the words in a sentence, the notes in a musical composition, the elements of a collage."[47] Unfortunately, many bricoleurs are dissuaded from using the computer by teachers who insist they follow a rule-driven system.

Turkle and Papert found that more girls than boys were bricoleurs. The issue of gender is salient in their work because feminist scholarship has been crucial in providing the research base for their argument. With Gilligan's counter to Kohlberg's hierarchy of moral values as an analogy,[48] they argue that girls' and women's preferred use of bricolage in programming is not less developed, merely different from boys' and men's preferred use of an abstract rule-system.[49]

The above discussion suggests that two approaches to issues of gender and technology in education will prove useful to increasing women's participation in new technologies: insure that new technologies, particularly computers and all the technologies associated with them, are not linked in people's minds only, or even primarily, to mathematics and science; and insure that the output from new technologies is not genderized, either by the terminology or by the types of materials.

Social and Ethical Issues Raised by New Technologies

Another issue for educators is whether those who use a given technology need to understand how it works, and if so, why. In this country, almost all people use electricity. Does that mean that everyone who does so understands how electricity works or needs to understand how it works? People drive cars to work or while on vacation. Do all drivers understand how a car works, or do they need to? Merely to ask is to realize that many people who use the technologies of our society understand neither their structure nor how they function.

However, the questions raise other issues. Were people to understand how a technology works, would they be better able to use it? Would they understand better both its capabilities and its limitations? To refer to the example cited earlier from Perry and Greber, people with a knowledge of computers *know* that adding a user-monitoring dimension to word-processing software is a deliberate choice. But a person can only understand the implications of that choice by using other knowledge than merely that of how a computer works. Thus, while from a technical perspective learning how something works may indeed help one better understand its capabilities or limitations, from the perspective of assessing the social impact of that technology, learning how it works is useful but not sufficient. To assess the social, political, and ethical capabilities and limitations of a technology, people have to be conversant with the values of their society and its members, and be able to judge the impact of a technology on those values. One does not learn how to assess merely from using a technology or from learning how it works.

In her discussion of computer ethics, Robinett claims that the computer's capacity to make decisions will force new ethical dilemmas on society. She comments that:

> the computer distances people from the work they do and from a sense of the people whom they serve. In much computer-based work, there is no sense at all of another person. This distancing makes it easy to relax ethical behavior. . . . When the other person is not present or is reduced to a two-line entry in a database, it might seem that there is no need to think about ethical behavior. It is exactly the same kind of distancing that occurs in the development of weapons which allow us to kill without having any personal contact with the person who dies. Protected from the reality and the consequences of what we are doing, we are capable of the most inhumane and terrible acts.[50]

In several occupations that became computerized, Shoshana Zuboff noted a similar distancing taking place between workers and the actual work of production.[51] Zuboff cited the frustration of workers passively watching data on a screen, workers whose skill had previously been measured by their ability to judge the state of a process through touching or smelling the raw materials as the machines transformed them. Robinett suggests the need to develop a new kind of ethics, so that all people who work with computers—"programmers, designers, software engineers, system managers, maintenance engineers, and office personnel at every level" and all others who use computers—understand that each of us depends upon personal integrity. "The same respect and care accorded to the physical person of fellow human beings must be extended to include the information that, in one way or another, describes and defines them."[52]

Already some computer systems are used for medical diagnoses, sales projections, and investment decision making. "As parallel processing, neural networks, and the art of programming continue to develop, other decision-making systems will take their places in our daily lives. It is altogether possible that in these areas we are facing something entirely new, something which older ethical guidelines are not equipped to deal with."[53]

Educators have a responsibility to teach girls and boys about the ethical issues spawned by new technologies. Such issues affect everyone. Each person in society, whether as a taxpayer, a word processor, a programmer, a person working the checkout at a supermarket, or a shopper, is likely at some time to encounter or work with computers. As Robert Morris demonstrated with his Internet worm, one person can cause chaos among networked machines nationwide.[54] There are educators who believe that only through strong sensory education do children learn what it means to hurt someone else or to be tender towards them, and that sensory education is more necessary now than ever before. Because this may be true it is essential that we do not become so attracted by the logic of symbols and two-dimensional pictures produced by computers that we neglect the teaching of sensory skills. This does not, however, negate the need for girls and boys and women and men to learn new ethical behaviors for a world dependent upon new technologies for communication.

Conclusion

In such an enterprise, what should be the role of educators? It should be to insure that all children, regardless of their gender, race, or socioeconomic status, have equal access to the new communication technologies and to assist in the creation and learning of a new ethics. At the moment we have few aphorisms, few metaphors, and few stories to illustrate a new ethics. We depend mostly upon what has been handed down to us from our premodern forebears, based upon a world view that does not encompass the changes that twentieth-century technologies have wrought or the social revolution in race and gender relations currently taking place. Our task as educators is to prepare students to envision the future, not only through knowledge of science and technology, but also by incorporating into that knowledge our understandings of diversity and equity.

I thank Amy El-Hindi, Wendy Pusch, and Michelle Maher for their assistance with the preparation of this chapter.

Notes

1. Alvin Toffler, *Power Shift: Knowledge, Wealth, and Violence at the Edge of the 21st Century* (New York: Bantam Books, 1991), p. 82.

2. Ruth Perry and Lisa Greber, "Women and Computers: An Introduction," *Signs: Journal of Women in Culture and Society* 16, no. 1 (Autumn 1990): 75. This article introduces a cluster of more specific articles on the topic.

3. Corlann Gee Bush, "Women and the Assessment of Technology: To Think, To Be; To Unthink, To Free," in *Machina Ex Dea: Feminist Perspectives on Technology*, edited by Joan Rothschild (New York: Pergamon Press, 1983), p. 163.

4. James J. Higgins, "Electronic Schools and American Competitiveness," *Business Week*, Special Advertising Section on "The Technology Revolution Comes to Education" (Fall 1990): 8, 10.

5. See Marlaine E. Lockheed's introduction to a special issue of *Sex Roles*, "Women, Girls, and Computers: A First Look at the Evidence," *Sex Roles* 13, no. 3/4 (1985): 115-122.

6. It has been suggested that "the temptation here is to call [an expert system or a neural network system] a 'machine,' but it seems that to apply the term 'machine' to systems of this complexity and sophistication is to deliberately evoke an outmoded

model and to make the same kind of mistake that we make in regarding the body as a machine. It begs the question by reducing these systems to something which they are not." Jane Robinett, "Computer Ethics Inside and Out," *Journal of Social and Biological Structures* 13, no. 3 (1990): 190.

7. See, for example, three chapters in *The Computer and Education: A Critical Perspective*, edited by Douglas Sloan (New York: Teachers College Press, 1985): Douglas Stone, "Introduction: On Raising Critical Questions about the Computer in Education"; Harriet K. Cuffaro, "Microcomputers in Education: Why Is Earlier Better?"; and Arthur G. Zajonc, "Computer Pedagogy? Questions Concerning the New Educational Technology."

8. A brief but useful survey of some research on visual texts may be found in Ann DeVaney Becker, "Picture as Visual Text," *Educational Considerations* 10, no. 2 (Spring 1983): 30-32. Becker refers to several authors who build upon the pathbreaking work of Roland Barthes in examining the social meaning of visual media, including John Fiske and John Hartley, *Reading Television* (London: Methuen, 1978) and Bill Nichols, *Ideology and the Image* (Bloomington, IN: Indiana University Press, 1981).

9. Sylvia Engdahl, "The Mythic Role of Space Fiction," *Journal of Social and Biological Structures* 13, no. 4 (1990): 292.

10. Ibid., p. 293.

11. Ibid., p. 295.

12. See particularly, Marshall McLuhan, *Understanding Media: The Extensions of Man* (New York: McGraw-Hill, 1964), chapter 4.

13. Ibid., p. 66.

14. I think of Sylvia Ashton-Warner, *Spearpoint: Teacher in America* (New York: Knopf, 1972), who wrote about her year of working with young children in the United States who were veteran TV watchers but lacked certain perceptual skills that the Maori children she had worked with in New Zealand (and had written about in *Teacher* [New York: Simon and Schuster, 1963]) had in abundance.

15. Joan Rothschild, "Technology and Education: A Feminist Perspective," *American Behavioral Scientist* 32, no. 6 (July/August 1989): 711.

16. For an interesting critique of recent government policy in India, see Padmini Swaminathan, "Science and Technology for Women: A Critique of Policy," *Economic and Political Weekly*, January 5-12, 1991, pp. 59-63. Swaminathan comments: "Given the 'male model of work', the partial services provided by the state and the almost static traditional role of men, very little change can be effected in the quality of women's lives, with the result that women are forced simply to do more and accept a double shift." (p. 62).

17. See, for example, Kay Deauz, "Self-Evaluations of Male and Female Managers," *Sex Roles* 5, no. 5 (October 1979): 571-580; Idy-Barasch Gitelson, Anne C. Petersen, and Maryse H. Tobin-Richards, "Adolescents' Expectancies of Success, Self-Evaluations, and Attributions about Performance on Spatial and Verbal Tasks," *Sex Roles* 8, no. 4 (April 1982): 411-419.

18. See Task Force on Women, Minorities, and the Handicapped in Science and Technology, *Changing America: The New Face of Science and Engineering*, Final Report (Washington, DC: U. S. Government Printing Office, 1989). The Task Force was established by Congress under Public Law 99-383.

19. Ibid., p. 13.

20. Judy Wajcman, *Feminism Confronts Technology* (University Park, PA: Pennsylvania State University Press, 1991), p. 34. For further discussion on the impact of environment on the acceptance of technologies, see Deborah Johnson, *Computer Ethics* (Englewood Cliffs, NJ: Prentice-Hall, 1985), chapter 5, and Joan N. Burstyn, "Introduction: The Promise of Desktop Publishing," in *Desktop Publishing in the University*, edited by Joan N. Burstyn (Syracuse, NY: Syracuse University School of Education, 1991).

21. Data gathered by Scholastic Aptitude Test scores, and J. Boli et al., "The Stanford Curriculum Study: Looking at Student Course Choices and How They Vary," *Campus Reports Supplement*, October 19, 1983, p. 13, as cited in Irene T. Miura, "The Relationship of Computer Self-Efficacy Expectations to Computer Interest and Course Enrollment in College," *Sex Roles* 16, nos. 5/6 (1987); 304.

22. Ibid., p. 310.

23. See Anthony Astrachan, *How Men Feel: Their Response to Women's Demands for Equality and Power* (New York: Doubleday, 1986), p. 170-174, for a discussion of negative and positive responses among male professionals to women's entry into their professions.

24. R. Howard, "Second Class in Silicon Valley," *Working Papers Magazine* 8, no. 5 (1981): 18. Referred to in Peter Watkins, *High Tech, Low Tech, and Education* (Victoria, Australia: Deakin Press, 1986).

25. Julia Kirby, ed., *Early Childhood Intervention: An Investment in the Future*, A Report to the Texas State Legislature (Austin, TX: Texas Interagency Council on Early Childhood Intervention, 1985), pp. 43-44.

26. See, for instance, the studies listed in Watkins, *High Tech, Low Tech, and Education*, pp. 35-39, including Roslyn L. Feldberg and Evelyn-Nakan Glenn, "Incipient Workplace Democracy among United States Clerical Workers," *Economic and Industrial Democracy* 4, no. 1 (February 1983): 47-67. See also, David Boddy and David Buchanan, *Managing New Technology* (New York: Blackwell, 1986), and Janine Morgall, "Typing Our Way to Freedom: Is It True that New Office Technology Can Liberate Women?", *Behavior and Information Technology* 2, no. 3 (July-September 1983): 215-226.

27. Perry and Greber, "Women and Computers: An Introduction," p. 82.

28. Michael W. Apple, "Teaching and Technology: The Hidden Effects of Computers on Teachers and Students," in *Crisis in Teaching: Perspectives on Current Reforms*, edited by Lois Weis, Philip G. Altbach, Gail P. Kelly, Hugh G. Petrie, and Sheila Slaughter (Albany, NY: State University of New York Press, 1989), p. 237.

29. See Eugene F. Provenzo, Jr., *Video Kids: Making Sense of Nintendo* (Cambridge, MA: Harvard University Press, 1991), pp. 108-9.

30. For a survey of research on the performance of girls and boys on standardized tests, the possible causes for the differences (especially the poorer performance of girls on mathematics and science tests), and suggestions for "rewriting the script," see a brief prepared by Kathy Vandell and Lauren Fishbein, *Equitable Treatment of Girls and Boys in the Classroom* (Washington, DC: American Association of University Women, 1989).

31. See Barbara Foorman, Hajime Yoshida, Paul Swank, and James Garson, "The Effect of Visual and Verbal Strategies on Children's Solutions of Figural Matrices in Japan and the United States" (Paper presented at the Annual Meeting of American Educational Research Association, Chicago, 1985). ERIC ED 266 194.

32. Ibid., p. 14.

33. See Irene T. Miura, "Gender and Socioeconomic Status Differences in Middle-School Computer Interest and Use," *Journal of Early Adolescence* 7, no. 2 (1987): 243-253.

34. Ibid., p. 252. Pamela E. Kramer suggests, however, that less affluent and minority girls may not benefit as much from computers that are available in schools as they could because of contextual factors, e.g., more than 50 percent of the teachers surveyed in 225 inner-city schools said they did not use computers, while 95 percent of them reported that computers *were* available in their school. See Pamela Kramer, *Final Report to the National Science Foundation*, Grant no. SER-8160408 (Washington, DC: National Science Foundation, 1987) as cited in Pamela E. Kramer and Sheila Lehman,

"Mismeasuring Women: A Critique of Research on Computer Ability and Avoidance," *Signs: Journal of Women in Culture and Society* 16, no. 1 (Autumn 1990): 159.

35. See Kramer and Lehman, "Mismeasuring Women," pp. 160-161, for a discussion of the literature on girls' reactions to being considered smart in mathematics.

36. For a useful review of this literature, see Lewis R. Aiken, "Sex Differences in Mathematical Ability: A Review of the Literature," *Educational Research Quarterly* 10, no. 4 (1987): 25-36.

37. Patricia Lynn Casserly, "Helping Able Young Women Take Math and Science Seriously in School," in *New Voices in Counseling the Gifted*, edited by Nicholas Colangelo and Ronald T. Zaffrann (Dubuque, IA: Kendall/Hunt, 1979) as cited by Kramer and Lehman, "Mismeasuring Women," p. 161.

38. See, for instance, Elizabeth Fennema, "Explaining Sex-Related Differences in Mathematics: Theoretical Models," *Educational Studies in Mathematics* 16, no. 3 (1985): 303-330; Elizabeth Fennema and Penelope L. Peterson, "Teacher-Student Interactions and Sex-Related Differences in Mathematics," *Teaching and Teacher Education* 2, no. 1 (1986): 19-42; and Penelope L. Peterson and Elizabeth Fennema, "Effective Teaching, Student Engagement in Classroom Activities, and Sex-Related Differences in Learning Mathematics," *American Educational Research Journal* 22, no. 3 (1985): 309-335.

39. See Marlaine E. Lockheed, "Reshaping the Social Order: The Case of Gender Segregation," *Sex Roles* 14, nos. 11/12 (1986): 617-628.

40. For a brief description of that and of another project, which was facilitated by Dr. Margaret Riel as part of the AT&T Long Distance Learning Network, see Dan Lake, "Two Projects That Worked: Using Telecommunications as a Resource in the Classroom," *The Computer Teacher* 17 (December/January 1988-89): 17-19.

41. Suzanne K. Damarin, "Unthinking Educational Technology," *Proceedings of the AECT: Selected Research Paper Presentations at the Convention of the AECT*, Anaheim, California, January 31-February 4, 1990 (Ames, Iowa: College of Education, Iowa State University, 1990).

42. Diane McGrath, "Eight Ways to Get Beginners Involved in Programming," *Women and Computers* 2, no. 1 (January 1990): 5-7. Reprinted from *The Computer Teacher* 18, no. 1 (August/September 1990).

43. See Sherry Turkle and Seymour Papert, "Epistemological Pluralism: Styles and Voices within the Computer Culture," *Signs: Journal of Women in Culture and Society* 16, no. 1 (Autumn 1990): 128-157.

44. See Sherry Turkle, *The Second Self: Computers and the Human Spirit* (New York: Simon and Schuster, 1984).

45. Turkle and Papert, "Epistemological Pluralism," p. 129.

46. Ibid., p. 131.

47. Ibid., p. 136.

48. See Carol Gilligan, *In a Different Voice* (Cambridge, MA: Harvard University Press, 1982).

49. Turkle and Papert, "Epistemological Pluralism," pp. 141-143.

50. Robinett, "Computer Ethics Inside and Out," p. 188.

51. See Shoshana Zuboff, *In the Age of the Smart Machine* (New York: Basic Books, 1989).

52. Robinett, "Computer Ethics Inside and Out," p. 190.

53. Ibid., p. 186.

54. For a description of the Morris case, see Harold L. Burstyn, "The Worm That Ate Internet," *Harvard Magazine* 92, no. 5 (May/June 1990): 23-28.

Section Four
GENDER AT WORK AMONG ADOLESCENTS AND ADULTS

CHAPTER VIII

Over Dinner: Feminism and Adolescent Female Bodies

MICHELLE FINE AND PAT MACPHERSON

> The experience of being women can create an illusory unity, for it is not the experience of being woman but the meanings attached to gender, race, class, and age at various historical moments . . . that [are] of strategic significance.
>
> Chandra Mohanty
> "Feminist Encounters"
> *Copyright* 1 (1987), p. 39

When we invited four teenagers—Shermika, Damalleaux, Janet, and Sophie—for a series of two dinners to talk with us about being young women in the 1990s, we could not see our own assumptions about female adolescence much more clearly than we saw theirs. By the end of the first dinner, however, we could recognize how old we were, how dated the academic literature is, how powerful feminism had been in shaping their lives and the meanings they made of them, and yet how inadequately their feminism dealt with key issues of identity and peer relations.

Only when we started to write could we see the inadequacies of our feminism to understand the issues of female adolescence they struggled to communicate. In this space of our incredulity, between

Michelle Fine is Professor of Psychology at the Graduate Center of the City University of New York. Pat Macpherson, a teacher of English at the Germantown Friends School in Philadelphia for thirteen years, is now a free lance writer.

our comprehension of their meanings and our *in*comprehension of how they could call themselves feminist, we are now able to see the configuration of our own fantasies of feminism for female adolescents. The re-vision that is central to feminist process gets very tricky when applied to adolescence, because our own unsatisfactory pasts return as the "before" picture, demanding that the "after" picture of current adolescent females measure all the gains of the women's movement. Our longing is for psychic as well as political completion. Michael Payne describes the fantasy of the Other: "What I desire—and therefore lack—is in the other culture, the other race, the other gender"[1]—the other generation, in our case. In the case of these four young women, to our disbelief, the desired Other is "one of the guys."

We grew convinced that we needed to construct an essay about these young women's interpretations of the discourses of adolescence, femininity, and feminism in their peer cultures. Barbara Hudson explains the incompatibility of femininity and adolescence:

> [F]emininity and adolescence as discourses [are] subversive of each other. All of our images of the adolescent—the restless, searching teen; the Hamlet figure; the sower of wild oats and tester of growing powers—these are masculine figures. . . . If adolescence is characterized by masculine constructs, then any attempt by girls to satisfy society's demands of them qua adolescents is bound to involve them in displaying notably a lack of maturity but also a lack of femininity.[2]

Adolescence for these four young women was about the adventures of males and the constraints on females, so their version of feminism unselfconsciously rejected femininity and embraced the benign version of masculinity that allowed them to be "one of the guys." They fantasized the safe place of adolescence to be among guys who overlook their (female) gender out of respect for their (unfeminine) independence, intelligence, and integrity. For them, femininity meant the taming of adolescent passions, outrage, and intelligence. Feminism was a flight from "other girls" as unworthy and untrustworthy. Their version of feminism was about equal access to being like men.

When we scoured the literature on adolescent females and their bodies, we concluded that the very construction of the topic is positioned largely from white, middle-class, nondisabled, heterosexual adult women's perspectives. The concerns of white elite women are represented as *the* concerns of this age cohort. Eating disorders are defined within the contours of what *elite* women suffer (e.g., anorexia and bulimia) and less so what nonelite women experience (e.g., overeating, obesity). The literature on sexual harassment is constructed from *our* age perspective—that unwanted sexual attention is and should be constituted as a crime—and not from the complicated perspectives of young women involved. The literature on disability is saturated with images produced by *nondisabled* researchers of self-pitying or embarrassed "victims" of biology, and is rarely filled with voices of resistant, critical, and powerfully "flaunting" adolescents who refuse to wear prostheses, delight in the passions of their bodies, and are outraged by the social and family discrimination they experience.[3]

We found that women of all ages, according to this literature, are allegedly scripted to be "good women," and that they have, in compliance, smothered their passions, appetites, and outrage. When sexually harassed, they tell "his stories."[4] To please the lingering internalized "him," they suffer in body image and indulge in eating disorders.[5] And to satisfy social demands for "attractiveness," women with and without disabilities transform and mutilate their bodies.[6]

We presumed initially that the three arenas of adolescence in which young women would most passionately struggle with gendered power would include eating, sexuality, and outrage. And so we turned to see what the literature said, and to unpack how race, class, disability, and sexuality played within each of these arenas. In brief, we saw in this literature a polarizing: (1) eating disorders appear to be a question studied among elite white women in their anticipated tensions of career *vs.* mother identities; (2) sexuality is examined disproportionately as problematic for girls who are black and underprivileged, with motherhood as their primary identity posed as "the problem"; and (3) young women's political "outrage" simply does not exist as a category for feminist intellectual analysis. The literature on adolescent women had thoroughly extricated these categories of analysis from women's lives. So, in our text we decided to rely instead upon the frames that these young women offered as they narrated their own lives, and on the interpretations we could generate through culture and class.

Our method was quite simple, feminist, and, ironically, anti-eating disorder. We invited the six of us to talk together over pizza and soda, while Sam—Michelle's four-year-old—circled the table. We talked for hours, two nights two months apart, and together stretched to create conversations about common differences; about the spaces in which we could delight together as six women; the moments in which they bonded together as four young women who enjoy football, hit their boyfriends, and can't trust other girls—"Not ever!"; and, too, the arenas in which the race, class, and cultural distances in the room stretched too far for these age peers to weave any common sense of womanhood. Collectively, we created a context that Shermika and Sophie spontaneously considered "the space where I feel most safe." We were together, chatting, listening, hearing, laughing a lot, and truly interested in understanding our connections and differences, contoured always along the fault lines of age, class, race and culture, bodies, experiences, and politics.

But we each delighted in this context differently. For Michelle and Pat, it was a space in which we could pose feminist intellectual questions from our generation—questions about sexuality, power, victimization, and politics—which the young women then turned on their heads. For Shermika (African-American, age 15) it was a place for public performance, to say outrageous things, admit embarrassing moments, "practice" ways of being female in public discourse, and see how we would react. For Damalleaux (African-American, age 14) it was a place to "not be shy" even though the group was integrated by race, a combination that had historically made her uncomfortable. For Sophie ("WASP," age 17), it was a "safe place" where, perhaps for the first time, she was not the only self-proclaimed feminist in a room full of peers. And for Janet (Korean-American, age 17), like other occasions in which she was the only Asian-American among whites and blacks, it was a time to test her assimilated "sense of belonging," always at the margins. In negotiating gender, race, ethnicity, and class as critical feminist agents, these four women successfully betrayed the academic literature, written by so many of us only twenty years older. Our writings have been persistently committed to public representations of women's victimization and structural assaults, and have consequently ignored, indeed misrepresented, *how well young women talk as subjects*, passionate about and relishing in their capacities to move between nexuses of power and powerlessness. That is to say, feminist scholars have forgotten to take notice of how firmly young women resist—alone and sometimes together.

The four young women began their conversation within this space of gendered resistance. Shermika complained, "Boys think girls cannot do *any*thing," to which Sophie added, "So we have to harass them." Shermika explained, "[Guys think] long as they're takin' care of 'em [girls will] do anything they want. And if I'm in a relationship, I'm gonna take care of you just as much as you take care of me. You can't say 'I did this'—No: 'We did this'. . . . Guys think you're not nothin'—anything—without them." Janet sneered, "Ego." Shermika recruited her friend into this conversation by saying, "Damalleaux *rule* her boyfriend (Shermika's brother)." Damalleaux announced her governing principle, "Boys—they try to take advantage of you. . . . As far as I'm concerned, I won't let a boy own me." Janet provided an example of the "emotionally messed up guys" she encounters: "I didn't want to take care of him. I didn't want to constantly explain things to him. . . . I want to coexist with them and not be like their mother. . . . It happened to me twice." And Sophie explained: "I'm really assertive with guys [who say sexist stuff]. If they have to be shot down I'll shoot them down. They have to know their place." The four expressed their feminism here as resistance to male domination in their peer relations. They applied the same principle in discussing how they saw careers and marriage. When Michelle asked about men in their future plans, Shermika laid it out in material terms: "I imagine bein' in my *own* house in *my name*. And then get married. So my husband can get out of *my house*." Sophie chimed in, "Seriously?" and Shermika nodded, "Yes, *very important*. So I won't end up one of them battered women we were talkin' about. I'm not going to have no man beatin' on me." Sophie offered her version: "You have to like, be independent. You have to establish yourself as your own person before some guy takes you—I mean—." Janet asserted her standard of independence: "I wouldn't follow a guy to college." Their feminism asserted women's independence from men's power to dominate and direct.

Class and cultural differences entered the conversations with their examples of domination and resistance. Shermika's example of guys materially "takin' care" of girls to establish dominance, and Damalleaux's resistance to male "ownership" reflected the practice of gift-giving as ownership, a norm of their local sexual politics.[7] Damalleaux explained that *respect* could interrupt this dominance structure: "How much respect a guy has for you—especially in front of his friends. . . . If a boy finds out you don't care how they treat you, and you don't have respect for your*self* . . . they won't have respect for you." Damalleaux turned to Shermika and said, "You try to teach me." Shermika's talk was full of lessons learned from her mother, and examples of their closeness. "My mom and me like this, 'cause she understands." Not talking "*leads* to problems. My mom tells me so much about life."

Sophie and Janet defined their resistance within their "professional class," peopled by "individuals," not relationships, who suffer from the dilemmas of "independence," typically explained in terms of psychology. Their isolation from their mothers and female friends enabled them to frame their stories alone, as one-on-one battles across the lines of gender and generations.

Ways of Talking: On Cultures of Womanhood

Herein lies a cautionary tale for feminists who insist that underneath or beyond the differences among women there must be some shared identity—as if commonality were a metaphysical given, as if a shared viewpoint were not a difficult political achievement. . . . Western feminist theory has in effect . . . [demanded that] Afro-American, Asian-American or Latin-American women separate their "woman's voice" from their racial or ethnic voice without also requiring white women to distinguish being a "woman" from being white. This double standard implies that while on the one hand there is a seamless web of whiteness and womanness, on the other hand, blackness and womanness, say, or Indianness and womanness, are discrete and separable elements of identity. If . . . I believe that the woman in every woman is a woman just like me, and if I also assume that there is no difference between being white and being a woman, then seeing another woman "as a woman" will involve me seeing her as fundamentally like the woman I am. In other words, the womanness underneath the black woman's skin is a white woman's, and deep down inside the latina woman is an Anglo woman waiting to burst through the obscuring cultural shroud. As Barbara Omolade has said, "Black women are not white women with color."[8]

At this moment in social history, when the tensions of race, class, and gender could not be in more dramatic relief, social anxieties load onto the bodies of adolescent women.[9] Struggles for social control attach to these unclaimed territories, evident in public debates over teen pregnancy, adolescent promiscuity, parental consent for contraception and abortion, date rapes and stories of sexual harassment, as well as in women's personal narratives of starving themselves or bingeing and purging toward thinness. For each of these social "controversies," there is, however, a contest of wills, a set of negotiations. Young women are engaged with questions of "being female"; that is, who will control, and to what extent can they control, their own bodies?

Threaded through our conversations at the dining room table, culture and class helped to construct at least two distinct versions of womanhood. It became clear that the elite women, for instance, constructed an interior sense of womanhood out of oppositional relations with white men. They positioned white men as the power group White Men.[10] And they positioned themselves in an ongoing, critical, hierarchical struggle with these men. Sophie, for example, often defined her feminism in relation to white boys; instead of "reinforcing guys all the time, I *bust* on guys. Because if you don't bust 'em they'll get ahead. You have to keep 'em in their place."

It was quite another thing to hear the sense of womanhood constructed horizontally—still in struggle—by African-American women, situated with or near African-American men. Given the assault on black men by the broader culture, it was clear that any announced sense of female superiority would be seen as "castrating," and unreconcilable with cross-gender alliances against racism.[11] So the construction of black womanhood was far less dichotomized and oppositional toward men, and far richer in a sense of connection to community.[12] In the context of being "deprived," then, of the traditional (oppositional to White Men) feminine socialization, women of color, like women with disabilities, may construct womanhoods less deeply repulsed by the traditional accoutrements of femininity, less oppositional to the cardboard White Male, and less assured that gender survives as the primary or exclusive category of social identity.

Among these four, then, we heard two quite distinct constructions of "being female." From the African-American women, both living in relatively impoverished circumstances, we heard a "womanhood" of fluid connections among women within and across generations; maturity conceived of as an extension of self with others; a taken-for-granted integration of body and mind; a comfortable practice of using public talk as a place to "work out" concerns, constraints, and choices; and a nourishing, anchored sense of *home* and *community*. bell hooks describes home as the site of nurturance and identity, *positive in its resistance* to racist ideologies of black inferiority.

> Despite the brutal reality of racial apartheid, of domination, one's homeplace was the one site where one could freely confront the issue of humanization, where one could resist. Black women resisted by making homes where all black people could strive to be subjects, not objects, where we could be affirmed in our minds and our hearts despite poverty, hardship, and deprivation, where we could restore to ourselves the dignity denied us on the outside in the public world.[13]

As the words of Damalleaux and Shermika reveal to us, however, the drawback of this centeredness in community is its fragility, its contingent sense of the future, terrors of what's "across the border," and the lack of resources or supports for planned upward mobility.

Indeed, when we discussed future plans, Shermika "joked" she'd be a custodian or bag lady. She "joked" she'd like to be dead, to see what the other world was like. She said she'd like to come back as a bird. "Not a pigeon, I hope," said Sophie. "Dove or peacock," Shermika decided, "something nobody be kickin' around all the time." Shermika finally confided in an uncharacteristic whisper that she'd like to be a lawyer, even the D.A. (the district attorney). What Shermika can be, could be, would like to be, and will be constitutes the terrain of Shermika's and Damalleaux's dilemma. Shermika doesn't worry that education would defeminize her, or that her parents expect something more or different from her career than she does. She quite simply and realistically doubts she'll be able to get all the way to D.A.

Nevertheless, Damalleaux and Shermika, on the other hand, expressed the connections with and respect for mothers found in Gloria Joseph and Jill Lewis's African-American daughters, "A decisive 94.5 percent expressed respect for their mothers in terms of strength, honesty, ability to overcome difficulties, and ability to survive."[14] Shermika's many examples of respect for her mother and Damalleaux's mother calling her "my first girl" suggest "the centrality of mothers in their daughters' lives."[15] In their stories, active female sexuality and motherhood are everywhere "embodied," while "career" is a distant and indistinct dream, marginal, foreign, and threateningly isolated.

In contrast, from the two privileged women, both living in relatively elite circumstances, we heard a "womanhood" struggling for positive definition and safe boundaries; a sharp splitting of body and mind; maturity as a dividing of self from family and school to find individual identity; an obsessive commitment to using privacy—in body, thought, and conversation—as the only way to "work out" one's problems; all nourishing a highly individualized, privatized, and competitive sense of home and community as sites which they would ultimately leave, unfettered, to launch "autonomous" lives as independent women. Materially and imaginatively these two women recognized an almost uninterruptable trajectory for future plans. Their "womanhood" was built on the sense of *self as exception*, "achievement" meritocratically determining how "exceptional" each individual can prove herself (away) from the group. Self-as-exception, for women, involves "transcending" gender. Rachel Hare-Mustin describes the illusion of gender-neutral choices:

> The liberal/humanist tradition of our epoch assumes that the meanings of our lives reflect individual experience and individual subjectivity. This tradition has idealized individual identity and self-fulfillment and shown a lack of concern about power. Liberalism masks male privilege and dominance by holding that every (undergendered) individual is free. The individual has been regarded as responsible for his or her fate and the basic social order has been regarded as equitable. Liberal humanism implies free choice when individuals are not free of coercion by the social order.[16]

The invisibility of women's "coercion by the social order" came out most clearly in Janet's and Sophie's relationships with their working mothers. They did not analyze their mothers' lives for power.

Sophie said, "My mom doesn't like her job but she has to work so I can go to college." Janet and Sophie said they were afraid of becoming their mothers, unhappy and overworked in jobs they hate, their workloads doubled with domestic responsibilities. "I fear I might be like her. I want to be independent of her," white middle-class women said of their mothers in the research of Joseph and Lewis.[17] Janet and Sophie said they didn't talk much, or very honestly, to their mothers, and didn't feel they could ever do enough to gain their mothers' approval. Janet said, "My mother [says] I really have to go to college . . . be a doctor or lawyer. . . . That's her main goal . . . job security. Then she wants me to get married and have a nice family, preferably Catholic. . . . Mom's got my life mapped out." Ambition and career "embody" this mother-daughter relationship, in a sense, while the daughter's problems with sexuality and power and with the mother *as woman*, are absent in the relationship Janet describes.

When discussing whom they would tell if they had a problem, Shermika immediately said "my mom" and Damalleaux said, "I tell Shermika almost everything before I tell my mother." Sophie and Janet agreed only in the negative. It would not be their mothers: "Don't talk to my mom."

> JANET: I can't tell my mother anything. If I told her something she would ground me for an entire century.
>
> SOPHIE: Once you tell them one thing, they want to hear more, and they *pry*. I keep my home life and school—social—life so separate.
>
> JANET: I'll be noncommittal or I won't tell her the truth. I'll just tell her what she wants to hear.

SOPHIE: I wish I could talk to my mom. It'd be great if I could.

SHERMIKA: It's the wrong thing to do [not talking], though. . . . It always *leads* to problems. My mom tells me so much about life.

Janet said her mother stares at her complexion [her acne] and says, "You're not going to get married, you're not going to have a boyfriend." "I get so mad at her," Janet said. She tells her mother either "I'm leaving, I'm leaving" or "Stop it! Stop it!" Later, when Pat asked whether self-respect was learned from the mother, Janet said her self-respect had "nothing to do with my mother. I used to hate myself, partly because of my mother. But not anymore. My mother's opinion just doesn't matter to me." Sophie said,

> My mother . . . nitpicks. . . . I'm sure it was like her mom [who] never approved anything about her. I get self-respect from my mom because she wants me to respect myself. . . . I don't think she respects herself enough. I respect her more than she respects herself. Her mother belittled her so much.

Later Sophie said, "I have the feeling that no matter what I do, it's not enough." Janet said her mother makes her and her sister feel like her mother's "racehorses":

> My mom *lives* through her kids. Two daughters: two *chances*. My sister wants to be an actress and my parents hate that [dykey] way she looks. . . . My mom: "You're just not *feminine* enough!" I'm just like, "Mom, grow up!" . . . She compares her daughters to everyone else's. [One example is] a straight-A student on top of all her chores . . . I know there's things in her personality that are part of myself. . . . We're just like racehorses. . . . "My daughter has three wonderful children and a husband who makes a million dollars a year."

For Janet and Sophie, their mothers were supports you get over, central to the life these daughters wished to escape, and to revise, in their own futures. Within their liberal discourse of free choice, the inequalities of power determining their mothers' misery were invisible to them, and their own exceptional futures were also unquestioned.

The Body: Boundaries and Connections

Over our dinners we created a democracy of feminist differences. That is, all four, as an age/gender cohort, introduced us to the female body in play with gendered politics. These young women consistently recast *our* prioritizing of sex at the center of feminist politics into *their* collective critique of gender politics. Using a language that analyzed dominance and power, they refused to separate sex from other power relations. Perhaps even more deeply Foucauldian than we assumed ourselves to be, they deconstructed our voyeurism with examples of sexuality as only one embodied site through which gendered politics operate. All four shared a distrust of men: "They think they have power." But they also distrusted female solidarity: "They back stab you all the time." Their examples overturned our notions of sisterhood by showing us that both young women and young men proficiently police the borders, and tenets, of masculinity and femininity among today's teens. They are often reminded of their bodies as a public site (gone right or wrong), commented on and monitored by others, both males and females. But as often, they reminded us, they forcefully reclaim their bodies by talking back, and by talking feminist. "It'd be harder not to talk," Sophie thought. "It'd be harder to sit and swallow whatever people are saying."

Resonating with much of feminist literature, when these four young women spoke of their bodies, it was clear that they found themselves sitting centrally at the nexus of race, class, and gender politics. *Gender* determines that the young women are subject to external surveillance and responsible for internal body management, and it is their gender that makes them feel vulnerable to male sexual threat and assault. *Culture and class* determine how, that is, determine the norms of body and the codes of surveillance, management, threat, assault, and resistance available to them.

Susan Bordo writes about body management as a text for control in the middle class.[18] Reflecting both elite material status and a pure, interior soul, this fetish of body management, operated by the "normalizing machinery of power," produces a desire to control flesh otherwise out of control, as it positions individuals within an elite class location. The tight svelte body reflects material and moral comfort, while the loose sagging body falls to the "lumpen." Bordo's cultural analysis of the representations and experiences of women's bodies and women's revulsion at sagging fat captures and yet too narrowly homogenizes what the four young women reported.

Each of the four, as Bordo would argue, was meticulously concerned with her body as the site for cataloguing both her own and others' "list" of her inadequacies. Indeed, each body had become the space within which she would receive unsolicited advice about having "too many pimples," "being too chocolate," "looking chubby," "becoming too thin," "looking like a boy," or in the case of a sister, dressing "very butch." The fetish to control, however, was experienced in ways deeply marked by class and race. While the elite women were familiar with, if not obsessed by, eating disorders now fashionable among their status peers, the African-American women were quite literally bewildered at the image of a young woman bingeing on food, and then purging. Therein lies a serious problematic in white feminist literature where class and culture practices are coded exclusively as *gender*, reinforcing hegemonic definitions of (white) womanhood, while obscuring class/culture contours of the body.

For these women, the female body not only signified a site of interior management vis-à-vis male attention or neglect. It was also a site for gendered politics enacted through sexual violence. Celia Kitzinger, in an analysis of how 2000 young women and men frame their personal experiences with "unfairness," found that 24 percent of interviewed girls spontaneously volunteered instances of body-centered unfairness, including sexual harassment, rape, and/or abuse.[19] So, too, stories of violence were offered by all four of the young women, each particular to her social context:

> DAMALLEAUX: When I got my first boyfriend [he] pressured me to have sex with him. That's why I didn't never go over his house.
>
> SOPHIE: I feel safe nowhere.
>
> SHERMIKA: When he pulled a gun on me, I said, "This is over."
>
> JANET: I know it's unlikely, but I am terrified of someday being date-raped. It's always been something I've been afraid of.

For Janet, violence is imagined as possible because of the stories of her friends. For Sophie, violence is encountered as harassment on the street. For Damalleaux and Shermika, violence is encountered or threatened in relations with boyfriends.

> MICHELLE: Is there any place where guys have more power than you?
>
> DAMALLEAUX: In bed.
>
> SHERMIKA: In the street. In the store, when he has all the money.
>
> DAMALLEAUX: And all the guys can beat girls. But I don't think it's true.
>
> * * *
>
> MICHELLE: Are you ever afraid that the hitting will get bad?
>
> SHERMIKA: Yeah, that's why I don't do so much hitting.

DAMALLEAUX: When I go out with a boy I hit him a lot to see if he's going to do anything. . . . You hit me once, I don't want anything to do with you.

* * *

SHERMIKA: Sometimes you can get raped with words, though. You feel so slimy. . . . The guy at the newspaper stand, I speak to him every morning. Then one day he said, "How old is you? I can't wait till you 16." And I told my mom, and she came [with me and told him off]. He lost respect. He didn't give me none. And that day I felt bad, what was I, bein' too loose? . . . You just can't help feelin' like that [slimy].

Liz Kelly offers this definition of sexual violence: Sexual violence includes any physical, visual, verbal or sexual act that is experienced by the woman or girl, at the time or later, as a threat, invasion, or assault that has the effect of degrading or hurting her and/or takes away her ability to control intimate contact.[20]

We found that the impression and/or experience of surviving male violence was indeed central. But class and race influenced its expression by the four young women. These fears and experiences were deeply traumatic to all the women, and yet the African-American women more frequently and more publicly, if uncomfortably, related them in the context of conversation. For the elite women the assaults and fears were more privatized and so left relatively unanalyzed, unchallenged, and in critical ways "buried." For example, Janet's story of a friend's date-rape contrasts radically with Shermika's stories of male violence and female resistance.

JANET: That happened to one of my friends.

SOPHIE: A date rape?

JANET: Sort of . . . He'd been pressuring her for a long time, and she's just "no no no no." She's at this party, her [girl] friend says, "Why don't you just do it?" and she says, "Because I don't *want* to." . . . She was drunk, puking. She fell asleep, and the next thing she knows she wakes up and he's on top of her and she's not really happy about it but she didn't do anything about it so she just let it happen. And . . . she was upset about it, she was really angry about it, but there was nothing she could *do* about it? [Janet's voice rises into a kind of question mark.] It didn't really bother her, but after that she totally knew who her friends were.

SOPHIE: She could've done something about it.

JANET: I guess we didn't talk about how she really really felt about it. She seemed really comfortable with it after it. She was upset for a while. After she . . .

SOPHIE: There's no way she was *comfortable* with it.

JANET: She's dealt with it in a way. She's gotten to the point where it doesn't really make her cry to talk about it.

Earlier in the conversation Sophie complained that the popular crowd got drunk at parties and had one-night stands. Somewhat defensive, Janet said aside to Sophie, "Hey, *I've* done that." Janet's story of the rape included Janet's anger at the girl's girlfriend: "Her *friend* was the hostess of the party and gave her the condoms and told her to go do it." Betrayal by the girlfriend and the boyfriend, a rape Janet calls "sort of" a date-rape, in a party situation Janet has been in many times, anger and helplessness, talking about it finally without tears: this worst-case scenario of women's sexuality and powerlessness is "dealt with" by *not* "talk[ing] about how she really felt about it." Janet's story was about the social and interior limits on one girl's control, before and after "sex" she didn't want.

In sharp contrast, Shermika offered a story of embodied resistance and resistance through public talk. Michelle asked, "Have you ever been in a relationship where you felt you were being forced to do what you didn't want to do?" Shermika's answer was immediate and emphatic, "Yeah, I quit 'em, I quit 'em." She followed with a story about what happened when she "quit" the boyfriend who was getting possessive:

SHERMIKA: I almost got killed. Some guy pulled a gun on me. . . . He put the gun *to my head.* I said, "You'd better kill me cause if you don't I'm gonna kill you." Then he dropped the gun. . . . I kicked him where it hurts. . . . hard, he had to go to the hospital. I was scared.

JANET: What happened? Have you ever seen him again?

SHERMIKA: I see him every day.

MICHELLE: Did you call the cops?

SHERMIKA: Yeah. He had to stay in jail [2 weeks] till I decided not to press charges. . . . Don't nobody around my way playin' like that with them guns.

Shermika's examples of male threat and violence all show her and her mother talking back, striking back, or disarming the man. The woman is embodied as her own best protector. Shermika followed up her first story (which stunned her audience into awed silence) with a second, another jealous boyfriend:

He told me if I went with anybody else he'd kill me. And he pulled a knife on me . . . "Stab me. Either way, you ain't gonna have me."

Later she told a story about her mother:

> My stepfather and my mother were fightin'—it's the only time they ever fought. And he stepped back and hit my momma with all his might. And he thought she was gonna give up. She stepped back and hit *him* with all *her* might—and he fell asleep. She knocked the mess outta him. He never hit her again.

And another about herself, with her mother as model:

> A guy tried to beat me with a belt, and I grabbed it and let him see how it felt to get beat with that belt. My mom wouldn't even take that.

The scars of actual and/or anticipated sexual violence were clear for each of the young women, and always culturally specific as encounter and resistance in the telling.

As with the violence of gender, the violence of racism on the female body was painfully voiced by the three women of color. Fears of attending a white prep school "where they'll ignore me," stories of fleeing an integrated school after three weeks and retrospective outbursts of anger at being "the only woman of color in my class!" showed a kind of agoraphobia which kept Shermika and Damalleaux in their wholly black communities, and, inversely, created in Janet deep assimilative wishes to disappear into the white suburbs. For Janet the "white church" in her elite suburban neighborhood—not the Korean church her parents attend—was the "safest place" she could imagine.

For Damalleaux and Shermika, the neighborhood and its school are clearly the only safe places. Damalleaux reported that she had lasted three weeks at an integrated school, "It was O.K. but I didn't feel right. I didn't know anybody. I don't like introducing myself to people, I'm too shy . . . I came back to the neighborhood school."

Shermika was offered a scholarship to go to a fancy private school in a white suburb. When discussing what scares us about the future, Shermika admitted she fears "being neglected. Not fitting in. One time I'm goin' in and nobody likes me." When Michelle asked if that was her fear about the prep school, Shermika said, "Not as far as the people. But I don't like travelling. And I'm not staying on the campus. . . . I ain't stayin' away from home, though." By the time of our second interview, Shermika had convinced her mother to delay her going to prep school, from mid-year until the next fall. Shermika said she feared she would not be able to keep her grades up in the new school. Shermika's reliance on nonstandard English meant she would have to manage a major cultural shift both academically and socially. Her only envy of Sophie and Janet's school was what she called its "socializing" function, which taught them "how to get along, socialize, fit in, knowin' the right thing to say and do." Shermika said that when she has a job she wants to stay in her neighborhood "where it all happenin' [not] where you won't fit in." Racial identity, segregation, and racism combine to reinforce the boundaries of Shermika's and Damalleaux's lives and futures, by defining where and who is "safe."

Shermika evidently decided our dinner table was a "safe" enough place to explore our own racial (and maybe racist) differences. Shermika asked Janet, "Are you Chinese?" and Janet said, "No, Korean," and launched into a story about Japanese racism, including the sale of "Sambo" dolls in Japan, and then a story about the 4,000-year-old hatred of Koreans for the Japanese. Shermika responded, "Well, I don't understand that. I mean, I'm supposed to hate somebody white because somebody I know was a slave?" Then Shermika put race and racism right on our dinner table:

SHERMIKA: I walk into a store and Chinese people be starin' at me. [Shermika was mistaking Korean for Chinese for the third time.]

JANET: My *mother* does that. I hate that, my *mother* does it. [Her mother runs a dry cleaner shop.] And I'm just like, "Mom, STOP it."

DAMALLEAUX: I leave [the store].

JANET: How do you feel when you're the only minority in a room?

DAMALLEAUX: I don't care.

SHERMIKA: I make a joke out of it. I feel like a zebra.

Unlike Janet's experience, the assaultive nature of Shermika's and Damalleaux's encounters with the white world had given them little encouragement to isolate themselves among a white majority. Shermika said her "darkness" meant she "looked like a clown" when they put on make-up for her local TV interview about the scholarship program she's in, then her pride and excitement about the video of herself on TV was clouded by family jokes about her dark skin making her "invisible" to the camera. Shermika reported plenty of harassment about her dark skin, from girlfriends and boyfriends, even those as dark as herself. "Choc-late!" was the common, hated term, and Shermika was troubled by its implied racial hierarchy and self-hatred. Atypically, she had no easy "come-back" for that one.

Race in Sophie's (WASP) experience is about being privileged, and feeling harassed for her blonde and blue-eyed good looks. Janet, for instance, annoys Sophie by calling her the "Aryan Goddess." Sophie is harassed on public transportation on her daily commute, where she is in the minority as a white woman. (Janet, in contrast, drives from suburb to school.) Sophie became exasperated in our interview when she felt targeted for white racism, and said she didn't "notice" race half as often as race identified her in public situations in which she is made to represent WASPhood or white womanhood.

Just as these women co-created for us a shared, if negotiated, sense of body politics, they separated along culture lines in their expressed reliance on social connections and surveillance of bodily borders. The African-American women, for instance, detailed deeply textured and relational lives. They not only care for many, but many also care for them. They give much to others, and receive much in return, but don't call it volunteer or charity work—simply "what I do." When they receive favors (from mothers and boyfriends), they feel neither "guilty" nor "obligated." Held in a complex web of reciprocal relations, they contribute, easily assured that "what goes around comes around." They resonate to ideas found in the writing of Robinson and Ward:

> Nobles' conception of "the extended self" is seen in the value structure of many black families. Willie argues that many African-American children are encouraged to employ their own personal achievements as a means to resist racism.[21] The importance of hard work and communalism is viewed threefold: as a personal responsibility, as an intergenerational commitment to family, and as a tie to the larger collective. A resistant strategy of liberation, in keeping with African-American traditional values, ties individual achievement to collective struggle. We maintain that in the service of personal and cultural liberation, African-American adolescent girls must resist an individualism that sees the self as disconnected from others in the black community and, as it is culturally and psychologically dysfunctional, she must resist those who might advocate her isolation and separation from traditional African-American cultural practices, values, and beliefs.[22]

The elite women, in contrast, deployed a language of bodily integrity, patroled borders, social charity, obligation, and guilt. As for any favors of gifts or time from mothers and boyfriends, they felt a need to "pay back." Bearing often quite deeply hostile feelings toward their mothers, they nevertheless both feel obligated to repay her sacrifices by fulfilling her expectations, often a professional career in return for a gigantic tuition bill. As vigilantly, they monitor their social and bodily boundaries for what and how much comes in and leaves: food, drink, drugs, exercise, money, sacrifices, and gifts. And they give back to community in the form of "charity." They live their connections almost contractually.

Related to these contrasting forms of body-in-relation, these two groups performed quite differently within our *public talk*. That is, they parted sharply in terms of how they hibernated in privacy, and how they revealed themselves through public talk. In numerous instances the white and Korean teens deferred to a "cultured privacy" in which "personal problems" were rarely aired, "personal grievances" were typically suffocated, "personal disagreements" were usually revealed "behind our backs." They often withheld juicy details of life, safe only in diaries or other private writings. Their bodies absorbed, carried, and embodied their "private troubles." These elite girls made it quite clear that their strategies for survival were interior, personal, and usually not shared. The costs of "privilege," as they revealed them, were in the internalizing, personalizing, and depoliticizing of gender dilemmas. Research makes evident these costs in anorexia, bulimia, depression, "talking behind each other's back," and even the "secrets" of rape or abuse survival stories. Socialized out of using public talk to practice varied forms of womanhood, while these women recognized collective gender power struggles, they retreated from women, and they embodied their resistance alone, through feminist individualism.

The individualism from which modern feminism was born has much to answer for but much in which to take pride. Individualism has decisively repudiated previous notions of hierarchy and particularism to declare the possibility of freedom for all. In so doing, it transformed slavery from one unfree condition among many into freedom's antithesis—thereby insisting that the subordination of one person to any other is morally and politically unacceptable. But the gradual extension of individualism and the gradual abolition of the remaining forms of social and political bondage have come trailing after two dangerous notions: that individual freedom could—indeed must—be absolute, and that social role and personal identity must be coterminous.

Following the principles of individualism, modern western societies have determined that the persistence of slavery in any form violates the fundamental principle of a just society. But in grounding the justification in absolute individual right, they have unleashed the specter of a radical individualism that overrides the claims of society itself. To the extent that feminism, like antislavery, has espoused those individualistic principles, it has condemned itself to the dead ends toward which individualism is now plunging.[23]

In contrast, the African-American women were publicly playful as well as nasty to each other, and about others, "because we love each other." Shermika told wonderful, vivid, outrageous tales, in part to "test" what the others would do, including, we believe, testing whether she was being classified as exotic, sexualized, or "other" as a specimen for the white women and the evening's analysis. Their school context made their bodies a matter of public talk. Exposed.

SHERMIKA: I don't like my rear end. Guys are so ignorant. "Look at all that cake."

PAT: Maybe it's their problem.

SHERMIKA: No, it *is* my problem. Because you see my butt before you see me.

Public talk could be aggression as well:

DAMALLEAUX: I wouldn't talk to him [a stranger] and he got mad.

SHERMIKA: I hate when they constantly talk to you and they get closer and closer.

The African-American women used and experienced conversation, public disagreements, pleasures, and verbal badgerings as ways to "try on" varied ways to be women.

During the second evening the four young women discovered and explored these differences through the metaphor of the "private" and "public" schools they attend.

JANET: I've got a question. At [your school, Shermika] are there kids who are like by themselves? Loners . . . who don't sit with anyone else, who nobody wants to sit with?

SHERMIKA: Yeah but they can't because there's somebody always messin' with 'em, tryin' to get 'em to do something. So if they wanted to be by themselves they couldn't.

JANET: At our school it's so easy to get shut out when you're by yourself.

SOPHIE: You just kind of—disappear.

JANET: They don't say it [criticism or insult] in front of your face.

SOPHIE: You insult someone by not considering them . . . You don't consider their existence.

SHERMIKA: Sometimes people need you to tell them how you feel.

JANET: For the most part when I'm mad at someone I don't say it to them.

SOPHIE: Only one on one. You don't say it to them in front of others unless you're joking. It's more private.

SHERMIKA: But if you say it *to* the person, you avoid fights. If they hear you saying it behind they back, they wanna fight.

The four pursued this discovered difference between the "private" and the "public" school.

SHERMIKA: Ain't nothin' private at my school. If someone got gonorrhea, everyone knows it.

SOPHIE: *Everything*'s private at my school.

JANET: Cause nobody really cares about each other at our school.

SHERMIKA: In our school, when I found out I had cancer, I heard about it on the loudspeaker. And everybody come and offer me help. When you're havin' problems in our school, people talk. That's why they're more mature at my school—excuse me. Say somebody poor, need name brand sneaks, they'll put they money together and give 'em some sneaks. And teachers do that too, if someone need food.

SOPHIE: We like to pretend that we're good to the neighborhood and socially conscious.

Over time, we came to see that "the facts" of these young women's lives were neither what we had invited them to reveal in our conversations, nor what they were giving us. Rather, we were gathering their interpretations of their lives, interpretations which were roaming within culture and class.

On Good and Bad Girls: Prospects for Feminism

"I consider myself a bad girl," Shermika explained, "but in a good sorta way."

Feminist scholars as distinct as Valerie Walkerdine, Carol Gilligan, and Nancy Lesko have written about polarizations of good girls and bad ones, that is, those who resist, submit, or split on the cultural script of femininity. Gilligan's recent essay, "Joining the Resistance," argues that at the outset of adolescence, young women experience a severing of insider from outsider knowledge, such that "insider knowledge may be washed away."[24] Gilligan and her colleagues have found that young women at early adolescence begin to submerge their interior knowledge, increasingly relying on "I don't know" to answer questions about self. They say "I don't know" at a rate amazingly greater the older they get—an average of twice at age seven, 21 times at age 12, 67 times at age 13. Gilligan and colleagues conclude, "If girls' knowledge of reality is politically dangerous, it is both psychologically and politically dangerous for girls not to know . . . or to render themselves innocent by disconnecting from their bodies, their representations of experience and desire."[25]

Nancy Lesko has written a compelling ethnography of gendered adolescents' lives inside a Catholic high school, where she unpacks a "curriculum of the body," mediated by class distinctions.[26] In this school, female delinquency was sexualized and "embodied." The genders segregated in high school by class, and created categories of behaviors to hang on to within these class groups. The rich and popular girls at her school paraded popular fashions, spoke in controlled voices, muted their opinions, and worked hard at "being nice." If they pushed the boundaries of wardrobe, it was always in the direction of fashion, not "promiscuity." The "burnouts," in contrast, were young women who fashioned their behaviors through smoking and directness. They rejected compulsions toward being "nice" and excelled at being "blunt." Refusing to bifurcate their "personal" opinions and their public stances, they challenged docility and earned reputations as "loose" and "hard" (like Leslie Roman's working-class women who displayed physicality and sexual embodiment[27]). Social class, then, provided the contours within which a curriculum of the body had its meaning displayed, intensifying within gender oppositions, and undermining possibilities for female solidarity.

Departing somewhat from Gilligan and Lesko, Valerie Walkerdine sees adolescence for young women as a moment not to *bury* the questioning female "self," but a time in which young women must *negotiate* their multiple selves, through struggles of heterosexuality, and critiques of gender, race, and class arrangements. In an analysis of popular texts read by adolescent women, Walkerdine finds that, "heroines are never angry; most project anger onto others and suppress it in self, yielding the active production of passivity."[28] She asks readers to consider that "good girls are not always good, [but] when and how is their badness lived?" Interested in the splitting of goodness and badness we, like Walkerdine, asked these young women that question. When Shermika said, "I consider myself a bad girl, but in a good sorta way," she was positioning herself in our collectively made feminist context where *good girls* follow femininity rules, and *bad girls* don't. This good kind of bad girl plays by male rules of friendship, risk, danger, and initiative.

Within five minutes of our first meeting, the four girls discovered they all liked football, *playing* football, and they eagerly described the joys of running, catching the ball, tackling, and being tackled. Only Janet drew the line at being tackled, citing a "300-pound boy" in her neighborhood. As an explanation for their preferred identities as "one of the guys," football exemplifies "masculine" values of gamesmanship. It is a game with rules and space for spontaneous physicality, with teamwork and individual aggression in rule-bound balance, and with maximum bodily access to others of both sexes, without fear about sexual reputation or reproductive consequences. When asked why they trust and like boys over girls, they cited boys' risk-taking making them more fun, their ability to "be more honest" and not backstab, "be more accepting." "You can tell when a guy's lyin'." "First of all they won't even notice what you're wearing and they won't bust on you." Shermika bragged that all of her boyfriends said they valued her most as a friend, not merely a girlfriend. The behavior, clothing, and values associated with such identification with boys and sports suggests both a flight from the "femininity" they collectively described as "wearing pink," "being prissy," "bein' Barbie," and "reinforcing guys all the time"—*and* an association of masculinity with fairness (vs. cattiness), honesty (vs. backstabbing), strength (vs. prissiness, a vulnerability whether feigned or real), initiative (vs. deference or reactionary comments), and integrity (vs. the self-doubt and conflicting loyalties dividing girls). The four girls' risk-taking behaviors—driving fast, sneaking out at night—reinforced identities as "one of the guys." Such are the Bad Girls.

But being "one of the guys" makes for a contradictory position of self versus "other girls." Sophie mocked the femininity of good girls, at its worst when she said dismissively, "You should sit and wait in your little crystal palace" rather than "chase after guys." This constructed difference between self (the good kind of bad girl) and other girls (the bad kind of good girl) is an essential contradiction of identity that all four girls were struggling with. Valerie Hey, in her study of adolescent female friendships, calls this "deficit dumping": "all the 'bad' bits of femininity, social and sexual competitiveness, placed upon the 'other'," that is, other girls.[29] Sophie, like the girls in Hey's study, excepted her best friend along with herself from the generality of femininity: "It's different though with best friends. I mean like girls in general." Shermika likewise excepted Damalleaux when Michelle asked whether *no* other girls were to be trusted. "She a boy," Shermika countered, raising a puzzled laugh. But when Shermika's boyfriend likened her to a body builder when she was running track, she felt ashamed to "feel like a boy . . . like a muscle man."

Sophie confessed ruefully, "I'm certainly no bad girl," and Janet taunted her, "Sophie has a little halo." Certainly Sophie's good grades, good works, politeness, friendliness, and trustworthiness were acceptably "good" to both adults and peers, even if the popular crowd had not approved or welcomed her. "I don't want that image," Sophie told Janet about the halo. Goody-goodyism would be unacceptable to *all* peers. Good-*girl*ism—Sophie's uncomfortable state—seems "good" for her conscience and adult approval, but "bad" for approval by the popular set, whose upper-class drink-and-drug-induced party flirtations and sexual liaisons Sophie disapproves of. The meaning of Sophie's good-girl image is, however, quite class-specific, as Mary Evans describes in her analysis of middle-class schooling:

> As far as possible a "good" girl did not have an appearance. What she had was a correct uniform, which gave the world the correct message about her, that is, that she was a well-behaved, sensible person who could be trusted not to wish to attract attention to herself by an unusual, let alone a fashionable, appearance.[30]

Signaling her acceptance of the career-class uniform, Sophie could not also signal her interest in boys. Indeed, she walked away from her body, except as an athletic court. "Other girls" dressed either "schleppy" (the androgynous or indifferent look) or "provocative." Sophie's neat, "sporty" look (tights and a lean body made her miniskirt look more athletic than hooker-inspired) seems designed to be comfortable and competent as one of the guys while ever so casually gesturing toward femininity (no dykey trousers). Her dress is designed to bridge the contradiction of middle-class education and femininity, as Evans describes it in her own schooling in the 1950s:

> To be a successful [prep] school girl involved, therefore, absorbing two specific (but conflicting) identities. First, that of the androgynous middle-class person who is academically successful in an academic world that is apparently gender blind. Second, that of the well-behaved middle-class woman who knows how to defer to and respect the authority of men.[31]

Feminists have altered, over history, their terms of deference to men, their ability to name sexism and resist. But our four young women do not seem to have revised the categories of "gender" or "body" at all. What seems intact from the 1950s is their terms of respect for the authority of men as superior and normal forms of human being. What seems distinct in the 1990s is that these young women think they have a right to be like young men too.

Damalleaux's example of her own goodgirlism shares some of Sophie's dilemma of being a good student at the expense of peer popularity. But Damalleaux resolved this tension differently, as Signithia Fordham would argue is likely to happen among academically talented low-income African-American students.[32]

DAMALLEAUX: I used to be a straight-A girl and now I'm down to B's and C's. I used to be so good it's a shame . . .

PAT: What changed?

DAMALLEAUX: I couldn't help it any more. When I got straight A's they'd call me a nerd and things. But I'd be happy because my mother would give me anything I want for it. Mom [would say to teasing brothers] "Leave my first girl alone!" [Then] I got around the wrong people, I don't study so much.

PAT: Is it uncool to be a girl and get good grades?

DAMALLEAUX: Yes, it is. I'll do my work and they'll say "Smarty Pants! Smarty Pants!"

Janet gave an example of "acting stupid" with peers, which seemed to be her manner of flirtation. Sophie pointed out that Janet could afford to because everyone already knew she was smart. Sophie clearly felt more trapped by being a smart and a good girl.

Girls can be good, bad, or (best of all) they can be like boys. This version of individualized resistance, or feminism, reflects a retreat from the collective politics of gender, and from other women, and an advance into the embattled scene of gender politics—alone, and against boys, in order to become one of them.

The End of the Second Pizza

We heard these four women struggling between the discourses of feminism and adolescence. Perhaps struggling is even too strong a word. They hungered for a strong version of individualistic, "gender-free" adolescence and had rejected that which had been deemed traditionally feminine, aping instead that which had been deemed traditionally masculine. Delighted to swear, spit, tell off-color jokes, wear hats and trash other girls, they were critical of individual boys, nasty about most girls, rarely challenging of the sex/gender system, and were ecstatic, for the most part, to be engaged as friends and lovers with young men. But we also heard their feminism in their collective refusal to comply with male demands, their wish for women friends to trust, their expectations for equality and search for respect, their deep ambivalence about being "independent of a man" and yet in partnership with one, and their strong yearnings to read, write, and talk more about women's experiences among women. They appreciated our creation of a context in which this was possible. "The women of Michelle's place," Shermika called us at the end of one evening, prizing our collectivity by adapting the title of a black woman's novel.

Barbara Hudson describes part of the task of feminist work with girls as follows:

> The public terms of the discourse of femininity preclude the expression of deviant views of marriage, motherhood, and the public terms are the only ones to which girls have access. Part of the task of feminist work with girls is thus, I would suggest, giving girls terms in which to express their experiential knowledge, rather than having to fall back into the stereotyped expressions of normatively defined femininity in order to say anything at all about areas of life which vitally concern them.[33]

Through *critical and collaborative group interview* we evolved a form of conversation (what Hudson might call feminist work) with these four young women which allowed us to engage in what we might consider *collective consciousness work* as a form of feminist methodology. Our "talks" became an opportunity to "try on" ways of being women, struggling through power, gender, culture, and class.

With Donna Haraway's notion of "partial vision" firmly in mind,[34] we realized that in our talk, no one of us told the "whole truth." We all occluded the "truth" in cultured ways. The conversation was playful and filled with the mobile positionings of all of us women. While we each imported gender, race, class, culture, age, and bodies to our talk, we collectively created an ideological dressing room in which the six of us could undress a little, try things on, exchange, rehearse, trade, and critique. Among the six of us we were able to lift up what had become "personal stories," raise questions, try on other viewpoints, and re-see our stories as political narratives.

As a critique of the excesses of individualism, feminism potentially contributes to a new conception of community—of the relation between the freedom of individuals and the needs of society. The realization of that potential lies not in the repudiation of difference but in a new understanding of its equitable social consequences.[35]

We could recount together how alone and frightened we have each felt as we have walked down city streets and are watched; how our skin tightens when we hear men comment aloud on our bodies; how we smart inside with pain when we learn that other women define themselves as "good women" by contrasting themselves with our feminist politics; how we make fetishes of those body parts that have betrayed us with their imperfection. Within the safety of warm listening and caring, yet critical talk, we attached each of these "secret" feelings to political spaces defined by culture, class, and gender contours of our daily lives. This method moved us, critically and collectively, from pain to passion to politics, prying open the ideologies of individualism, privacy, and loyalty which had sequestered our "personal stories."

After our second dinner, stuffed and giggly, tired but still wanting just one more round of conversation, we (Pat and Michelle) realized that the four young women were getting ready to drive away. Together and without us. Before, Pat had driven Shermika and Damalleaux to and from Michelle's home. But now they were leaving us behind. Stunned, we looked at each other, feeling abandoned. We thought we were concerned about their safety. Four young women in a car could meet dangers just outside the borders of Michelle's block.

We turned to each other realizing that even our abandonment was metaphoric, and political. These four young women were weaving the next generation of feminist politics, which meant, in part, leaving us. We comforted ourselves by recognizing that our conversations had perhaps enabled this work. No doubt, individual interviews with each of the four would have produced an essay chronicling the damages of femininity: eating disorders, heterosexual traumas, perhaps some abuse or abortion stories—deeply individualized, depoliticized, and atomized tales of "things that have happened to me as an adolescent female." What happened among us instead was that a set of connections was forged between personal experiences and political structures, across cultures, classes, and politics, and within an invented space, cramped between the discourses of a rejected *femininity*, an individualized *adolescence* and a collective *feminism as resistance.*

Resistance is that struggle we can most easily grasp. Even the most subjected person has moments of rage and resentment so intense that they respond, they act against. There is an inner uprising that leads to rebellion, however short-lived. It may be only momentary, but it takes place. That space within oneself where resistance is possible remains: it is different then to talk about becoming subjects. That process emerges as one comes to understand how structures of domination work in one's own life, as one develops critical thinking and critical consciousness, as one invents new alternative habits of being and resists from that marginal space of difference inwardly defined.[36]

In our finest post-pizza moment, we (Pat and Michelle) realized that as these women drove off, they were inventing their own feminist legacy, filled with passions, questions, differences, and pains. We were delighted that we had helped to challenge four young women's versions of individualistic feminism, without solidarity, by doing the consciousness work of our generation. We taught, and relearned, feminism as a dialectical and historical discourse about experience and its interpretation, a collective reframing of private confessions. As we yelled, "Go straight home!" to their moving car, for a moment we felt as if the world was in very good hands.

The authors acknowledge with many thanks the patient assistance of Elizabeth Sayre.

Notes

1. Michael Payne, "Canon: The New Testament to Derrida," *College Literature* 18, no. 2 (1991): 18.

2. Barbara Hudson, "Femininity and Adolescence," in *Gender and Generation*, edited by Angela McRobbie and Mica Nava (London: Macmillan Publishers, 1984), p. 35.

3. Michelle Fine and Adrienne Asch, eds., *Women with Disabilities: Essays in Psychology, Culture, and Politics* (Philadelphia: Temple University Press, 1988); Gelya Frank, "On Embodiment: A Case Study of Congenital Limb Deficiency in American Culture," in *Women with Disabilities*, edited by Michelle Fine and Adrienne Asch, pp. 41-71; Kathryn Corbett, with Susan Klein and Jennifer L. Bregante, "The Role of Sexuality and Sex Equity in the Education of Disabled Women," *Peabody Journal of Education* 64, no. 4 (1987): 198-212.

4. Linda Brodkey and Michelle Fine, "Presence of Mind in the Absence of Body," *Journal of Education* 170, no. 3 (1988): 84-99.

5. Susie Orbach, *Hunger Strike: The Anorectic's Struggle as a Metaphor for Our Age* (New York: W. W. Norton, 1986).

6. Susan Bordo, "Reading the Slender Body," in *Body/Politics: Women and the Discourses of Science*, edited by Mary Jacobus, Evelyn Fox, and Sally Shuttleworth (New York: Routledge, 1990), pp. 31-53.

7. See Elijah Anderson, *Streetwise: Race, Class, and Change in an Urban Community* (Chicago: University of Chicago Press, 1990).

8. Elizabeth Spelman, *The Inessential Women* (Boston: Beacon Press, 1988), p. 13.

9. Michelle Fine, *Framing Dropouts: Notes on the Politics of an Urban High School* (Albany, NY: State University of New York Press, 1991); J. Halson, "Young Women, Sexual Harassment, and Heterosexuality: Violence, Power Relations, and Mixed Sex Schooling," in *Gender, Power, and Sexuality*, edited by Pamela Abbott and Claire Wallace (London: Macmillan Publishers, 1990).

10. Houston Baker, personal communication, 1989.

11. bell hooks, *Feminist Theory from Margin to Center* (Boston: South End Press, 1984); Paula Giddings, *When and Where I Enter: The Impact of Black Women on Race and Sex in America* (New York: Bantam, 1984).

12. And, although not at the table, it is still another thing to construct a sense of womanhood by and for women whose disabilities socially and sexually "neuter" them, propelling them out of any presumed relation with men, and depriving them of the many burdens of being female, including the privileges that come with those burdens, in experiences such as sexual harassment, motherhood, sexuality, having others rely on you, etc. Disabled women's identities are rarely positioned under, against, or with men's. As Kathryn Corbett, Adrienne Asch and Michelle Fine, Harilyn Rousso, and others have written (see Adrienne Asch and Michelle Fine, "Shared Dreams: A Left Perspective on Disability Rights and Reproductive Rights," in *Women with Disabilities: Essays in Psychology, Culture, and Politics*, edited by Michelle Fine and Adrienne Asch [Philadelphia: Temple University Press, 1988], pp. 297-305), it is no blessing for the culture to presume that because you are disabled, you are not female; not worth whistling at; not able to love an adult man or woman; not capable of raising a child; not beautiful enough to be employed in a public space.

13. bell hooks, *Yearning: Race, Gender, and Cultural Politics* (Boston: South End Press, 1990), p. 42.

14. Gloria Joseph and Jill Lewis, *Common Differences: Conflicts in Black and White Feminist Perspectives* (Boston: South End Press, 1981), p. 94.

15. Ibid., p. 79.

16. Rachel T. Hare-Mustin, "Sex, Lies, and Headaches: The Problem Is Power," in *Women and Power: Perspectives for Therapy*, edited by T. J. Goodrich (New York: Norton, 1991), p. 3.

17. Joseph and Lewis, *Common Differences*, p. 125.

18. Bordo, "Reading the Slender Body."

19. Celia Kitzinger, " 'It's Not Fair on Girls': Young Women's Accounts of Unfairness in School" (Paper presented at the British Psychological Society Annual Conference, University of Leeds, April, 1988).

20. Liz Kelly, *Surviving Sexual Violence* (London: Basil Blackwell, 1988), p. 41.

21. Charles Vert Willie, *Black and White Families: A Study in Complementarity* (Bayside, NY: General Hall, 1985).

22. T. Robinson and J. Ward, "A Belief in Self Far Greater than Anyone's Disbelief," in *Women, Girls, and Psychotherapy*, edited by Carol Gilligan, A. Rogers, and D. Tolman (New York: Harrington Park Press, 1991), p. 9.

23. Elizabeth Fox-Genovese, *Feminism without Illusions* (Chapel Hill: University of North Carolina Press, 1991), pp. 240-241.

24. Carol Gilligan, "Joining the Resistance: Psychology, Politics, Girls, and Women" (Essay presented as the Tanner Lecture on Human Values at the University of Michigan, Ann Arbor, MI, March 1990).

25. Carol Gilligan, Janie Victoria Ward, and Jill McClean Taylor, *Mapping the Moral Domain* (Cambridge, MA: Harvard University Press, 1988), p. 33.

26. Nancy Lesko, "The Curriculum of the Body: Lessons from a Catholic High School," in *Becoming Feminine: The Politics of Popular Culture*, edited by Leslie G. Roman, Linda K. Christian-Smith, and Elizabeth Ellsworth (Philadelphia: Falmer Press, 1988), pp. 123-142.

27. Leslie G. Roman, "Intimacy, Labor, and Class: Ideologies of Feminine Sexuality in the Punk Slam Dance," in *Becoming Feminine: The Politics of Popular Culture*, edited by Leslie G. Roman, Linda K. Christian-Smith, and Elizabeth Ellsworth (Philadelphia: Falmer Press, 1988), pp. 143-184.

28. Valerie Walkerdine, "Some Day My Prince Will Come: Young Girls and the Preparation for Adolescent Sexuality," in *Gender and Generation*, edited by Angela McRobbie and Mica Nava (London: Macmillan Publishers, 1984), p. 182.

29. Valerie Hey, " 'The Company She Keeps': The Social and Interpersonal Construction of Girls' Same Sex Friendships" (Doctoral thesis, University of Kent at Canterbury, England, 1987), p. 421.

30. Mary Evans, *A Good School: Life at a Girls' Grammar School in the 1950s* (London: Women's Press, 1991), pp. 30-31.

31. Ibid., p. 23.

32. Signithia Fordham, "Racelessness as a Factor in Black Students' School Success," *Harvard Educational Review* 58, no. 1 (1988): 54-84.

33. Hudson, "Femininity and Adolescence," p. 52.

34. Donna Haraway, *Primate Visions: Gender, Race, and Nature in the World of Modern Science* (New York: Routledge, 1989).

35. Fox-Genovese, *Feminism without Illusions*, p. 256.

36. hooks, *Yearning: Race, Gender, and Cultural Politics*, p. 15.

CHAPTER IX

Mothers' Gaze from Teachers' Eyes

SARI KNOPP BIKLEN

When white middle-class mothers and their children's female elementary school teachers come into conflict they both grapple with the same concern though it plays out in contrasting ways in their lives. Both mothers and elementary teachers share social and gendered positions because of their relationship to children. They also share the desire to better position paid or unpaid work that is connected to children, even though each group often feels great hostility toward the other. They both attempt to resist the devaluation of work labeled "domestic." Within the construct of school-family relations, however, they resist traditional images of domesticity through conflict with each other, the teachers by resisting mothers' demands and the mothers by attempting to insert their knowledge into the pedagogical arena. While each group can give the other headaches, while each can behave in outrageous ways in relation to the other, the same social problem, the devaluation of work with children (traditional women's work), underlies their conflict. In this chapter, I examine, from teachers' points of view, how female teachers and middle-class white mothers negotiate their relationship, focusing particularly on tensions and conflict. I look at what teachers choose to tell as well as how they structure their stories. What are the effects of these narrative structures? What assumptions undergird their relationship? What are the politics of this discourse?

This research emerges from a larger study in which I examined the perspectives of women teachers on their work. The data on which this argument rests were gathered through participant observation and interviewing over an eighteen-month period between 1980 and 1982. I spent two-thirds of the time at Vista City Elementary School, a school in a mid-sized northeastern city which served eight hundred children.[1] I observed teachers in the lunch room, at meetings, in the

---

Sari Knopp Biklen is Associate Professor in the Department of Cultural Foundations and Curriculum, School of Education, Syracuse University.

halls, at staff development sessions. I interviewed them and the principal as well as ten parents, both mothers and fathers. The other third of my time I spent observing and interviewing teachers at a contrasting school in the city. Whereas Vista City had the best scores in the city on reading and achievement tests, and was known for its high morale, Archduke had the lowest scores and was located in the poorest neighborhood. (Because this chapter focuses on relationships between teachers and middle-class white parents [of which there were none at Archduke], little mention will be made of this second site except for the reputation that the Vista City parent-teacher relationship had there.) Many university professors and other professionals and their families lived in the neighborhood in which Vista City was located. The school was also integrated through busing, so that there was a mixture of social classes as well as races at this school. "Mixture" may suggest an arrangement that was not always present at the school during this time. While little *overt* hostility occurred between African-American and European-American children, tracking and friendship patterns tended, although not absolutely, to follow racial lines. There were, in other words, patterns of segregation within an integrated school. Also, only four of approximately forty positions in this school were held by African-Americans: one teacher, one specialist, and two administrators.

There is nothing new about conflict between parents and teachers. Researchers have long recognized its presence and see it as reflecting the considerable hostility that exists between the parties. In the 1930s, Willard Waller called teachers and parents "natural enemies," though he suggested that the conflict benefits rather than harms children. Howard Becker argued that teachers labeled parents' entrance into schools as "potentially dangerous"; Seymour Sarason referred to parent-teacher relations as a "cold war"; and Gertrude McPherson attended to the "hostility between parents and teachers."[2]

Many other writers examine the sources and nature of this troubled relationship, though some focus on mothers and some on parents. There is disagreement on what to call the participants. References to "parents" could mean interchangeable talk about either mother or father. My research at Vista City suggests that when teachers talk about parents they generally mean mothers. This view is revealed in many examples throughout this chapter. Most teachers' comments began with the word "parents" but then focused on mothers. For example, "The parents of the downtown kids and the black parents are just fine. The parents in this neighborhood are very social. They are wives of university professors, and they are just so sure that their kids have to be bright and do well because of the families they come from." I do not mean to suggest that teachers do not have conflict with fathers. But encounters are gendered. Fathers, in the case study data I report, tended to get more involved in schoolwide problems, like a school renovation that occurred, leaving the classroom concerns to mothers. That was not always the case, however, and teachers came to fear fathers with degrees in psychology who carried a repertoire of IQ measuring skills to chart their children's progress.

Others have remarked on these parental issues. Miriam David critiques researchers as well for their use of this problematic term: " 'Parent' is used for both mothers and fathers where their roles might not be interchangeable. It is also used as if it were a social category."[3] In a discussion of parent-teacher relations, Ray Rist also uses the word "parents" in describing conflicts. When he directly quoted the teacher referred to in the example, however, she said: "This damn group of meddling mothers has gotten me so mad I feel like leaving this school."[4] In this chapter I refer both to mothers and parents, as the teachers did, but always mean mothers. When teachers refer to parents and not mothers, they attempt to avoid the gender issues which connect them. The gendered positions of both mothers and teachers always lurk as the subtext to each encounter.

Relationships between Mothers and Teachers

The history of the relationship between middle-class white mothers and teachers reflects the lack of partnership between these two groups and the lines of argument each group employed with the other. William Reese argues that during the Progressive era middle-class mothers thought that schools should be extensions of "ideal" middle-class American homes. School people were not any less drawn to middle-class norms than the mothers, but wanted parents to be well aware that teachers and parents could not be equal partners. Parents had to respect the teacher as an expert professional. When parents organized around an issue, educators attacked them as "meddlers, malcontents, and the worst enemies of the public schools." When school people espoused a vocabulary of "cooperation," they generally meant "parent submission"; then parents and teachers could get along. An anecdote Reese tells reflects parents' refusal to accept the limits of professional authority with their children: "A Chicago principal who regularly interacted with parent groups stated that they simply never understood that the world was run by professionals." Teachers' desire to have parents recognize them as professionals and parents' resistance to that wish has a long history.[5]

What started as the National Congress of Mothers was transformed in 1908 to the National Congress of Mothers and Parent-Teacher Associations, and in 1924 to the National Congress of Parents and Teachers. While the mothers who started the National Congress of Mothers had taken a charity perspective (the better-off helping the less fortunate) to help educate schools and families so as to reflect a more middle-class orientation, the new name developed because relations between schools and the community came to be seen as more important than the education of parents.[6]

Much of the research on relationships between mothers and teachers focuses on the detrimental effects of a "discontinuity" between family and school. Hence, studies of relationships between schools and less powerful groups such as working-class families, poor families, and families from various racial and ethnic groups have examined the negative effects of the lack of parental involvement (a) on children's performance and (b) on the racist, Eurocentric, and class-consciousness characterizations teachers and parents can have of each other.[7] These characterizations are interactive.

The tensions between middle-class white mothers and teachers have been characterized as more subtle than the direct racism or paternalism present in the relationships between teachers and working-class parents or poor parents. Teachers see working-class parents as not providing a good "foundation" at home for the children. Working-class parents see teachers as not expecting anything of their children. White middle-class parents, on the other hand, criticize teachers as too "rigid and uncreative" while teachers criticize these parents as too "pushy."[8] The relationship between teachers and mothers of poor, working-class, and African-American children has been characterized as "worlds apart."[9]

Some explanations of the conflict apparent in the mother-teacher relationship include gender, while others do not. Teachers have universalistic expectations of their students, needing to spread their attention over a group. Mothers, on the other hand, have a particularistic focus on their own children. Additionally, the mother's relationship to her child is primary, while the teacher's is secondary.[10] Social class, ethnicity, race, and language also provide important sources for the conflicts between mothers and teachers.[11]

Neither have scholars ignored the gendered aspects of the relationship. Madeleine Grumet suggests that "gender contradictions, the simultaneous assertion and denial of femininity, have served to estrange teachers of children from the mothers of those children. Instead of being allies, mothers and teachers distrust each other."[12] The social construction of gender puts women, as teachers and as mothers, at odds with one another. Lightfoot reflects this concern when she argues that "mothers and teachers are caught in a struggle that reflects the devaluation of both roles in this society."[13] One might wish that mothers and teachers were collaborators over children's interests, and in many cases they are. The literature on parent-teacher relations can be divided into that which discusses how parents and teachers work together and that which emphasizes the conflicts.[14]

In studying the structure of women's everyday worlds, Dorothy Smith looks at "how the organizational practices of the school penetrate and organize the experience of different individual women as mothers." Using interviews with both mothers and the women who teach their children, Smith shows how mothers (attempt to) read the desires and expectations of teachers in order to work with their children at home. The work of the teachers, on the other hand, rests on the work mothers have already done with their children. Smith avoids pitting woman against woman because she embeds her discussion in the structure of school days and school practices. Her examples, however, reflect discord.[15]

Relationships between Mothers and Teachers at Vista City Elementary School

The theme of parent-teacher conflict came up in most conversations I had with Vista City teachers. It took me a while, however, to understand how the conflict was gendered. I was cued by a teacher who started talking about "parents" and concluded that she was not like those "mothers who sit around the kitchen table with a coffee cup in their hands criticizing teachers." A review of the data revealed that though examples of teachers' annoyance or anger with parents consistently began with the more gender-neutral term of "parent," each example that teachers (but not the principal) gave specified mothers.

The relationship between women who taught at Vista City Elementary School and the mothers of children in their classes reflected interdependence as well as the hostility they most frequently voiced. Many teachers depended on volunteer help from parents in order to structure their classes in ways that fit their educational goals. Teachers made statements like, "I can't run the kind of program that I want without a lot of hands." Mothers, particularly, helped in classrooms by bringing their own talents and expertise to improve what might be offered to their own and other children. They helped in this way by running weekly mathematics groups, by doing science lessons—activities that enriched and advanced the curriculum. Whatever the subject matter, whether reading or mathematics or science, mothers could be counted on to volunteer their help. These mothers valued schooling and had expertise to offer. The pool of mothers was such that some mothers could be counted on for education or experience in all these areas. Mothers also volunteered to tutor groups who were behind, to accompany classes on trips, and to organize parties for the class. They helped outside the classrooms in the school at large as well through such activities as running the RIF (Reading Is Fundamental) program, by organizing fund-raising activities including an annual carnival, and by helping in the large musical productions that different grades sponsored several times a year. Some teachers complained that they could not depend on parents in quite the same way as they had even several years before. A third-grade teacher said, "I've been fortunate in the past to have parents come in, three or four parents on a regular basis for an hour or two a day so that I have a lot of extra help in the classroom." The teacher attributed declining parental help to "more and more working parents. And I put out these pleas to my kids. 'Somebody come in and help us do this, that, or the other thing.' And kids look at me sadly and say, 'My mom's working.' " The children knew how to interpret the teacher's call for parental help. They read it as mother's help, and they read it correctly. Teachers liked the help that mothers provided.

Teachers developed ways of thinking about how mothers and teachers are connected to each other. They called on their common interests to do this. Both were interested in the child's welfare. Both believed in the value of education for the child's future. Each needed the other's help to develop an educated child. They had to work as a team.

Teachers also developed ways of thinking about how mothers and teachers were in conflict with each other. For this purpose, they called upon how they had opposing views in relation to classroom needs. Teachers constructed the conflict over the power to define; mothers could not refuse to accept the authority of the teacher. Put another way, even though mothers and teachers had to work as a team, teachers had to be the team leaders.

Teachers not only valued mothers; they also strongly criticized them. The mothers they particularly disliked (who were also the mothers from whom they accepted volunteer help) were the neighborhood mothers, to whom they referred as "pushy parents" and "professional parents." They were sometimes called "the intellectual or pseudointellectual ones." Who were these "parents"? "They're wives of university professors, and they're just so sure that their kids have to be bright and do well." Teachers ardently criticized mothers' intensity and determination about their children's achievement. Many teachers described the "pressure" this achievement orientation created. They felt like mothers were "on their backs." One teacher described this orientation of mothers as "self-centered interest" because they were "only concerned" with the achievement of their own child, not with the welfare of the class as a whole or, for that matter, with the teacher's welfare. As one fifth-grade teacher admitted, "It's boring to talk about some kid's math for a whole hour. Some of these parents are too concerned about how their kids do." Teachers criticized parents for an overemphasis on their children's accelerated achievement.

Some teachers suggested that too often many parents ignored the close relationship between the situation of the class as a whole and the position of their child. If a mother thought more expansively about others and about the whole class, teachers suggested, the mother's child would benefit. Interestingly enough, some parents who volunteered in classrooms did so with this very goal in mind: improving the class as a whole improved their own child's prospects for a valuable educational experience.

Another kind of complaint teachers made about parents centered on mothers' challenges to their professional identity and reflected teachers' insecure status regarding their roles. Teachers often felt that mothers did not trust their abilities to teach: to diagnose, to develop curriculum, to stimulate their children. This lack of trust, teachers felt, reflected mothers' diminished respect for their abilities as individuals and for the occupation of teaching generally. Teachers complained when mothers wanted to look over their lesson plans, when they stopped in to talk after school without making an appointment, saying, "It will only take five minutes," and then "proceeding to talk for an hour." When mothers did not make appointments or value teachers' time, they showed, from teachers' perspectives, that they did not respect teachers. A common refrain was, "Don't they know we're professionals!"

Teachers had to face parents who wielded impressive educational vocabularies. Some mothers commonly used phrases like "instruction time" and "large muscle activities" in their discussions of teachers' strengths and weaknesses. Data collected for this project confirmed teachers' complaints that neighborhood parents spent a lot of time talking about individual teachers. Teachers could say about mothers that they either took the education of their children seriously or that they were "busybodies." Teachers said both, but were critical of what they saw as maternal "overinvolvement" in their children's education.

Middle-class white parents made two kinds of objections to teachers' practices. *Principled objections* centered around the morality or justice of particular practices. Some mothers, for example, strongly criticized as "sexist" a musical production that a novice teacher had spent many hours preparing. The teacher and her co-producers had taken Richard Rodgers' songs and strung them into a play for kids. The mothers were particularly upset that the song "There Is Nothin' Like a Dame" was included. The teacher reacted angrily: "Can't everybody realize that it's just Richard Rodgers? That's just how it was then, and that's how we're using it." She threatened to quit if anyone tampered with the play. The teacher had looked at the material in one way and wanted others to see it in the same way, refusing to recognize any broader dimensions. At the same time, teachers felt that when parents made principled objections, unfair outside concerns were often dragged in, providing parents with ammunition that teachers had difficulty challenging.

Individual objections, on the other hand, centered around actual teachers' practices with mothers' own children. If principled objections were made in the name of the good of all children, individual objections could (but did not always) separate the needs of particular children from others in the class. These were the most frequent kinds of objections mothers made to teachers. In these kinds of objections mothers wanted to make sure that the teacher did not treat all children in the class the same. One mother described a point in a difficult year with a teacher when she went in to talk to the teacher about her daughter's unhappiness in the classroom: "She [the teacher] really didn't know the kids individually at all. She talked about the whole group. It was very hard to get Heather to focus in on Margaret." Teachers often worried that too many demands by mothers would multiply; hence, they read this sort of objection as greatly increasing their work load in the face of diminishing resources.

Not all teachers were equally critical of parents. Some had only praise for mothers' involvement in the school: "They're very concerned about their kids' education and very involved in it." Many teachers who withheld criticism had either had worse experiences with parents in other schools, or had young children of their own at the time and were personally familiar with the parental role in schools. These teachers, however, were in the minority. Most teachers wanted parents to help in the classroom activities and in ways that teachers determined or of which they approved, and at the same time they criticized mothers for "pounding down our doors."

Teachers' Stories about Mothers

The content of the stories teachers told about mothers was also informed by their narrative construction. Though what teachers said about mothers varied, though some were more or less critical than others, two lodestars guided the stories. I will describe the forms, try to account for these constructions, and discuss their effects.

One way teachers organized their stories of parents employed what I have come to call the "juvenile delinquent" approach, since just as all juveniles are not delinquent, neither are all parents difficult. But the few can give a reputation to the many. That is, after describing difficulties they have had with particular parents, or talking in general about parent-teacher relationships at Vista City Elementary School, teachers would say, "It's really just a few parents." Here are more examples of this construction:

- One experienced teacher said that for all the years that she has been at the school "there might have been five parents who were absolutely difficult, just impossible."
- "It's really only a few parents who cause problems, but these parents make life miserable for the teachers."
- Many people exaggerate and then end up gossiping about what the parents are like, "but in fact it is only very few parents who are so intrusive and busybodyish."
- "Actually, just a few parents give the parents a bad name. Only a few of them make trouble."

The behavior of some parents came to represent and stand in for the possible behavior and potential threat of all middle-class parents. This characterization reflects the notion that a few rotten applies spoil the rest.

These comments about parents (read "mothers") never came at the beginning of a story about parent-teacher relationships. They came after some negative comments: a particularly vehement criticism, a depiction of a series of incidents that described run-ins with mothers, some sweeping statement that generalized parent behaviors. The teachers seemed to regulate their critical stance toward the mothers by these statements. They also showed that they could differentiate among kinds of middle-class parents with whom they came into contact. But by suggesting that parents come to be represented by those who behaved inappropriately, they insisted that parents were the problem.

The juvenile delinquent approach also provided a way to categorize parents as "good" parents or "bad" parents. Both good and bad parents had a classroom presence. Good parents volunteered in the classroom under the teacher's structure. Bad parents intruded in the classroom to observe and monitor the teacher's competence. Both good and bad parents saw the teacher's position in the classroom as privileged. Good parents respected the teacher's abilities or at least understood how the difficulties of a particular class interfered with good teaching. Bad parents questioned or challenged the teacher's authority, competence, and abilities, perhaps blaming the teacher for a child's unhappy school year. Both good and bad parents communicated information and feelings about family life to the teacher although in different amounts. Good parents shared with the teacher family difficulties (like divorce) that might be occurring, or problems a child might be having outside of school. Good mothers, in other words, were willing to be vulnerable. Bad parents, on the other hand, postured the ideal world of family and behaved in a closed fashion. They covered up. Bad parents revealed little, and teachers had a hard time believing what they did tell.

When teachers took the juvenile delinquent approach, they were also communicating to me that I was not one of *those* parents. By differentiating the majority good parents from the minority bad parents, teachers were permitted to criticize all parents to the parents they liked, and then qualify their remarks as only applying to certain "bad" parents. It also meant that "horror stories," rather than cooperative alliances, came to represent normative relationships.

The juvenile delinquent approach also had an "essentializing" effect on teachers' vision of the mother-teacher relationship. Teachers could develop a characterization of what neighborhood mothers were "essentially" like. If mothers in the neighorbood came to be known by the rotten apples, then teachers acted as if mothers were "essentially" pushy and demanding. Mothers who cooperated, volunteered, and made few demands were distinguished as different, even though they were in the majority. Hence, teachers were on the defensive with mothers and were unable to articulate the class issues which existed.

A second construction of teacher narratives about neighborhood parents distanced the individual teacher from other teachers in the building, from a reputation of teachers-in-general that revealed teachers' vulnerability. The outline of this construction followed a basic pattern: "Others have problems with difficult parents though I do not. But their difficulties show me that it could be me." Another feature of this narrative included a discussion of the teacher's strength or self-confidence which prevented her from having difficulties. At the same time, narrators would contradict these statements by presenting situations where their interpretations of parents' words or behaviors caused them to feel like objects rather than subjects. Or observations of the teacher's "shaking voice" in front of parents suggested fear rather than self-confidence.

Some examples of this kind of narrative structure reveal teachers differentiating themselves from other teachers as they position themselves in opposition to mothers. One teacher distanced herself from other teachers because she depended on daily parental help, while "most teachers do not want parents around in the classroom." In other words, while other teachers might feel self-conscious under a mother's gaze, she did not. She also did not have personal problems with mothers: "Just by being strong, I don't usually get friction, like the parents bothering me. I don't feel any problem with them." Yet before and after this statement, this teacher had described conflicts with parents that made her feel she had no control, that she was an object to them. Before this statement, she criticized parents for "pounding on our doors," and not making appointments to see teachers but "just stopping by" to talk: "The parent feels no need to stop at the office and say, 'Would it be all right if I went down to the classroom?' or to call the teacher the night before or send a note [saying]: 'I would like to come,' or 'Can I come in?' or 'When can I talk to you?' or whatever. Just feeling they have complete open entrance."

After making her statement that she did not have friction with parents, this teacher subsequently described an incident which made her feel like an "object." A mother took a child out of her mathematics class without even talking to her about it because the child, another teacher told her, was afraid of her. The teacher had no opportunity to negotiate the incident. To make matters worse, she only heard the reasons secondhand.

Another teacher said that it was the parents who made teaching most difficult for her and made her feel most pressure. As examples of this pressure, she said that parents sometimes came in and wanted to see her lesson plans or wanted to observe in her class. The teacher proudly showed a letter she carried with her. The letter told how much the mother appreciated the teacher and how wonderful her daughter thought her as well. The mother had written, "As you know, we've had many ups and downs with Ginger this year and being in your class has been a wonderful experience for her." The teacher said that she actually got quite a few letters like this and personally had very few problems with parents. Yet earlier she had described parents as "really pressuring," as people who came in and made her life difficult. The exaggerated importance of parent praise was the flip side of parent criticism.

A teacher in the primary grades with a reputation for leadership and strength talked in many interview sessions about parents. At the same time she said that she never had any difficulty with parents, but a lot of other teachers had. She did not like it when parents challenged her competence. She said a number of times, "I'm a professional. I'm trained [in my area] and I make judgments on this basis." When parents come in and argue with her, she wants to make it clear that she has the files, that she sees the child daily, that she "knows the score." She noted many cases where parents have given "absolute grief" to teachers by demanding things of them. Many other teachers, however, do not have her self-assurance and "give in." She then told a story of a difficult mother who criticized her methods for teaching reading, and of another who had challenged her warm relationship with children. In this latter instance, the parent had said to someone (and this comment had come back to the teacher), "I hear she makes them march." The principal reported that the teacher had been "devastated." The teacher, however, said only, "Many of the parents are surprised because I am a very structured person and structured in the class, but I have a very warm, wonderful relationship with the kids." At a recent roller-skating party, the kids were "hanging all over" her and prevented her from skating. She also told a "horror story" of a mother who came in to observe the class. During the instructional time the parent rifled through lesson plans and papers on the teacher's desk. Her self-confidence helps her to handle situations like this, but these conflicts with parents devastate teachers with less confidence. Her narrative construction positioned her as capable of overcoming any difficulties a parent might pose.

A teacher in the upper elementary grades said that she had never had problems with parents, perhaps because she has made a point of having an open classroom and because she does not want to be "either on the offensive or the defensive with parents." Yet an observation of this teacher in a meeting with parents had revealed her "shaking voice." She had sworn to a "good" parent before the meeting, "These goddamned parents. I'm not going to go in there." The good parent, who had set up the meeting to encourage dialogue between teachers and parents, reported that she literally held her up, supporting her body, as she said to the teacher: "You can do it, Ellen. If you don't want to say anything, that's all right. I'll sit next to you or you can sit next to one of the other teachers and someone else can say something for you." The teacher did not like that idea. She decided she would say something.

The contrast between the teacher's comments to me about not having any problems with mothers, and her high level of anxiety before the meeting (which went well), not only reflect the power that middle-class white parents have in teachers' eyes, but also the shame involved when teachers consider their relationships with mothers problematic. Novice teachers might be allowed problems with women who were mothers but the expert, professional, experienced teachers should not have such problems. Hence Ellen could not refuse to speak with parents and have someone else speak for her; the shame would be too great. Mothers might make life difficult, but not being able to handle them meant you were not a professional.

Teachers agreed that one needed to be strong and have self-confidence to manage parents. A second-grade teacher said, "Confidence helps me deal with the parents because I don't doubt myself when they come in." In addition to confidence, experience provided leverage. "When I had all these highly skilled kids in my class, the parents would come to the door. I would see them standing there with worried looks on their faces. When they found out this was my eighth year teaching, their faces visibly relaxed."

A sixth-grade teacher had said to me in the teachers' room, "You're interested in what concerns us. I guess one thing is parents." The afternoon before she had had a conference with a child's parents and the child's psychiatrist that had greatly upset her. She also reported an incident where a mother, whose daughter said that the teacher had lost her homework, had pressured her terribly (and the daughter had not done the homework). Yet, in an interview with this teacher several weeks later, she reported that she had very few problems with parents "herself." She has a way of dealing with them: she shapes the relationship. She cannot blame parents for advocating for their children because "we all want the best for our children."

Why do teachers tell their stories of parents in this way? Why do they distance themselves from "problems" with parents and then give examples from their own experiences which contradict the assertion? Is it humiliating that mothers' activities, viewpoints, and words have the power to affect them so deeply? Do they see other teachers as weak and want to avoid identification with that weakness? Do they want to dissociate themselves from other teachers because they have internalized social devaluations of teaching? Is the dissociation similar to the way that professional women dissociate themselves from housewives or moderate feminists distance themselves from radical feminists because they do not want the more "fringe-identified" group to represent what they are?

Vista City teachers see good teachers moving through stages. As a novice one has problems with parents, but as an experienced and expert teacher one does not. Most teachers structured their narratives to reveal that they were no longer novices. The one novice teacher who reported parent problems identified herself as a new teacher. She expected to have parent problems. It was not that problems went away, but teacher narratives did not make room for vulnerability.

Teachers have internalized the negative value accorded their occupation. Many teachers said if they had to do it again, they would go into management in order to gain more status and more financial security. Hence they call on professionalism to defend their decisions involving children, and in order to separate *their* relationship with children, which rests on professional training, from mother's relationships and advice, which rest on the purely personal. Complicating matters at this school were the educational credentials of some of the mothers.

Effects of Teachers' Constructed Narratives

The effects of structuring their narratives about parents as they did led to the mystification of the parent-teacher relationship. Parents' image as unpredictable and demanding meant that teachers could never really know what parents wanted. As one teacher said, "Some mothers say, 'You're giving my kid too much homework; my kid's up till ten o'clock doing your homework,' and other parents say, 'Gee, why doesn't my kid get any homework from you?' These conflicting demands are hard to take." If some parents want one thing (an open classroom) and other parents want something else (a fast-paced class), then the teacher cannot please them all. Hence she can follow the curriculum. The teacher presents herself caught in a world which makes no logical sense. If some want this, and some want that, what can she do? She can do what serves her interests. The school principal participated in the mystification of middle-class white parents in her assertion that one could not predict how mothers would respond to changes in a classroom. The same incident will please some and anger others.

Teachers resist mothers' interference in the classroom because they see it as a challenge to their professionalism. Rightly perceiving their flimsy status in the occupational world, they envision an old-fashioned professionalism, untouched by consumer movements, as the potential rescuer from this situation. They resist mothers' interference because they want their work taken seriously, and they see mothers' activities not as a parallel effort but as a challenge to this desire.

Both teachers and white middle-class mothers call upon traditional ideologies of professionalism. These assumptions about what a profession is interfere with their collaboration because, ironically, both understand professionalism similarly. The mothers want teachers to have more of the training and abilities of doctors. The teachers want the mothers to act more like patients, making appointments and respecting their expertise with children. So they share the same definition of professionalism even as they lament each other's participation.

Teachers' relationships with parents are embedded in a web of other relationships and material conditions of school life, including their relationships with the principal and with each other, parents' relationships with other parents, the amount of the school budget, the attitudes and behaviors of the central administration, and the curriculum. Teachers' understanding of the expertise on which curriculum development rests differentiated their perspectives from those of the upwardly mobile middle-class parents.

How teachers thought about the curriculum influenced how they evaluated parental demands. Reactions varied. Those who took the curriculum for granted as an expert-developed measure of how much their students should accomplish for the year fussed when parents wanted more and more challenging assignments. They saw the students as "two years ahead of themselves" or as "way beyond grade level" already. Hence they could not understand why parents were "so worried" about how their children did in class.[16] Teachers who saw the curriculum as a guideline did not object to mothers' concern for their children's achievement if mothers were, at the same time, cooperative and available.

When they thought about mothers, in general, teachers worried that mothers would not think of them sympathetically, that they would not understand what was "legitimately" difficult about teachers' work. Teachers needed legitimation from others around the point that when they faced difficulties in the classroom, it was not just a matter of their skill levels (say, not enough large-group instruction), but because the composition of the class was challenging.

How parents were categorized was also not always the result of single, individual encounters. The school culture supported a warning system for self-protection so that teachers could advise each other about particularly troublesome parents. Parents had developed citywide reputations at Vista City Elementary School which magnified what they did. When Mrs. DeFrancisco demanded more homework, everyone knew about it. When Sally Martin made "outrageous" comments to a teacher, the others commiserated. The teacher who had the children of one of these parents in her class could depend on the support of other teachers to criticize and, in a way, dismiss these parents' concerns.

I have worried that examination of the conflicts between mothers and teachers sets up the classroom as a site where women struggle with each other for status and control. I emphasized conflict rather than cooperation because teachers highlighted conflict with parents as a major problem for them. The difficulties in their relationship center on a socially devalued domesticity associated with the education and care of young children. How teachers construct and structure their stories reveals the tenuous hold teachers have, if they have it, on respectable work when read against middle-class rather than working-class social mobility.

Needed: A Model that Allies Mothers and Teachers

At the opening of this chapter I suggested that mothers and teachers are in the same predicament: society devalues the work they do with young children. Teachers and mothers, then, struggle against the same obstacles even though it appears as if they vie with each other for status and control. They need, however, to name these obstacles and to recognize the similarities of their positions.

I take the risk of appearing to hold a kind of essentialist position. This position would describe teachers as if they were all alike, rather than examining their class, race, ideological, and other differences. Teachers are not alike. We must continually emphasize this point. They do, however, have a standpoint shaped by the particular social contexts from which they view mothers. At Vista City the commonality of position among teachers in relation to parents was noticeable. Teachers who called themselves feminists as well as others who were "progressive" educators joined with more conservative teachers in their criticisms of mothers' behaviors in the school. At other schools in the city where staff struggled to involve parents, teachers shared the concerns of those at Vista City Elementary School.

Teachers' position of vulnerability leads them to what we might also call an essentialist view of parents. But their daily experience challenged this approach; teachers depended on parents, teachers liked many parents, teachers had good relationships with many parents. So to avoid this position teachers developed a way of talking about parents that categorized them as good or bad. Talking as if most parents were "bad" when they were really "good," or fitting parents into only one (or the other) category was a form of needed self-protection that was ultimately self-damaging. In daily life they easily negotiated with and distinguished among mothers individually. They were caught in a contradiction.

Social class shaped teachers' reading of middle-class white mothers. Teachers' discussion of pressure suggests that they saw mothers' demands as the desire for preference. The stronger the working-class background of the teacher, the more clearly she read it this way. Teachers from middle-class backgrounds could accept this view even if they fought it. Connell and his colleagues noted similar emphases in their study in Australia. Upper-middle-class mothers showed their "class fear" when asserting that an education could not be taken away from their children, therefore implying that other family possessions could be.[17]

Teachers' lack of control over the conditions of their work makes them vulnerable to demands of white middle-class mothers. At Vista City they recognized their vulnerability but their way of thinking about their positions pushed this recognition to the background where it went underground.

Both mothers and teachers wanted to change the social configuration of their work. Teachers wanted to be considered full-fledged professionals with all of the privileges that status entails, while middle-class white mothers wanted recognition that the bearing and nurturing of children does not render mothers vacuous. At the same time, valuing the domestic as a complementary sphere leaves women powerless. Many of the women who taught felt that distancing themselves (and their professional credentials) from the mothers (with their commonsense understandings of child development) would enhance their own professional credibility. But this view did not recognize the gender link. Calling the problem "parents" rather than "mothers" might mystify the question, might detract from centering gender, but its consequences were that the analysis always missed the mark. Teachers need a model that allies them with rather than separates them from mothers.

Notes

1. All names of teachers, parents, administrators, and children have been changed, as well as some identifying characteristics, e.g., sometimes grade level.

2. Willard Waller, *The Sociology of Teaching* (New York: Wiley, 1932), p. 68; Howard Becker, "The Teacher in the Authority System of the Public School," in *Sociological Work* (New Brunswick, NJ: Transaction Books, 1970), p. 155; Seymour Sarason, *The Culture of Schools and the Problem of Change*, 2nd ed. (Boston: Allyn and Bacon, 1982); Gertrude McPherson, *Small Town Teacher* (Cambridge, MA: Harvard University Press, 1972).

3. Miriam E. David, "Schooling and the Family," in *Critical Pedagogy, the State, and Cultural Struggle*, edited by Henry Giroux and Peter McLaren (Albany: State University of New York Press, 1989), p. 51.

4. Ray C. Rist, *The Invisible Children* (Cambridge, MA: Harvard University Press, 1978), pp. 60-61. See also Malcolm Levin, "Parent-Teacher Collaboration," in *Critical Pedagogy and Cultural Power*, edited by David W. Livingstone (South Hadley, MA: Bergin and Garvey, 1987), p. 275.

5. William Reese, "Between Home and School: Organized Parents, Club Women, and Urban Education in the Progressive Era," *School Review* 87 (November 1976): 4, 13.

6. Steven Schlossman, "Before Home Start: Notes toward a History of Parent Education in America, 1897-1929," *Harvard Educational Review* 46 (August 1976): 443.

7. David, "Schooling and the Family"; Don Davies, "Poor Families and Schools: An Exploratory Study of the Perspectives of Low-income Parents and Teachers in Boston, Liverpool, and Portugal" (Paper presented at the Annual Meeting of the American Educational Research Association, New Orleans, 1988) ERIC ED 294 939; A. Henderson, *The Evidence Grows* (Columbia, MD: National Committee for Citizens in Education, 1985); Annette Lareau, "Social Class Differences in Family-School Relationships: The Importance of Cultural Capital," *Sociology of Education* 60 (April 1987): 73-85; Levin, "Parent-Teacher Collaboration"; Sara Lawrence Lightfoot, *Worlds Apart: Relationships between Families and Schools* (New York: Basic Books, 1978), especially chapter 2, "The Other Woman: Mothers and Teachers."

8. Levin, "Parent-Teacher Collaboration," p. 274.

9. Lightfoot, *Worlds Apart: Relationships between Families and Schools.*

10. See McPherson, *Small Town Teacher* and Lightfoot, *Worlds Apart.* Both draw upon the functionalist views of Talcott Parsons, "The School Class as a Social System," *Harvard Educational Review* 29 (Fall 1959): 297-318.

11. Lareau, "Social Class Differences in Family-School Relationships"; Levin, "Parent-Teacher Collaboration."

12. Madeleine Grumet, *Bitter Milk: Women and Teaching* (Amherst: University of Massachusetts Press, 1988).

13. Sara Lawrence Lightfoot, "Family-School Interactions: The Cultural Image of Mothers and Teachers," *Signs: Journal of Women in Culture and Society* 3 (Winter 1977): 404.

14. Joyce L. Epstein, "Parents' Reactions to Teacher Practices of Parent Involvement," *Elementary School Journal* 86 (January 1986): 277-294.

15. Dorothy Smith, *The Everyday World as Problematic* (Boston: Northeastern University Press, 1987), p. 187.

16. It should be noted that teachers also pressured teachers of lower grades to make sure they did not encroach on the higher grade's turf by teaching beyond a certain level. Kindergarten and first-grade teachers engaged in heated dialogue over reading levels. First-grade teachers did not want kindergartners to go beyond reading readiness levels. So it was an issue of work load as well.

17. Robert W. Connell, Dean J. Ashenden, Sandra Kessler, and Gary W. Dowsett, *Making the Difference: Schools, Families, and Social Division* (Sydney: George Allen & Unwin, 1982), p. 141.

Section Five
GENDER IN CLASSROOM AND SCHOOL POLICY

CHAPTER X

Making It Happen: Gender Equitable Classrooms

ELOIS SCOTT AND HEATHER MCCOLLUM

In 1972, women were encouraged by the passage of Title IX of the Education Amendments which prohibited sex discrimination in education. Title IX was quickly followed in 1974 by the Women's Educational Equity Act (WEEA) which required states to work to eliminate sex bias from their vocational education programs and provided funds for model sex equity programs. Women believed that the passage of these pieces of legislation would provide them with access to nontraditional fields of education and thus lead to a decrease in sex segregation by occupation that accounted for much of the wage gap between men and women. As we view the effect of this legislation today, we find that indeed there has been an increase in women's access to education. However, increased access has not led to major changes in the degree to which women receive the educational preparation needed to broaden their occupational choices.

We believe that the limited impact of Title IX is due in large part to learned behaviors resulting from classroom instruction which subtly teaches "appropriate" behavior for boys and for girls. According to a brief of the American Association of University Women (AAUW), *Equitable Treatment of Girls and Boys in the Classroom* (1989), girls' everyday interactions with teachers and with

---

Elois Scott is with the U. S. Department of Education. Heather McCollum is Senior Research Associate with Policy Studies Associates, Washington, DC. The views expressed are those of the authors writing in their private capacities. No official support by the U.S. Department of Education is intended or should be inferred.

other students contribute significantly to the slow change that has occurred in sex equity.[1] According to authors of the report,

> Too often, classroom dynamics are laced with unconscious sex stereotypes, as when teachers spend more time with boys in math classes and more time with girls in reading classes. Such subtle but powerful messages have been shown to circumscribe girls' and women's choices regarding academic preparation, achievement, and careers (p. 3).

To provide better opportunities for both girls and boys, teachers today must learn how to implement effective strategies for providing quality education for children who as adults will live and work in a very pluralistic society. Research has shown that teaching behavior is largely influenced by how teachers were taught, and yet school populations today are often much different from those that teachers knew as children and from those they learned about in schools of education. Teachers must learn how to address the multiple needs arising because of gender, class, ethnicity, language, and location.

Issues of fairness and equity, which have often been overlooked because they were considered unimportant or no longer issues,[2] are now considered by some to be paramount because of the economic necessity to provide an effective education to all students. According to statistics from the U.S. Department of Education, 45 percent of our current work force is female and, of the women in the work force, 51 percent are mothers with children under the age of three. It is projected that by the year 2020, 40 percent of the U. S. population will be minorities.

These data support the view of Harvey and Noble, who find that the economic and legal status of women now forms the programmatic basis for sex equity.[3] For example, the year-to-year stability of sex differences in wages and in types of occupations where women are employed means that fewer resources are available for women to deal with the day-to-day impact of changing family structures. The economic future of the United States depends largely on the ability of teachers to construct learning environments that provide encouragement, resources, and opportunities to girls and boys from all backgrounds.

In the first section of this chapter we explore current research on variations in teaching practice that result in inequities between girls and boys and between minority and nonminority groups and we examine the consequences of these inequities. In the second section we review the research on changing institutional behavior and we tie what is known from research about institutional change to how we can change teachers' behavior to bring about better practice. In the third section we use the research on effective teaching to suggest strategies for teachers that will facilitate a more equitable classroom environment for all students. Finally, we draw upon a recent report of the National Coalition on Women and Girls in Education that shows how reaching the National Education Goals for the year 2000 is contingent upon making sure that the educational needs of girls and women are met.

Inequities in Educating Girls and Boys

Lockheed and Klein, reporting the well-known fact that a child's educational achievement is closely linked to the level of education attained by her or his mother, conclude that raising the educational status of girls is essential for long-term achievement gains.[4] They also believe that subtle inequities remain in coeducational classrooms, despite the fact that public schools are prohibited by law from providing different services to boys and girls. They consider some of the subtle factors which may lead to an inequitable classroom environment and eventually to the perpetuation of sex inequities in general. They mention, for example,

> the physical characteristics of the room, such as its location and the size and location of its furniture; . . . the pedagogical material used in class; . . . [the] verbal and nonverbal messages from the teacher, such as her or his use of praise, eye contact, or the direct content of instruction; . . . [the] verbal and nonverbal messages from the student's classmates; and . . . the general organizational context in which the classroom is located, including such characteristics of the school as its staff, rules, or even the playground or special instructional facilities.[5]

These factors are particularly important at the preschool and kindergarten level where most children begin their formalized education. Classrooms that are arranged into gender-stereotyped play areas, such as a cooking corner for girls and a building-blocks corner for boys, reinforce the notion that some activities are for boys and others are for girls. These physical separations make it difficult for children to diversify their play without regard to gender. Moreover, since the teacher arranges the play areas, the lesson children learn is that this is how they are supposed to behave. Further, the physical arrangement of classrooms in this manner supports segregation, which is most often voluntarily initiated by children themselves, with boys choosing to play and talk with boys and girls preferring to interact with other girls.

Teachers have many opportunities to encourage cross-sex interactions so that sex stereotypes may be confronted by contradictory evidence and thus minimized. For example, they can make sure that the curriculum as well as the materials displayed in the classroom show both boys and girls engaged in similar highly valued activities.

The manner in which teachers interact with students can serve as a positive role model showing how students should interact among themselves. They should, for example, send the same signals to both boys and girls, as in discouraging inappropriate classroom behavior equally in boys and girls. Loud boisterous behavior should be tolerated neither for girls nor boys, just as passive children of both sexes should be challenged and encouraged to speak up. Teachers should provide all children with opportunities for engaging in and receiving praise for such behaviors as curiosity, cooperation, assertiveness, and helpfulness. In this manner, the teacher demonstrates appropriate school behavior, not gender behavior.

The distribution of resources is also an area in which frequent distinctions are made between girls and boys. The clearest and most evident example of this is the amount of money that is available for male sports compared to that available for sports for females. A similar example is the amount of laboratory equipment that is provided for activities in subjects in which males are especially encouraged to participate such as science and computer technology.

Although in many classrooms the environment is more equitable today than ten years ago, this change has been due primarily to the efforts of a few individual teachers who are attempting to be fair to students of both sexes. Practices that appear to be somewhat successful are the use of curriculum materials that focus on equity and the arrangement of seating and work groups to avoid the possibility of same-sex selection. While such practices are helpful, they are insufficient to combat the pervasiveness of messages regarding sex differences—messages that are passed along informally in institutions, families, and other social organizations. For sex-fairness practices to be effective they must be sustained by efforts of the entire school staff, not just by a few individual teachers.

Research on Sex Inequities in Classrooms

Lockheed and Klein report that there is little evidence of differences in achievement between boys and girls in the early grades, but there is substantial evidence of behavioral differences.[6] Girls are less disruptive than boys and speak out less often than boys. Studies have shown that teachers interact differently with girls and boys—calling on girls more than on boys or selectively ignoring certain male behavior. In fact, interactions between teachers and students often contain subtle messages that affect how girls see themselves and how they feel about themselves.

Hall and Sandler summarized teacher behaviors that communicate sex-differentiated expectations.[7] They noted that teachers may devalue the work of female students relative to males and may encourage female helplessness by solving a problem posed by girls, while explaining to boys how to solve the problem. They also noted that in interactions with postsecondary or adult students, teachers call on, or make eye contact with, male students more frequently than with female students.

Research by Lee and Gropper shows that teachers perceive the ideal student to be orderly, conforming, and dependent.[8] These are characteristics which often fit female students. Because the behaviors are seen as "ideal" teachers tend to give less attention to students who exhibit them, most frequently girls. On the other hand, boys who do not conform to the ideal pupil role are disciplined, getting more attention when they misbehave. Sadker and Sadker found that when both boys and girls are misbehaving, teachers are three times as likely to discipline the boys rather than the girls,[9] thus continuing to provide more attention to boys even though the context is negative. (This finding held across racial and ethnic lines.) These findings were supported by the research of Eccles and Blumenfeld, who reported that teachers initiated 10 percent more communication with boys than with girls, again strengthening the boys' sense of dominance and importance.[10]

Not all teacher interaction with boys is negative. Sadker and Sadker found that teachers asked boys more complex, abstract, and open-ended questions.[11] They were also more likely to give detailed instructions to boys on class projects and assignments while they were more likely to complete the task for girls. The Sadkers also found that teachers differentiated between boys and girls in the type of activity they praised. Ninety percent of the praise given to boys was directed at the intellectual content and quality of their work (rather than its form or neatness), whereas girls were praised for the content and quality of their work only 80 percent of the time. On the other hand, approximately 90 percent of the criticism of girls' schoolwork was focused on its intellectual content and quality, compared to 50 percent of such criticism received by boys. Furthermore, teachers often told boys that they did not do well because they did not try hard enough, whereas the connection between effort and outcome was rarely made with girls.

The result of differential treatment for boys and girls plays out in academic classes in a variety of ways. For example, Hallinan and Sorensen's research on the relationship of ability grouping to mathematics achievement found that even when boys and girls had similar mathematics scores, boys were assigned to the highest ability group more frequently than girls.[12] Rennie and Parker examined student behavior as boys and girls worked together on science projects.[13] They observed that girls spent 25 percent less time than boys manipulating the equipment and four times as much time watching and listening.

The manner in which teachers interact with students also varies by race. While Sadker and Sadker found that minority students of both sexes received less attention from the teacher than nonminority students,[14] Damico and Scott surveyed the literature on teacher interaction with black and white, male and female students, and reported the following:

- Despite similarity in achievement of white males and black females, teachers reinforced academic behavior only of the white males.
- Teachers reinforced academic behavior among white females and social behavior among black females.
- Teachers called on black females to help classmates with nonacademic tasks and white females to help with academic tasks.
- Teachers viewed black females as socially mature but not cognitively mature.[15]

These teacher behaviors resulted in black females having lower academic self-esteem than their classmates, including black males (despite the females' academic performance, which was higher than that of black males and comparable to that of white males). The black females also saw themselves as less powerful than other students are in their relationships with teachers and peers.

In summary, research on teacher interactions indicates that teachers' positive reinforcement of "ideal" behaviors and their lack of attention to girls discourages girls from learning more active and assertive learning styles, which in the long run tend to get students farther along. While these findings hold true for girls as a group, they are more pronounced for black girls than for white girls. Lockheed and Klein acknowledge that praising, criticizing, asking questions, and interacting are practices that maintain classroom discipline as well as providing instruction.[16] They caution, however, that it is inappropriate to try to assess whether teachers respond inequitably to girls versus boys without identifying and controlling for the antecedent student behaviors (or contingencies) that precipitate teacher response.

Peer interaction is an important source of sex inequities. Although peer contacts account for 29 percent of all experiences of a child in a typical classroom, according to Lockheed's estimate,[17] relatively little research has been conducted on unstructured peer interaction in the classroom. Some research on unstructured interaction between boys and girls has shown that in many school activities children self-select sex segregation. For example, Serbin, Tonick, and Sternglanz found a low rate of cooperative cross-sex play in two nursery school classes,[18] and Grant reported that cross-sex helping was rarely observed in first grade.[19] The lack of spontaneous cross-sex academic helping behavior was observed by Damico in an ethnographic study of one classroom of students aged eight to ten.[20] This lack continues to persist among boys as they grow older. Webb found that girls in a homogeneously grouped high school mathematics class responded to requests for help from other girls and boys, whereas boys primarily responded only to other boys.[21]

Lockheed and Hall[22] conducted a review of the research on mixed-sex discussion groups and made the following generalizations:

- Men are more verbally active than women; that is, the average man initiates more verbal acts than the average woman (p. 112).
- Men are more influential than women; a woman is more likely to yield to a man's opinion than vice versa (p. 113).
- Men initiate a higher proportion of their acts than women in task-oriented categories of behavior, whereas women initiate a higher proportion of their acts in social-emotional categories (p. 114).

Just as sex inequities in society are reflected in classroom climate and organization, so too are inequities related to race, ethnicity, and perceived ability. Thus, studies indicate that minority girls experience a different classroom environment from minority boys or nonminority girls.[23]

In summary, the research on peer interaction shows that throughout schooling classroom interaction between boys and girls is infrequent. A consequence of this lack of interaction is the reinforcement of stereotypes about sex-segregated activities.

Changing Schools and Teacher Behavior

We turn now to some of the literature on how schools and the behavior of teachers can be changed. The assumption is that broad-based changes must occur before schools and classrooms become sex equitable.

Change processes in the school culture. Creating sex-equitable learning environments in classrooms requires more than changing the behaviors of individual teachers. Perspectives on gender, race, and ethnicity emerge from strongly held norms and beliefs that may not always be conscious. Because many unfair arrangements may be firmly embedded in traditional practice, real change will most likely be part of a more comprehensive process of school reform. The results of several decades of efforts to reform schools have taught us that achieving structural and attitudinal change is not a trivial endeavor. Accordingly, for our purposes it will be instructive to review the growing evidence on how real change happens in schools.

Until the 1970s, many reformers believed that the way to increase student achievement was to bring teacher behavior in line with tested and proved "best practice" of various kinds. School change was viewed as a matter of reforming the individuals closest to the students—the teachers—by providing access to better instructional techniques. Problems that occurred in implementing best practice were viewed by these researchers in terms of teacher "resistance," and educational reformers became interested in discovering how teachers could become more receptive to behavioral change. From researchers such as Lortie, we learned that teachers as a whole are largely conservative and defensive of the status quo.[24]

According to Baldridge and Deal, this emphasis on changing teachers was analogous to an approach taken in organizational behavior studies in which change in institutions is effected by manipulating the individuals within them.[25] These models of the change process were drawn from innovations in fields such as agriculture and medicine. Examples are (a) research that focuses on the kind of farmer who would accept and use advances in soil technology and (b) research focusing on the characteristics of individuals seeking vaccinations. The recipients of new knowledge were generally viewed as independent of formal institutions. Katz and Kahn refer to this earlier line of thinking as the "psychological fallacy" because it ignores the social and structural context.[26] The focus on the individual rather than the organization as a whole led to the search for new and better technologies and more effective ways to convince people to bring their behavior in line with improved knowledge about what works best.

The implementation perspective. A number of authors have noted the gradual shift from this individualistic basis to a more structural approach.[27] A new interest emerged in the structure of institutions and the roles played by individual actors within them. House describes an analogous shift from a technical perspective to one that examines both the political and cultural aspects of organizations.[28] Attention to the ways people behave in institutions casts new light on the difficulties encountered in changing individual actions within them. For example, Weatherley and Lipsky described the gap between mandated policy in theory and policy in practice as a function of the discretion exercised by "street-level bureaucrats" over their various responsibilities.[29] Further, examination of their structural characteristics led to the characterization of schools as "loosely coupled" organizations,[30] in which teachers behind closed doors could be relatively autonomous and impervious to policy mandates. This transition in theoretical approach was reinforced by the burgeoning research on efforts to change schools. One of the most ambitious attempts to examine the implementation of promising strategies, the series of RAND volumes known as the "Change Agent Study," looked at the progress of several hundred federally funded projects and concluded:

> Despite considerable innovative activity on the part of local school districts, the evidence suggests that: No class of existing educational treatments has been found that consistently leads to improved student outcomes. . . . "Successful" projects have difficulty sustaining their success over a number of years. . . . [They] are not disseminated automatically or easily, and their "replication" in new sites usually falls short of their performance in the original sites.[31]

One of the key findings of the RAND work emphasized the lack of uniformity in implementation approaches. Indeed, while the project had been designed to compare the effectiveness of particular intervention strategies, the authors of the study found more variation across classrooms within each model than among the different models themselves. The authors concluded that program replication was simply not occurring as planned, and they coined the term "mutual adaptation" to describe the interactive, reciprocal process between policy and practice that better characterizes innovation efforts. Berman further describes the change process as inevitably "implementation-dominant," that is, events occurring after the adoption of the program determine the outcome, and these events cannot be predicted by the content of the technology itself.[32]

The overriding importance of the local context thus emerged as a key determinant in the success of school reform efforts. Many of the findings of the original Change Agent Study have been reinforced by the results of school improvement projects in the years since its publication. In a recent review of the study's conclusions, McLaughlin noted that many of its assertions were still valid twelve years later. Those that have withstood the test of time especially well include: (a) implementation dominates outcome, local choices have more influence than technology or design, and change continues to be a problem of the smallest unit; (b) because of the determining effect of local capacity and will, policy "can't mandate what matters"; and (c) local variability is the rule, and uniformity is the exception.[33]

The implications of these conclusions for strategies to change schools are clear: policymakers must pay attention not only to program design but to the local setting as well. This entails an examination of the ways people live and work in organizations and requires a willingness to learn from the school context.[34] The shift from change agent as dispenser of proved knowledge to a more explicitly reciprocal arrangement led in turn to a new interest in the culture of the school.

The cultural perspective. Sarason's analysis of incomplete efforts to change schools emphasized the importance of institutional norms and ways of operating, which he calls the "regularities" of schooling, in defeating ambitious innovations.[35] Other authors have also underscored the centrality of teachers' own interpretations of the meaning of initiatives for school change. However, the most widely publicized examination of the power of organizational culture came from outside education. The publication of Peters and Waterman's *In Search of Excellence* in 1984 brought new attention to this overlooked aspect of organizational life: the way people in institutions understand and interpret the meaning and significance of their work.[36] Organizational cultures are powerful and resilient; workers use symbols and stories to guide their actions and commitments. The good news is that cultures are dynamic as well as stable, and thus are susceptible to transformations under appropriate circumstances. For many, understanding how school cultures evolve and change holds the key to lasting school reform. This is especially true today, when many school improvement efforts are more ambitious in scope and involve far more than the successful dissemination of instructional strategies.

Definitions of culture and theories about its development have varied over the last century and across disciplines. For our purposes, we draw from classical anthropology and define culture as the social legacy an individual acquires from a group: a way of thinking and interpreting the environment and a mechanism for the normative regulation of behavior. Put more simply, culture represents socially transmitted knowledge that provides a guide for action.[37]

Why does culture matter to investigations of school reform strategies? As Fullan notes, "educational change depends on what teachers do and think—it's as simple and complex as that."[38] An understanding of culture provides important clues to the shared understanding and beliefs of teachers, which in turn help us to predict more accurately how various change initiatives might be received. Some reform initiatives, such as the introduction of new instructional materials, may conflict with norms and goals. Those that ask more of teachers—reforms that require shifting priorities and changed attitudes—have a much better chance of success if they are introduced with a clear understanding of the normative setting. Sergiovanni argues in support of this perspective, noting that while schools are indeed loosely connected in a management sense, they are tightly connected in a cultural sense. Thus he warns that comprehensive reforms which ignore the cultural dimension are problematic:

> What matters most are the norms of the work group and the individuals' beliefs, values, patterns of socialization, convictions, and commitments. Management systems and related patterns of control, which are easily circumvented, are less important. The theories that often drive school improvement efforts are based on the opposite premise: they give too much attention to managerially oriented systems of control and not enough to the human factors associated with increased performance.[39]

Rossman, Corbett, and Firestone examined three school improvement projects in the light of this perspective. They noted that most literature on school change looks at the political or technical reasons for failure without taking into account the fit between the desired behaviors and the culture's normative core—the accustomed ways of believing and behaving. In their view, "successful change must either accommodate that core or engage in the difficult enterprise of reinterpreting, redefining, or reshaping it."[40]

Where there is strong consensus among staff members around certain central norms (e.g., high expectations for all students), the introduction of appropriate technology (e.g., a new set of instructional materials) to reach those goals may be well received. Thus not all reform efforts need to address cultural change. However, in the most sweeping reforms—those that affect staff roles and responsibilities—leadership that is sensitive to cultural factors becomes much more essential.

Encouraging teachers to provide a more just structure of opportunity in the classroom is a good example of a change that requires a cultural shift. Fundamental reform in lifelong habits and patterns of interaction cannot be achieved through administrative fiat. Top-down efforts in this direction are likely to be resisted; results will be superficial and short-lived. Ideally, teachers should work together, explore their own strengths and weaknesses, and collaborate in developing plans to realize high expectations for all students.

The research we have cited on institutional change demonstrates the importance of culture and cultural norms in the introduction of change. As mentioned earlier, teachers tend to teach the way they were taught and tend to be conservative and reflect cultural norms. We need to examine the role that culture plays in defining how children see themselves and consider how culturally learned behaviors are mediated through the classroom behaviors of both the teacher and the student. In other words, in order to effect positive change in teachers we must take into account not only individual behavior but also organizational behavior and the cultural milieu in which they exist. This will be a very difficult task.

However, we should not be overly discouraged. It is possible to implement programs which are more sex equitable if strong support is provided. This leadership can come from teachers, but most generally should come from the principal, who as instructional leader is in a position to affect the school ethos. Without strong support from the beginning, the implementation of classroom change may tend to be watered down and modified to the extent that it is no longer what was intended. In addition, it should be recognized that support will have to be continued after initial implementation if change is expected to persist.

Strategies for Creating Gender-fair Education

Needed changes in teacher education. We often erroneously assume that by simply increasing the number of women in a field we will automatically make that field more gender equitable. This ignores the fact that most elementary teachers and a significant portion of those in the later grades are women. Studies have shown that education schools do not provide future educators with either the training or the experience they need to create a gender-fair, multicultural education system.[41] It is crucial that teacher education, both preservice and in-service, provide teachers with the skills and strategies they need to ensure gender-fair education for girls and boys from all cultures. These skills include the following:

- The ability to assess, select, and implement a curriculum that reflects the pluralistic context of our society and presents fairly the contributions of women and minorities as doers and decision makers rather than victims, including the use of an integrated curriculum which strengthens the link between students' schooling, work, and their cultures.
- The ability to implement teaching strategies which are appropriate for all learners, including abandoning tracking and working with mixed-ability groups in cooperative learning settings; using interactive learning methods that develop critical thinking skills through questioning and dialogue; modeling appropriate behaviors.

Strategies for classroom teachers. Among the strategies that can be implemented by classroom teachers are the following:

- Eliminate the assignment of sex-stereotyped tasks; provide opportunities for all children to participate in all activities.
- Teach good practice by modeling sex-equitable behavior.
- Challenge misconceptions of race and gender by raising these topics in class discussions.
- Organize classes so that students do not segregate themselves by sex.
- Eliminate direct instruction and/or interpersonal interactions which support learning only traditional sex roles; provide opportunities for children to explore a variety of areas and to see role models in a variety of professions.
- Examine instructional materials to determine if they are sex biased, sex fair, or sex affirmative.

- Participate in revising school rules and making suggestions on the physical arrangements of classrooms to ensure that they are sex fair.
- Encourage girls to play with equipment that is typically reserved for boys.
- Structure group projects so that girls will have an equal opportunity to participate.
- Provide opportunities for cooperative learning activities to take place with groups of boys and girls.

Suggestions for administrators. Teachers cannot do it alone. The school must have the support of an administrator who is an advocate for gender equity. The administrator can support gender equity by

- Supporting the faculty when they try to implement gender-equitable strategies.
- Promoting a school culture in which gender and ethnic bias is tolerated neither by the teachers nor by the students.
- Providing equal access to all resources for girls and boys, including the provision of a variety of role models in everything from faculty and staff hiring to textbook selection to the designation of speakers at assemblies.

Conclusion

The need to restructure our schools to meet the needs of the students and to meet the social and economic needs of our country as we approach the twenty-first century is being given considerable time and thought by educators and state and federal political leaders. In February 1990, the National Governors' Association and the Bush Administration jointly published *Education 2000*, a statement of national education goals. The National Coalition on Women and Girls in Education carefully analyzed the goals and assessed their implications for gender equity in public education. In a report issued in May, 1990, the Coalition argued that meeting the stated goals by the year 2000 is contingent upon making sure that the needs of girls and women are met.[42] The American Association of University Women (AAUW) summarized these needs as follows:

GOAL 1: *By the year 2000, all children in America will start school ready to learn.* Requires enhancing the ability of female-headed households to prepare children for school, including achievement of adequate living standards and access to parental leave, child care, Head Start funding, and adult female literacy programs.

GOAL 2: *By the year 2000, we will increase the percentage of students graduating from high school to at least 90 percent.* Requires addressing factors that have a particular impact on keeping girls in school, including provisions of gender-fair curricula and instruction, pregnancy prevention programs, and assistance to pregnant and parenting teens.

GOAL 3: *By the year 2000, American students will leave grades four, eight, and twelve having demonstrated competency over challenging subject matter, including English, mathematics, science, history, and geography, and every school in America will ensure that all students learn to use their minds well, so they may be prepared for responsible citizenship, further learning, and productive employment in our modern economy.* Requires gender-fair curricula, teaching methods attentive to learning styles of individual students, and methods of assessing competency that do not rely on standardized tests, which can contain race and sex biases.

GOAL 4: *By the year 2000, U. S. students will be first in the world in mathematics and science achievement.* Requires developing interventions at key junctures in girls' academic lives to increase their participation and success in these subjects.

GOAL 5: *By the year 2000, every adult American will be literate and will possess the knowledge and skills necessary to compete in a global economy and exercise the rights and responsibilities of citizenship.* Requires gender-fair programs in vocational education and training programs including postsecondary training for technical and professional careers.

GOAL 6: *By the year 2000, every school in America will be free of drugs and violence and will offer a disciplined environment conducive to learning.* Requires ensuring safety from sexual and racial harassment and assault in the schools.[43]

As we move into the twenty-first century, we can no longer ignore the miseducation of girls and minorities. If our nation is to continue to be a leader, we must attend to the needs of all of our citizens.

Notes

1. Kathy Vandall, *Equitable Treatment of Girls and Boys in the Classroom* (Washington, DC: American Association of University Women, June, 1989), ERIC ED 326 477.

2. "Women: The Road Ahead," *Time Magazine* 136, Special Issue (Fall 1990).

3. Glen Harvey and Elizabeth Noble, "Economic Considerations for Achieving Sex Equity through Education," in *Handbook for Achieving Sex Equity through Education*, edited by Susan S. Klein (Baltimore, MD: Johns Hopkins University Press, 1989).

4. Marlaine E. Lockheed, with Susan S. Klein, "Sex Equity in Classroom Organization and Climate," in *Handbook for Achieving Sex Equity through Education*, edited by Susan S. Klein (Baltimore, MD: Johns Hopkins University Press, 1989).

5. Ibid., pp. 189-190.

6. Ibid., p. 196.

7. Roberta M. Hall and Bernice R. Sandler, *The Classroom Climate: A Chilly One for Women* (Washington, DC: Project on the Status and Education of Women, Association of American Colleges, 1982).

8. Patrick C. Lee and Nancy B. Gropper, "Sex-Role Culture and Educational Practice," *Harvard Educational Review* 44 (August 1974): 370-371.

9. Myra P. Sadker and David M. Sadker, *Sex Equity Handbook for Schools* (New York: Longman, 1982), p. 105.

10. Jacquelynne Eccles and Phyllis Blumenfeld, "Classroom Experiences and Student Gender: Are There Differences and Do They Matter?" in *Gender Influences in Classroom Interaction*, edited by Louise Cherry Wilkinson and Cora B. Marrett (Orlando, FL: Academic Press, 1985), p. 84.

11. Sadker and Sadker, *Sex Equity Handbook for Schools*.

12. Maureen T. Hallinan and Aage Sorensen, "Ability Grouping and Sex Differences in Mathematics Achievement," *Sociology of Education* 60 (1987): 67.

13. Leonice J. Rennie and Lesley H. Parker, "Detecting and Accounting for Gender Differences in Mixed-Sex and Single-Sex Grouping in Science Lessons," *Educational Review* 39 (1987): 67-68.

14. Myra P. Sadker and David M. Sadker, "The Treatment of Sex Equity in Teacher Education," in *Handbook for Achieving Sex Equity through Education*, edited by Susan S. Klein (Baltimore, MD: Johns Hopkins University Press, 1989), pp. 147-149.

15. Sandra B. Damico and Elois Scott, "Behavior Differences between Black and White Females in Desegregated Schools," *Equity and Excellence* 23 (1988): 63-66.

16. Lockheed, with Klein, "Sex Equity in Classroom Organization and Climate."

17. Marlaine E. Lockheed, "Sex Equity in Classroom Interaction Research: An Analysis of Behavior Chains" (Paper presented at the Annual Meeting of the American Educational Research Association, New York, 1982).

18. Lisa A. Serbin, Illene J. Tonick, and Sarah H. Sternglanz, "Shaping Cooperative Cross-Sex Play," *Child Development* 48 (1977): 924-929.

19. Linda Grant, "Sex Roles and Statuses in Peer Interactions in Elementary Schools" (Paper presented at the Annual Meeting of the American Educational Research Association, New York, 1982).

20. Sandra B. Damico, "Sexual Differences in the Responses of Elementary Pupils to Their Classroom," *Psychology in the Schools* 12 (1975): 462-467.

21. Noreen Webb, "Interaction Patterns: Powerful Predictors of Achievement in Cooperative Small Groups" (Paper presented at the Annual Meeting of the American Educational Research Association, New York, 1982).

22. Marlaine E. Lockheed and Katherine P. Hall, "Conceptualizing Sex as a Status Characteristic: Applications to Leadership Training Strategies," *Journal of Social Issues* 32, no. 3 (1976): 111-124.

23. Damico and Scott, "Behavior Differences between Black and White Females"; Grant, "Sex Roles and Statuses in Peer Interactions in Elementary Schools"; Thomas L. Morrison, "Classroom Structure, Work Involvement, and Social Climate in Elementary School Classrooms," *Journal of Educational Psychology* 71 (1979): 471-477.

24. Dan Lortie, *Schoolteacher* (Chicago: University of Chicago Press, 1975).

25. J. Victor Baldridge and Terrence E. Deal, eds., *Managing Change in Educational Organizations: Sociological Perspectives, Strategies, and Case Studies* (Berkeley, CA: McCutchan Publishing Corp., 1975).

26. Daniel Katz and Robert Kahn, "Individual and Small Group: Organizational Change," in *Managing Change in Educational Organizations: Sociological Perspectives, Strategies, and Case Studies*, edited by J. Victor Baldridge and Terrence E. Deal (Berkeley, CA: McCutchan Publishing Corp., 1975), pp. 35-74.

27. See, for example, Baldridge and Deal, eds., *Managing Change in Educational Organizations*; Gretchen B. Rossman, H. Dickson Corbett, and William A. Firestone, *Change and Effectiveness in Schools: A Cultural Perspective* (Albany, NY: State University of New York Press, 1988).

28. Ernest R. House, "Three Perspectives on Educational Innovation: Technological, Political, and Cultural," in *Improving Schools: Using What We Know*, edited by Rolf Lehming and Michael Kane (Beverly Hills, CA: Sage, 1981).

29. Richard Weatherley and Michael Lipsky, "Street-level Bureaucrats and Institutional Innovation: Implementing Special Educaton Reform," *Harvard Educational Review* 47, no. 2 (1977): 171-197.

30. John W. Meyer and Brian Rowan, "Institutionalized Organizations: Formal Structure as Myth and Ceremony," *American Journal of Sociology* 83 (1977): 340-363.

31. Paul E. Berman and Milbrey W. McLaughlin, *Implementing and Sustaining Innovations*, vol. 8 (Santa Monica, CA: Rand Corporation, 1977), pp. 1-2.

32. See Paul Berman, "Educational Change: An Implementation Paradigm," in *Improving Schools: Using What We Know*, edited by Rolf Lehming and Michael Kane (Beverly Hills, CA: Sage, 1981).

33. Milbrey W. McLaughlin, "The Rand Change Agent Study Revisited: Macro Perspectives and Micro Realities," *Educational Researcher* 19 (December 1990): 12.

34. See, for example, William H. Clune, "Three Views of Curriculum Policy in the School Context: The School as Policy Mediator, Policy Critic, and Policy Constructor," in *The Contexts of Teaching in Secondary Schools: Teachers' Realities*, edited by Milbrey W. McLaughlin, Joan E. Talbert, and Nina Bascia (New York: Teachers College Press, 1990).

35. Seymour B. Sarason, *The Culture of the School and the Problem of Change* (Boston: Allyn and Bacon, 1974).

36. Thomas J. Peters and Robert H. Waterman, Jr., *In Search of Excellence: Lessons from America's Best-Run Companies* (New York: Harper and Row, 1982).

37. See Clyde Kluckhohn, as cited in Clifford Geertz, *The Interpretation of Cultures* (New York: Basic Books, 1973), pp. 4-5.

38. Michael Fullan, *The Meaning of Educational Change* (New York: Teachers College Press, 1982).

39. Thomas J. Sergiovanni, "What Really Counts in Improving Schools?" in *Schooling for Tomorrow: Directing Reforms to Issues That Count*, edited by Thomas J. Sergiovanni and J. H. Moore (Boston: Allyn and Bacon, 1989).

40. Rossman, Corbett, and Firestone, *Change and Effectiveness in Schools*, p. 18.

41. M. Gail Jones, "Gender Issues in Teacher Education," *Journal of Teacher Education* 40 (January/February 1989): 33-38; Sadker and Sadker, "The Treatment of Sex Equity in Teacher Education."

42. National Coalition on Women and Girls in Education, *Education for All: Women and Girls Speak Out on the National Education Goals* (Washington, DC: National Coalition on Women and Girls in Education, 1990).

43. Kathy Vandall, *Restructuring Education: Getting Girls into America's Goals* (Washington, DC: American Association of University Women, August, 1990). ERIC ED 326-476.

CHAPTER XI

It Happens Here, Too: Sexual Harassment and Child Sexual Abuse in Elementary and Secondary Schools

NAN D. STEIN

I begin this chapter with two scenarios:

Scenario A. A female high school student claims that the school's band director touched her during practice sessions at school, and has hinted at his interest in having sex with her when the band plays at school-sponsored musical events away from the school. At first, she complains to the high school principal, who responds by telling her that it is her word against the band director's word. Furthermore, he tells her that the band director has always received excellent evaluations. The young woman decides to file a law suit claiming sex discrimination.

Scenario B. A young woman in the ninth grade, one of the few females in an auto mechanics course, is subjected to dirty, sexist jokes by classmates. The teacher never intervenes even though he seems to overhear some of the banter. The other girls in the class seem oblivious or unaffected by the jokes, but this one young woman can't block out the jokes or the stares; she feels generally uncomfortable. Although she tries to stay focused on her projects, she finds it hard to pay attention, and soon the quality of her work declines. She receives a less than satisfactory grade in the first marking period, and is advised to drop the course, which she does.

In this chapter I will define and describe sexual harassment in schools as it occurs between students and between staff and students. I will demonstrate that sexual harassment is a rampant yet largely

After more than a decade as the sex equity/civil rights specialist with the Massachusetts Department of Education, Nan Stein is presently with the Center for Research on Women at Wellesley College, where she directs a research project on sexual harassment and child sexual abuse in schools.

unrecognized problem with deleterious effects on its subjects/victims. (The words "subject/victim" will be used in tandem when referring to the subject or recipient of unwanted attention: "subject" to indicate that anyone can be a subject of such attention, and "victim" because it is a legal notion, albeit often with paralyzing psychosocial consequences.) I will chronicle the reckless indifference manifested by school administrators toward this problem in schools, and I will then conclude with proposals for action and intervention at various levels.

Defining the Problem

Scenarios such as those represented at the beginning of this chapter are sadly frequent in school life, yet are startlingly absent from the literature on education, and from the recent national discourse on sexual harassment. Assuming that one is able to identify these descriptions as "child sexual abuse," or "sexual harassment," one would have great difficulty finding published literature on the existence of these problems and strategies for eliminating them from elementary and secondary schools.

Sexual harassment in elementary and secondary schools does not look the same (albeit with younger actors) as it does in higher education. With children age twelve and older, sexual harassment is all too often dismissed as "typical adolescent behavior," and misconstrued as a normal rite of passage, as awkward "getting-to-know-you" behaviors. Instead of being carefully defined and communicated to students, teachers, and administrators, sexual harassment is trivialized, condoned, or described as "flirting" or "initiation rites."

SEXUAL HARASSMENT: A RAMPANT PROBLEM

Sexual harassment occurs in the mundane, daily matters of school life: in the corridors and stairwells; in the cafeteria; in the chemistry laboratory as well as in the carpentry shop; in the gym and the parking lot; on school buses, in the driver's education car, and on the practice fields for extracurricular sports. This universal presence of sexual harassment in schools is apparent from the few surveys about sexual harassment in schools which have been undertaken. In 1980, the Massachusetts Department of Education, with assistance from a now defunct organization, the Alliance Against Sexual Coercion, conducted the first survey on sexual harassment in high schools. The sample of approximately 200 male and female students from across Massachusetts included culturally and racially diverse students from urban, suburban, and rural schools, attending both public and private schools. In addition, in-depth interviews were conducted between 1979 and 1982 with sixty young women who were enrolled in courses that were previously considered nontraditional for their sex (such as auto body, auto mechanics, plant maintenance, plumbing and air conditioning, metal fabrication.)[1]

The research revealed the following:

- Young women are much more likely to be victims of sexual harassment, especially in the more severe forms of unwanted physical attention, than their male counterparts.
- Sexual harassment is a problem for many students in both academic and vocational high schools. It is not the case that sexual harassment only occurs when young women are in the minority, as they often are in vocational schools or in courses which have been previously considered sex role nontraditional. Sexual harassment is a typical part of the fabric of daily life in schools where young women comprise 50 percent of the school population.
- Student-to-student sexual harassment is more prevalent than teacher-to-student sexual harassment.
- Peer-to-peer sexual harassment ranges from verbal and written comments to physical assault and attempted rape.
- Sexual harassment on the job is not unfamiliar to high school students, whether the jobs are part of the school curriculum, as in "co-op" jobs supervised by school personnel, or whether the jobs are acquired independently of the school.

EFFECTS OF SEXUAL HARASSMENT—KNOWN AND UNKNOWN

This survey as well as other attempts to collect data by state sex-equity specialists in California, Hawaii, Washington, and Minnesota have shown that sexual harassment has an adverse effect on teaching and learning, and on psychosocial development of adolescents in the classroom and outside it. Students who have experienced sexual harassment have reported an array of examples of it, as well as of its consequences. Among the direct and immediate effects were feelings of embarrassment, fear of retaliation, anger, powerlessness, loss of self-confidence, and cynicism about education and teachers. Students also identified physical symptoms, including insomnia and listlessness. They also reported a reduced ability to perform school work and excessive absenteeism or tardiness. Some also indicated that sexual harassment led them to transfer from particular courses or majors, and in some cases, to withdraw from school. Indeed, such consequences constitute a denial of equal educational opportunity, and the presence of a "hostile environment."

More subtle experiences of harassment produced less tangible results. Students who felt betrayed, discredited or compromised by peers, and unsupported by school staff seemed less trusting of people in general, and less enthusiastic about pursuing their education. Victims/subjects of sexual harassment, as well as the bystanders and witnesses to incidents of sexual harassment, expressed a loss of confidence in the effectiveness of school policies. In fact, positive feelings and beliefs about justice and caring may be in jeopardy if such a "poisoned environment" is allowed to exist through the tolerance of sexual harassment.[2] Such a loss of community, let alone the hope for a just and caring community, may have a greater impact upon young women than upon young men, whether or not these young women are victims of sexual harassment.

A more recent survey was conducted in 1986 in Minnesota with male and female juniors and seniors, ages sixteen to eighteen, who were enrolled in a predominantly white, middle-class secondary vocational center.[3] This study found that of the 133 females questioned, depending on the courses in which they were enrolled, 33 to 60 percent reported incidents of sexual harassment, while only one out of 130 males reported that he had been a victim of sexual harassment. Additional data were obtained at a Minnesota State Sex Equity Student Leadership Conference held in May 1986. Eighty percent of the participants indicated that they were aware of sexual harassment in their schools, the preponderance of those incidents occurring between students.

In elementary and secondary schools as well as in higher education, sexual harassment is against the law and is a form of sex discrimination, a violation of Federal Title IX of the Education Amendments of 1972, and Title VII of the Civil Rights Act (1964 amended 1972), and may also violate state criminal and civil statutes. Some forms of sexual harassment may also be actionable as child abuse, sexual assault, rape, pornography, criminal or civil libel, slander or defamation of character. Victims, as well as educators or community members acting on the victim's behalf, may file sexual harassment complaints.

Unlike higher education where sexual harassment is a widely researched and discussed phenomenon, in elementary and secondary schools it remains largely unexplored and unacknowledged. Occasionally, sexual harassment is reported to those rare school officials who do indeed believe that such allegations warrant pursuit, but who often find themselves "ad-libbing," inventing a system of investigation and adjudication. At other times, these same school officials, frustrated by their institutions' inability or unwillingness to pursue these allegations, may turn to those state agencies charged with resolving complaints of sex discrimination (agencies such as the state education department or the state human rights commission). At the very least, an intervention from an outside agency may escalate the situation, and often leads to more litigious remedies than those which might have been applied successfully had they occurred at the school level at an earlier stage of the conflict.

In cases of alleged child sexual abuse of a minor by a school employee, reports to those agencies charged with protecting children from child abuse and neglect are usually dropped after a required period of investigation. These state agencies have responsibility for child welfare and protection. But in addition to constant staff shortages and high case loads, their authority is limited to the removal of children from abusive and neglectful homes. Thus, insult is added to injury when there is an attempt to report the alleged occurrence of child sexual abuse in a school setting: jurisdictional confusion, gaps in policy, and a virtual "no man's land" exist, thus vitiating most allegations of child sexual abuse in schools. Meanwhile, back at the school, the presenting problem and conditions fester, spawning an atmosphere that permits and tolerates at a minimum sexual harassment and discrimination, denying students the right to an equal educational opportunity and equal protection under the law. "Other more cynical lessons are also taught by such behaviors: schools become an unsafe place; students lose confidence in school policies and trust for school officials. These consequences are felt not only by the victim/subject, but also by the bystanders, both 'innocent' witnesses and colluders, who have now, too, tasted the bitter lessons of sexual harassment."[4]

When the specter or hint of a sexually tinged relationship between a minor and an adult in a school setting emerges, confusion or cover-up seems to be the typical response.[5] Because the sexual harassment has entered a new domain, that of child abuse and criminal felonious behavior, more is at stake. Despite the lack of extensive documented occurrences in public schools, incidents of sexual abuse and sexual harassment do occur, and the offenders are frequently clustered in a few particular capacities within the school community. Such roles as coach, driver education teacher, and extracurricular adviser often require individual contact with students, often in private settings, and often in a capacity that can build trust and intimacy. Although these same adults may serve in a dual capacity as classroom teachers, examples suggest a less frequent occurrence of physical sexual harassment by these individuals when they are in their classroom roles as opposed to their adjunctive roles.[6]

The Mobile Molester and the Conspiracy of Silence

Recently, a new avenue for the adjudication of sexual harassment and child abuse of minors by school personnel was created in a precedent setting case heard before the U. S. Court of Appeals for the Third Circuit. In this case, *Stoneking v. Bradford Area (PA) School District*,[7] the court held that public school officials had violated a student's 14th Amendment right to "liberty" when they failed to protect her from sexual abuse by school employees. This 1989 decision paved the way for the former high school student to sue a Pennsylvania school district and individual school officials for negligent supervision of a band director who had sexually assaulted her during school-sponsored events and trips, and sometimes on school property. The two other original plaintiffs in this case, who had also been subjected to sexual pressure and assault by the band director, had settled out of court with the insurance company for the sum of $700,000 in 1987 when the case was first heard at the District Court level.

This case is salient and illuminating for several reasons. Foremost is the prototypical role the harasser had in the school community. Once again, the harasser had power and prestige, gleaned from the accomplishments of individual band members who were extremely successful in regional and national competitions, and from the overall status of the band which became the pride and joy of the school and of the community.[8] This case parallels another very similar one in the Philadelphia Public Schools, which began in the late 1970s and continued until the young women came forward with their stories in the late 1980s, years after some of them had graduated from high school. Again, a band director who had brought national acclaim to a school orchestra was the harasser. "(Jones) did not simply create an exceptional music program; he created an elite corps of musicians within the school. Jones's orchestra became something to aspire to, and music students would practice even in the hallways and stairwells, using every bit of available space and filling (the school) with sound." Concurrent with these accomplishments were his behaviors toward his students during their private music lessons, held in the secluded location of his office. "Private lessons would often start with a hug, . . . and comments about (my) hair or clothes, and (ask) questions about (my) friends or boyfriends. . . . Gradually, the hugs would get longer and more intimate. Then, there would be kisses."[9] Sometimes, he would brazenly display such affectionate behaviors in front of other students, like having female students sit on his lap, or kissing students on their necks in the hallways. Clearly this man knew no limits; nor were any imposed by the school officials. His reign of terror and accomplishments coexisted with impunity.

These two cases of band directors who terrorized and sexually abused their students stand out, but do not stand alone. There are countless more cases of school employees, especially those who hold power over the futures of their students in their hands (scholarships, exposure to prestigious competitions, recommendations to colleges and summer institutes, etc.) who abuse their authority and trust. Their transgressions and their subjects/victims, as well as bystanders and witnesses who were damaged in less direct ways, call out for a higher level of scrutiny and continuing oversight by school authorities over school employees. Measures must be created and applied to protect all students, not just female students. For example, attaching chaperones to every female student, or requiring only female students to work in pairs when they are alone with a male teacher, would be unacceptable because as remedies they reintroduce and reenforce sex discrimination into the solutions. In the quest to rid schools of sexual harassment, there cannot be a return to measures conceived in the name of protecting only females.

The second salient feature of *Stoneking* and the Philadelphia cases is the route to resolution of the complaints chosen by the school districts. In both cases, and in countless others, the teacher is typically confronted with allegations of sexual misconduct and is asked to resign, thereby avoiding a lengthy hearing or trial. In essence, a plea bargain has been worked out. There is no termination hearing at the local level, no revocation of the teacher's license at the state level, and more often than not, no criminal charges brought by the young women and their families.

In *Stoneking*, the band director, Edward Wright, was suspended in March, 1986, and when faced with termination proceedings he resigned his position. In November 1986, he pled guilty to criminal charges, but was able to plea-bargain the felony charges to misdemeanor convictions and was fined $2,500, sentenced to three years' probation, and ordered to complete 300 hours of community service and to continue to undergo psychological evaluation. According to a report by the state of Pennsylvania principals' association, the assistant district attorney has appealed this sentence.[10]

In the 1988 case of the Philadelphia band director, when Mr. Stephen Clayton Jones was confronted with the allegations and was handed the students' signed statements, "he turned in his letter of resignation to the Board of Education. He never confirmed or denied the allegations. Nor did he fight for his job. The school district began proceedings to revoke his teaching license due to immorality. He surrendered his license in 1989, in lieu of revocation, and notification of that fact was sent to the department of education of every state in the country. Because Jones chose to resign and gave up his license voluntarily, there was never a formal hearing before the Board of Education or the state to determine if he was culpable."[11]

In both cases the school board got what they wanted—the eventual removal of the teacher from their district. The unusual feature of both *Stoneking* and the Philadelphia cases described above *was* that there were institutional responses: a trial in the first case and an attempt to revoke a teaching license in the second case. Neither occurs in most cases because plea-bargaining arrangements have been worked out between the school board and the accused. There are no official termination hearings at the local level, and the superintendent and school board agree to keep the entire matter confidential and not to pursue revocation of the teacher's license with the state's department of education. Thus, in the more typical sequence of events, the teachers become "mobile molesters": they resign and just move along to another community where they repeat the alleged behaviors all over again. The culprit in these prototypical scenarios is not merely the harassing, abusive teacher, but also the superintendent and school board who collude in this conspiracy of silence by passing along a harasser because it is easier, more expedient and cheaper than going forward with dismissal proceedings. Clearly, such negligence must be stopped, and if need be, prosecuted.

Potential Remedies

In December 1991 the United States Supreme Court heard oral arguments in *Franklin v. Gwinnett County (GA) Public Schools*, a case that involved a female high school student who had alleged intentional gender discrimination (in this case, sexual harassment) by a teacher/coach. As a fifteen-year-old sophomore at North Gwinnett High School in suburban Atlanta, Christine Franklin was the subject of unwanted sexual attention from a social studies teacher. Initially, the attention was flattering. She was often asked by him to grade papers and tests. However, his attention turned obsessive. He would wait for her outside her classes or in the parking lot, and would call her at home. He began to make suggestive sexual remarks during the course of the next year, and on three occasions pressured her into having sex with him on the school premises. Although seeming to comply with rather than to resist his sexual demands, she did not keep silent. She informed the school officials and filed a complaint with the U.S. Department of Education's Office for Civil Rights.

According to Ms. Franklin the school officials did nothing to stop the harassment, and also tried to dissuade her from filing charges. The teacher ultimately resigned on condition that the charges against him be dropped. Once he left the school the Office for Civil Rights declared that since he was gone they could not proceed with their investigation.

In 1988, Ms. Franklin and her lawyers sued the school district in federal court, but her suit was dismissed because the judge ruled that she could not collect damages under Title IX. The U.S. Court of Appeals for the 11th Circuit affirmed the dismissal.

In February 1992, the Supreme Court ruled for the first time, and in a unanimous decision, that compensatory damages are available under Title IX. This decision has enhanced Title IX's stature as an avenue for redress for sexual harassment, and has also opened the gate for victims of other intentional discrimination (e.g., on grounds of race or disability) to recover compensatory damages from school systems. Organizations which had filed amicus briefs in support of the petitioner included the National Women's Law Center, American Association of University Professors, American Civil Liberties Union, Coalition of Labor Union Women, National Council of La Raza, the National Education Association, and many other advocacy groups. These groups as well as school districts throughout the country now realize that this stunning decision holds major legal and fiscal implications for school districts. Ms. Franklin and her lawyers return to federal district court in Georgia for trial in 1993.

Promoting Awareness of Sexual Harassment in Schools

In the aftermath of the lessons given to the country by the Anita Hill-Clarence Thomas hearings on sexual harassment in the workplace, and by the decision in *Franklin*, we need to provoke a national awareness that sexual harassment exists in elementary and secondary schools also. One route to this awareness is to use curriculum materials which highlight the problem of sexual harassment in schools. Several products in print and in audio-visual form already exist, targeting different audiences and age groups. The first product created about sexual harassment in schools was *Who's Hurt and Who's Liable: Sexual Harassment in Massachusetts Schools*,[12] developed by the Massachusetts Department of Education. First written in 1979, and currently in its fourth edition (1986), this curriculum and resource guide for school personnel contains classroom activities, guidelines for discussing sexual harassment with staff and students, sample policies and grievance procedures, and an extensive bibliography. Several other state departments of education, most notably Minnesota, Washington, and New Jersey, have produced derivative curriculum materials, relying heavily on the pioneering effort of the Massachusetts Department of Education.[13]

The highly original booklet, *Tune in to Your Rights: A Guide for Teenagers for Turning off Sexual Harassment*,[14] was created in 1985 by the Programs for Educational Opportunity at the University of Michigan. This readable and compelling text reads as a teenager's journal, with information on sexual harassment alternating with entries in a female student's diary. It is available in English, Spanish, and Arabic, and has sold over 160,000 copies.

In addition to these print materials, there are three media productions on the subject of sexual harassment in schools. *No Laughing Matter: High School Students and Sexual Harassment*,[15] developed by the Massachusetts Department of Education in 1982, uses docudrama vignettes about three young women's experiences with sexual harassment: the first, in a traditionally male vocational school, is subjected to teasing and demeaning behaviors by other students and teachers; the second attends a regular, comprehensive high school and is harassed by a male student; and the third experiences sexual harassment on the job. Interspersed throughout these vignettes are interviews with real teachers, administrators, and students, confirming the existence of sexual harassment in schools.

This twenty-five-minute videotape has been sold to approximately 200 school districts, colleges, state and federal agencies, and advocacy organizations. A second media production on the subject of sexual harassment was developed by the Sex Equity Office of the California Department of Education in 1985. The two filmstrips, *It's Not Funny If It Hurts* and *Think About It—It Won't Go Away*,[16] provide summaries of the relevant laws, geared in the first instance to students, and in the second to school staff. About 200 copies have been sold to school districts both in and outside of California. A third videotape, produced in 1984 and distributed by the Northwest Women's Law Center in Seattle, Washington, discusses adult-to-student sexual harassment in schools and sexual harassment among employees in schools.[17] This is a videotape particularly suitable for adult audiences who need an introductory lesson on the subject.

Another route to provoking national awareness of the problem of sexual harassment in schools is to include discussions of it in teacher preparation programs. Preservice teachers need to understand their responsibilities to intervene in order to discourage discrimination and harassment. Beyond this understanding, they need to develop strategies for intervention and various models for resolution of the problem.

Likewise, in-service programs for all school personnel must be developed and conducted. Everyone in the school community, from the custodian and bus driver to the classroom teacher, coach, and extracurricular advisor, to the superintendent and school board members must be trained to recognize sexual harassment, become knowledgeable about their responsibilities to report it to the proper individuals, and create strategies to prevent and eliminate it. Particularly useful would be the development of nonlitigious remedies which could remediate sexual harassment incidents before they escalate.

Finally, policymakers must extend this national lesson beyond one of mere awareness into the domain of regulation and legislation. First and foremost, they must disentangle the jurisdictional confusion about which state agencies have authority over complaints of sexual harassment and child sexual abuse in schools, and then publicize those lines of authority to the public. In addition, they must design models for public policy, procedures, regulations, and delivery of services to ensure that children who experience sexual abuse and sexual harassment in school settings are heard and protected.

By implementing these varied suggestions we can turn the fleeting national exposure given to sexual harassment in the workplace into substantive and qualitative changes in the cultures of schools. It is time to recognize that sexual harassment, a pervasive, pernicious problem, is an obstacle to receiving equal educational opportunity. Our neglect and denial can no longer be allowed to silence the victims/subjects of sexual harassment or to condone the institutions and individuals which permit it to exist, and even flourish. In order to achieve real justice for all, we must take action to prevent and eliminate sexual harassment in schools.

I would like to thank Joe Blatt, Janet Kahn, Freada Klein, and Margaret Weir for reading and discussing earlier versions of this chapter, and Alan Rom for offering mid-course corrections, both legal and editorial.

Notes

1. Nan Stein, *Sexual Harassment of High School Students: Preliminary Research Results* (Quincy, MA: Massachusetts Department of Education, 1981).

2. Eleanor Linn, Nan Stein, and Jackie Young, with Saundra Davis, "Bitter Lessons for All: Sexual Harassment in Schools," in *Sexuality and the Curriculum*, edited by James T. Sears (New York: Teachers College Press, 1992).

3. Susan Strauss, "Sexual Harassment in the School: Legal Implications for Principals," *National Association of Secondary School Principals Bulletin* 72 (March, 1988): 93-97.

4. Linn, Stein, and Young, "Bitter Lessons for All," p. 159.

5. Dan Wishnietsky, "Reported and Unreported Teacher-Student Sexual Harassment," *Journal of Educational Research* 84, no. 3 (January/February, 1991): 164-169; Audrey Cohan, "Child Sexual Abuse within the Schools" (Doctoral dissertation, Hofstra University, 1991).

6. Linn, Stein, and Young, "Bitter Lessons for All."

7. *Stoneking v. Bradford Area (PA) School District*, 882 F. 2d 720 (3rd Cir. 1989).

8. Perry Zirkel, "Wrong by Wright: Liability for Sexual Abuse," *Phi Delta Kappan* 69 (February, 1988): 451-452.

9. Dale Mezzacappa, "When the Music Stopped," *Philadelphia Inquirer Magazine*, 19 May 1991, pp. 25-37.

10. Zirkel, "Wrong by Wright: Liability for Sexual Abuse."

11. Mezzacappa, "When the Music Stopped," p. 34.

12. Nan Stein, ed., *Who's Hurt and Who's Liable: Sexual Harassment in Massachusetts Schools* (Quincy, MA: Civil Rights/Chapter 622 Project, Massachusetts Department of Education, 1986). Originally published in 1979.

13. Laura Kiscaden, *It's Not Fun/It's Illegal. The Identification and Prevention of Sexual Harassment to Teenagers: A Curriculum* (St. Paul: Minnesota Department of Education, 1988); Northwest Women's Law Center, *Sexual Harassment in the Schools*, Multicultural Resource Series (Olympia, WA: Office of Equity Education, Department of Public Instruction, 1984, 1992); New Jersey Department of Education, *Sending the Right Signals: A Training Program about Dealing with Sexual Harassment* (Trenton, NJ: New Jersey Department of Education, 1990).

14. Programs for Educational Opportunity, University of Michigan, *Tune in to Your Rights: A Guide for Teenagers about Turning Off Sexual Harassment* (Ann Arbor, MI: University of Michigan, 1985).

15. Massachusetts Department of Education, Bureau of Educational Resources and Television, *No Laughing Matter: High School Students and Sexual Harassment* (Quincy, MA: Massachusetts Department of Education, 1982).

16. California Department of Education, Sex Equity Office, *It's Not Funny If It Hurts* and *Think about It . . . It Won't Go Away* (Sacramento, CA: California Department of Education, 1985).

17. Northwest Women's Law Center, "Sexual Harassment in the Schools," videotape (Seattle, WA: Northwest Women's Law Center, 1984).

CHAPTER XII

Gender and Public Education: From Mirrors to Magnifying Lens

MEG CAMPBELL AND DIANA LAM

This chapter reflects our experience as educators in the Boston Public Schools and most recently in the Chelsea (Massachusetts) Public Schools. By any measure, the Chelsea school system has been in crisis with a teen pregnancy rate of one in four and dropout rates of 52 percent. The school population is 54 percent Latino, 12 percent Southeast Asian, 5 percent African American, and 29 percent white. In 1989, Boston University entered into a historic agreement to manage the Chelsea public schools for a ten-year period. Diana Lam served as the first superintendent hired by the Boston University Management Team and Meg Campbell served as Special Assistant to the Superintendent.

We believe that our experience, imagination, and knowledge, as well as other women's, not only matter but illuminate our way. We think of Alice standing before the looking glass, and like her, we step through and across the divide into another world of possibility. The fact that our world is the world of urban public education does not matter in the final analysis. The way we see—the eyes we bring, the curiosity and the willingness to take all of ourselves as females through the glass with us—defines our perspective. How we see and the lenses we enlist—from magnifying to bifocal to telescopic—to expand our vision are what count.

We have never been content with mirrors, society's one dimensional definition of how we should view ourselves. Our anger at the inequities we witness and the falseness which too often passes for educating children is too strong to be confined to a flat plane. While we

---

Meg Campbell is Director of the Expeditionary Learning Project, Cambridge, Massachusetts, a project funded by the New American Schools Development Corporation. Diana Lam is Superintendent of Schools in Dubuque, Iowa. They are founding partners in Voyager Associates, an educational consulting firm in Boston, Massachusetts.

value humility, a willingness to take risks, and an attitude of lifelong learning, we also allow ourselves the full rein of our own ambitions. This is not yet a path well worn by women in public education.

Carolyn Heilbrun defines power in this way: "Power is the ability to take one's place in whatever discourse is essential to action and the right to have one's part matter. This is true in the Pentagon, in marriage, in friendship, and in politics."[1] It is also true in schools and school systems. We step forward to exercise power and to claim that our parts matter.

We know we are "in the water" with others who also share this vision of change and urgency. We are reminded of the image of dolphins giving birth. When a dolphin gives birth, other female dolphins close in to support her during labor—literally, to keep her afloat so her air passage will remain unobstructed. When the laboring dolphin needs oxygen the most, it is the females in her community who lift her up. They do not talk about offering help; they do not circle round or make great arcs in the air for attention or sport; they know where they are needed and go. They heave to and swim under.

No person—man or woman—arrives at a moment of sunshine, a mantle of authority, or a life of accomplishment unassisted. In our own careers, we have often felt ourselves dolphins giving birth to change. We have been keenly aware of those colleagues, primarily women, who have offered us support to keep our air holes, our lifelines, open to another world of possibility. Because we are members of an expanding team, we are able to accelerate the change process and leapfrog over and, when necessary, around the barriers in institutions which have come to function more often as patronage-riddled employment agencies than as coordinated systems of family-centered schools dedicated to the exemplary education of every child.

According to the American Association of University Women, "approximately 5 percent of the school superintendents in the United States today are women."[2] Of that 5 percent, the majority are superintendents in affluent suburban districts where a majority of school board members are women. There is no other profession or field in the United States which has an equivalent history of numerical domination by women coupled with a continuing legacy of exclusion of women from key decision-making roles. For example, nursing (primary and secondary teaching's closest cousin), succeeded in erecting a separate structure of education and supervision which, while predicated on support of and deferral to doctors who were almost all men, still established and fostered the separate tradition and profession of "nursing" and promoted women from within those ranks to administrative professions.

Public education in this country, caught as it is in the vortex of property tax financing and local control, most often reflects the prevailing views of the decision makers of the community it serves. When the time comes to look for a superintendent, a community rarely looks for an educational leader grounded in teaching any more than it looks for its best firefighter to head the fire department or best police officer to head the police department. Political considerations must be taken into account. The common pathway to the superintendency has been through the position of high school principal, a position in turn filled from the pool of those who almost always have also had significant athletic coaching experience.[3]

School systems reflect the traditional nuclear family, with most classes headed by a "Mom" and nearly every school and school system headed by a "Dad." Since the white male in this paradigm represents success, other expressions, cultures, or values are measured against that standard and found lacking. Contrary to the popular myth that "girls do better in school," the long-term effects of catapulting females into college and graduate education were negligible until the resurgence of the women's movement in the mid-1970s. Girls may have appeared to be doing better, but the boys were still walking away with the power and financial security that a complete education can leverage.

Being in a position of power and responsibility, one is constantly faced with the choice of effecting change or continuing the status quo. The first litmus test for women in authority in public education, particularly because there are still so few relative to their numbers in the field, is whether or not these women who have "made it" promote and mentor other women or whether they adopt more of the old boys' values and network than many of the old boys themselves. A token female in power does not address underlying power inequities; strong representation of women in power can *begin* to redress the imbalance. Our view challenges the traditional conception of power as a limited commodity to be hoarded and guarded. We view power as elastic and inclusive—rather yeast-like—which can grow and expand as the proper ingredients are combined and given time and nutrients to multiply.

This view presupposes that the only true source of power must come from within, from the character and integrity of the individual who is exercising influence or power and who is realizing her vision.

The vision that is shared has a brighter and stronger arc of light and influence than the vision flickering alone. Power is not seen here as most efficiently hierarchical, though lines of authority and accountability are important safeguards for the exercise of power. Our view of power pivots on the importance of relationships and the invisible agenda and culture of individuals and organizations. The sheer force of personality cannot be underestimated; but the multiplication of that force in a group which works within the parameters of a shared vision, trust, respect, and hard work is truly energizing and liberating. It is this force which men have rhapsodized about and tried to recapture from their adolescent or college days of team sports. It is this force which, in the stultified setting of an urban school bureaucracy, can breathe fresh air and hope. It is the magnificent strength of unified numbers. In our case, as women in public education, it is long overdue.

Political Responsibility and Gender Equity

Across continents and cultures, women have for centuries been socialized to resist accepting what Vaclav Havel, human rights activist and former president of Czechoslovakia, calls "the burden of political responsibility." For centuries, our other responsibilities—survival and traditional motherhood—have left us with few other options. For those of us who have had access to education—and only a tiny portion of females on the globe have that opportunity even today—the burden of political responsibility weighs heavier.

The first Latin American to win the Nobel Prize in Literature was a Chilean woman, Lucila Godoy de Alcayaga. Because she was an elementary school teacher and was concerned about what people might think of her poems, she took a pen name, Gabriela Mistral. When she heard the news of the Nobel Prize, she responded, "Perhaps I was chosen because I was the candidate of the women and children."

As educators, our goal is to be worthy of the title, "candidates of the women and children." Accepting the burden of political responsibility means speaking up, speaking out, and acting on what we see. We have a responsibility to work to change the agenda and priorities for what is decided at the table as well as a responsibility to change the composition of the decision makers at the table. There are countless examples of how those power relations play out in public education. What does political responsibility mean day-to-day?

1. *Political responsibility means speaking up on behalf of ourselves and other women, being willing to reach for the brass ring, realizing each stretch involves a risk.*

Diana Lam recalls her experience in the Boston Public Schools:

In 1985, when I was a principal of an elementary school in Boston, I attended a meeting with the Deputy Superintendent. At that time, two of the seventeen high schools were headed by females and one of the twenty-three middle schools had a female principal. I urged the Deputy Superintendent to consider appointing women to these positions, especially because a middle school principalship had just opened.

"Would you be interested?" he asked in a tone of disbelief.

Quite frankly, I had not asked on my own behalf and I had assumed my next position would be a principalship in a large elementary school although I had experience working in kindergarten through grade twelve. Like most women in education, I had not thought about becoming a middle school principal and like most men, he had pegged me into a limited role. Men are groomed for positions of leadership; women must be assertive and meet higher standards of competency and talent.

Still, he had asked. The question dangled before me. I reached for the brass ring. "Yes," I answered quickly. "I would be."

While I was a middle school principal in Boston, there was an opening for an assistant principal. I interviewed many candidates with the help of teachers and parents, and selected the best person—an African-American woman. The superintendent told me I could not hire her because he could not allow an all-female administrative team although nine of the twenty-three middle schools had all-male administrative teams. The unspoken assumption was that if I did not hire a man, who would handle discipline in the middle school? Younger children, well, that was one matter. Middle school students are older; many are overage for their grade. They're big. I'm physically small. How could a woman handle disciplining the boys?

I left the position of assistant principal vacant rather than hire anyone else. I also filed a sex discrimination complaint with the City of Boston Human Rights Commission; three years later they ruled in my favor. This case spotlighted the need to promote women at the secondary level, whether as department heads or principals. In the years since, significant progress has been made in Boston on this score; today there is not a single all-male administrative team at any middle or high school. Litigation was a tool which opened the doors for other women.

Did I challenge the rules? Yes, because I believed the rules were unfair. Was there a cost for my actions? There is always a cost within an institutional bureaucracy for one who steps outside the prescribed roles and shouts, "The emperor is wearing no clothes." Like many other women, I remain convinced that I had to be more qualified for equivalent positions held by men. I valued and appreciated my allies—my network of support—but I was honest in my appraisal that my actions had also alienated some in positions of authority who might not have short memories. For example, there were people in the school department who called our middle school "the Amazon school."

In 1987, I was appointed District A Superintendent in Boston, responsible for twenty-three schools (pre-K to 12) and a district staff. Our staff of ten women included Hispanics, African Americans, and Anglos, some with years of educational experience and some new to the field. Our personalities were as different as any gathering of ten women could be. At a staff meeting one morning, the Deputy Superintendent for Operations walked into our office and then quickly backed out, nervously laughing that he hadn't meant to walk in "on all women." We were perhaps a formidable group simply because we did function effectively as a team and we were comfortable and proud to be women. I was struck by his being flustered because I could remember the frequent experience of being the only female, and often the only Hispanic as well, at high level school department meetings.

After we had been working together for five months in District A, we held a one-day retreat at a local University. Some women, knowing we were to dine in the faculty club for lunch, dressed up for the day; others, including me, took advantage of the day away from the office to dress casually. I wore a brightly colored running suit.

Mid-morning, I received a phone call from the Superintendent instructing me to come immediately for an emergency meeting; he would send a car to pick me up. I was distressed. How could I wear sweat pants and sneakers to this important, emergency meeting?

Within moments, someone had suggested that the group dress me. One woman offered her suit, another her shoes and stockings. A third woman lent her blouse. These are personal items, and yet, they were being peeled off, there in our seminar room, and swapped with my shoes, socks, and running suit. The shoes were a little too big, the suit wasn't something I ordinarily would have worn. It didn't matter. In a matter of moments, I was transformed. Colleagues had lifted me up to keep my air hole open. In a very real sense, every woman accompanied me to that meeting; I carried their presence with me.

When is one "ready" to reach for the brass ring? Women are expected to wait much longer, even lifetimes, to advance. I find it ironic that the chief criticism I continue to hear is that I have "moved too quickly" in my profession. I have never heard that criticism leveled against a man; in fact, it is considered a bonus for a man to "be on the move" within his profession, regardless of the field. There remains the clear expectation—and this is one way the "glass ceiling" stunts so many women's careers—that I should have stayed longer in each position than a similarly talented man would have been expected to stay. As a Hispanic and female, I was supposed to wait docilely, regardless of intelligence and skills. The brass ring does not fall by itself; one must reach.

2. *Political responsibility means taking women's ideas seriously and supporting them.*

Meg Campbell speaks:

In the fall of 1988, Diana had asked me to go with her to a planning meeting to do something, for the first time in Boston schools districtwide, for Women's History month. I had previously worked at the State House as Research Director for the Health Care Committee and on my lunch breaks had wandered the Freedom Trail and African-American Heritage Trail on and near Beacon Hill. I had searched the State House for a tribute to women's contributions and had found only the statues of the Civil War nurse tending a soldier and Mary Dyer, "hanged on Boston Common for her beliefs." This grand building—our own temple of democracy, as it were—was festooned with paintings and sculptures of white men.

I was planning my return to education and on those walks I daydreamed of a class project where my future students and I would research and create a Women's Heritage Trail, uncovering where author Margaret Fuller had walked or where Mary Eliza Mahoney, an African-American, had been one of the first nursing students in 1878 with Dr. Marie Zakrewska at the New England Hospital for Women and Children. I knew women of all races and ages had made significant contributions and they were there to be honored. They were simply hidden from view and therefore not part of our common understanding.

Diana shared with the committee the notice of a federal sex equity grant that she wanted us to pursue. Isabel Mendez, Assistant Principal of the Agassiz Elementary School, had been most insistent about the need for the committee to meet and "do something" to celebrate women's history and promote girls entering mathematics and science. Isabel hoped the grant could fund an adventure—an overnight experience for her female fifth graders at the Museum of Science.

Looking at the guidelines and based on my own fund raising experience, my hunch was that we needed something more catchy and different from the overnight. We kicked around different ideas and I finally shared my idea for a Boston Women's Heritage Trail. Diana immediately saw its potential. Isabel Mendez demonstrated her leadership by exercising flexibility and throwing her enthusiasm behind the idea for a Women's Heritage Trail.

Charlotte Harris, Director of External Funds for the Boston Public Schools, consultant Stephen Holt (who was later elected to the Boston School Committee), and I wrote and submitted a grant to create the Boston Women's Heritage Trail, a gift to the City of Boston created by students and teachers in grades four through eight of the Boston Public Schools. The grant was funded for $150,000 during the school year 1989-1990 and the Women's Heritage Trail, the first in the nation, was formally unveiled in May.

In the intervening months, selected teachers and their students participated in workshops and primary document research, preparing students to vote knowledgeably about the more than 300 women who had been nominated to the trail. According to Women's Heritage Trail director, Dr. Patricia Morris, "We kept uncovering more and more remarkable women. In designing the tour, we decided also to honor the fifty-nine educational, cultural, medical, and social service institutions founded by or for women. These range from the Christian Science Church founded by Mary Baker Eddy to the Museum of the National Center for Afro-American Art founded by Elma Lewis. Fifteen women were selected for the first downtown walking trail, and plans were under way to extend the trail into Boston's neighborhoods in the future.

A nonprofit board has been created to continue the Women's Heritage Trail mission of promoting the inclusion of multicultural women's studies into curriculum and honoring the many contributions of women of all races to the city of Boston and the nation. *Boston Magazine* voted the Women's Heritage Trail the "Best of Boston" Walking Tour for 1990.

I think the Women's Heritage Trail was a great idea. I know that without the initial support of District Superintendent Diana Lam—who, in very practical terms, could redirect me to work on this project—the idea would have remained just an idea. With the creation of the Board of Directors and the hiring of a Director, the Women's Heritage Trail has become an institution for and on behalf of women of all races in its own right.

March 1989 saw the first districtwide celebration of Women's History Month in Boston Public Schools as District A hosted a conference for teachers voluntarily attended by over 300 persons, including male administrators from the central office and other districts. This event was significant as the first time an entire district staff within the Boston schools worked together to organize a conference which brought together curriculum development and teacher training in women's studies for a wide audience. The fact that the conference was so well attended affirmed the work of many individuals who had long worked in isolation. The Massachusetts Department of Education in 1989 honored District A teachers who had developed curriculum packets on women's studies for their classrooms.

In 1990, Stephen Holt, a new member of the Boston School Committee, successfully sponsored the passage of a resolution that every school in Boston honor Women's History Month thereby extending the district recognition of women to the entire school system. The March 1991 systemwide celebration included a teacher conference cosponsored by the Women's Heritage Trail and the Boston Teachers Union.

Strong leadership encourages teachers to participate in the development and implementation of multicultural women's studies at the school, district, and systemwide levels. This never happens spontaneously; someone or some group makes it happen first by articulating it as a priority for teachers and administrators.

Good ideas work like yeast, expanding, pushing out the boundaries, and giving an inviting aroma so that others join in the feast.

3. *Political responsibility means examining symbols, including words, recognizing their power and using them with care and fairness. It means holding a magnifying glass to everyday speech because what we say and what others say matters.*

The most obvious change in the culture of the Chelsea Public schools since our arrival has been the near abandonment of the use of the word "girls" to describe adult working women. This term was previously used frequently by females and males and applied to clerical, teaching, and administrative staff. Culture is automatic reflex and works without thinking. It is the soda you grab from the refrigerator.

Asking people to substitute something healthier and more edifying is, predictably, initially met with resistance.

"What difference does it make?"

"We like to think of ourselves as girls because we feel younger."

"He means no harm."

Raising the issue invites and even legitimizes reflection. If it is one's supervisor raising the question, the process of change is greatly accelerated. On numerous occasions, we both had the opportunity to call attention to the issue, preferring to use directness without a sledgehammer.

In her opening day speech, "The Rings of Saturn," to Chelsea teachers and staff in September 1990, Diana noted:

> I see the rings of Saturn in Chelsea in our rising self-esteem as educators, no longer tolerating that our work and our dignity be devalued by referring to any one of us as "girls." Instead we view ourselves as talented, committed adult women and men who are making a difference.

"Diana doesn't want me calling the clerks 'girls' anymore. I forget sometimes but I'm getting better," the male Business Manager noted soon after. "She's right. I don't call the men 'boys'." The Business Manager subsequently came into the Superintendent's office with a notice for a conference aimed at attracting females into computers and science. "I thought you'd like this," he said.

Women in positions of authority can set a tone, a direction by reinforcing the values of gender equity. Clearly, men have the same responsibility to do likewise and there are examples of men who shine in this regard; they remain the exception. Too often, the language itself is trivialized and demeaned—with the undercoating of alleged humor or conviviality—and how women view and name themselves is diminished.

Take the case of high school headmasters. Tradition weighs in here—a male tradition. When Dr. Elsa Wasserman was appointed to head Chelsea High School in September 1990, she asserted, "I won't use the term *headmaster*. I prefer to be *principal*." Her two assistants, both men, also agreed to change their titles from *submasters* to *assistant principals*. "We're a team," Dr. Wasserman explained. "That master stuff smacks of plantations."

These are small changes, perhaps, and yet they are indicative of a new way of looking at ourselves within the still remarkably insulated field of urban education.

When the stacks of fliers for the Miss Latin American contest crossed the desk of Dr. Wasserman she bundled them together and sent them down to the Superintendent's office with a note, "Do you want to make this package available to students?" In the past, they had been routinely handed out at the high school. Again, there was not any particular malevolence here. This was a chance for girls to win cash. Why deny them? It took a female in a position of authority at the school site to question the practice: "What message are we, the school department, sending girls and boys when we hand out beauty pageant brochures to our female students?" The fliers were not distributed.

While walking down the hallway at Chelsea High with an assistant principal, one of us noticed a glossy pin-up calendar on the wall of a woodshop room. The conversation was brief and nonjudgmental.

"What message does that give students?"

"I didn't notice it. I'll take care of it," he replied.

With the best of intentions, a male principal and female teacher of one of the elementary schools in Chelsea compiled a 1989-1990 year-end anthology, "Memories and Reflections," for students. The anthology began with two poems, both called "IF", one directed to girls and the other directed to boys.

"To the girls" ended:

If you can strive, not caring who gets credit,
And work at building bridges and not walls,
You'll be a woman, and all those around you
Will be the richer for your womanhood!

While "To the boys" ended:

If you can dream—and not make your dreams your master,
If you can think—and not make thoughts your aim,
If you can fill the unforgiving minute
With sixty seconds' worth of distance run,
Yours is the Earth and everything that's in it,
And—which is more—you'll be a Man, my son!

For those of us with a commitment to gender equity, reading such damaging dribble passed like candy to unsuspecting children in the late twentieth century makes us scream or weep. Or it makes us angry.

We have every right to our anger, of course, but unless it is productively channeled it festers. Each of us has frequent opportunities to "stop the line" for the sake of gender equity in urban education. It remains an unrecognized issue. In all the articles and reports on the necessity for restructuring public schools, there has been no call for gender balancing of authority, structures, and curriculum. "Restructuring" is the frequent focus of conferences for educators and these almost always include the theme of "recognizing diversity," but in the main, they fall short of crossing the gender line, defining diversity exclusively in racial, ethnic, and linguistic terms. These are crucial, we agree. But where are women's distinct voices in this chorus calling for change?

In the spring of 1990 teachers at Chelsea High School developed an idea for a school-within-a-school to be called "The Renaissance School." The school was to have an interdisciplinary focus. Meeting with teachers and administrators over dinner, we were studying the course catalog and schedule to see how it would need to be changed to support the proposed restructuring which had the aim of eliminating tracking by race and ability. We turned to the business department offerings and came across a course called "Charm and Personality."

"What's this?" Diana asked.

"There's a problem with this course because no boys sign up. We should change the name," argued the male director of guidance.

"What is the course content?" Diana continued.

"How to have charm and personality in the business setting," we were informed. Gender tracking had been rampant.

"Drop the course," Diana decided on the spot.

As part of restructuring Chelsea High the eighth and ninth grades were clustered with the introduction of algebra as a requirement for all students. Females and minority males had been underrepresented in advanced mathematics and science classes; getting through the algebra "gate" is an important equalizer for later opportunity. Additionally, classes in wood shop, electronics, and home economics were required of all students. When these courses were offered as electives they had been effectively gender tracked. Only the few females who took these introductory courses were able to pursue the more advanced courses in shop and electronics at the upper grades.

4. *Political responsibility means creating alternate structures in which students and teachers, regardless of gender, can flourish.*

We cannot expect our female students to achieve in school or on the playing field when we are telling them in elementary school "not to care who gets credit" while we are telling boys "the earth is theirs." Before the Boston University-Chelsea Public Schools partnership became effective in July 1989, the sports program for boys had many more offerings than the sports program for girls. This imbalance has begun to be redressed. For example, the first girls' volleyball team was organized (it won first place in its division in 1990) and a two-week sports clinic specifically for girls aged eight to fourteen was sponsored. Athletics, where females have the experience of testing and stretching their physical limits, are an important dimension of a full education.

Another school-within-a-school, the Voyager Alternative Academy, opened in September 1990 to serve approximately twenty-five youth who were seriously at risk of dropping out due to being overage for their grade level. In one class, team-taught by Maggie Lodge and Juan Casillas, Voyager students combine physical education and science through weekly rowing sessions in Boston Harbor through the Hull Lifesaving Museum. Voyager students were invited to cohost the first rowing race on Chelsea Creek, with competitors coming from area high schools. Voyager students democratically elected their coed team and conferred the honor of coxswain on a female. After rowing to an upset victory, they hoisted their coxswain on their shoulders in jubilation. None had ever before participated on a team, let alone a *winning* team.

Younger males use primary schooling as an opportunity to mentor or bond with each other through team sports or the camaraderie of the discipline "bench." Less likely to choose disruptive behavior and hence less likely to be sent out of class for disciplinary reasons, females have few times when they are together as a "single sex" in school. It was with pleasure, then, that we watched a special needs female high school student, who had previously been in a substantially separate class, participate in our after-school courses for credit in the spring of 1990. She looked younger than the other girls in her High Expectation Learning Program (HELP) course which featured small classes with an experiential component. Participation and discussion were important features of the class. Several of the other girls reached out to this special needs student in very tangible and thoughtful ways. Their actions prompted us to reflect on ways in which schools might promote that sense of inclusive community. We might talk about the theory of integrating special needs students with regular education and bilingual students. These girls were living it to a degree rare in urban high schools today. They were a living example to us that it was truly possible.

5. *Political responsibility means carving out listening time as an integral part of an inclusive leadership style.*

Diana Lam speaks:

The president of Iceland, Vigdis Finnbogadottir, holds open office hours every week where any citizen in her country may stop by to talk. As Chelsea superintendent, I wanted to emulate that practice, so I scheduled separate monthly coffees for teachers and parents. If we truly value the rich expertise garnered only from field experience, then we had better build into our schedules a mechanism for insuring the constant flow of those ideas and concerns. These regularly scheduled "drop-in" coffees have served a valuable communication purpose.

The attitude of listening is an important one to model and foster. When I taught one of the science HELP courses, I told the students they were welcome to come by my office outside of class.

One day, one of the students came insistently looking for me. She was referred to Meg who realized I would want to be interrupted from my meeting.

"My boyfriend wants to marry me but I don't want to, but I don't know what to do," she said.

"Why do you think he wants to marry you?" I asked.

"To control me," she replied. "Will you talk to him? I think I should finish my education."

I not only spoke to the young man, I also spoke to his headmaster in Boston. The wedding was delayed.

For most women in urban education, even raising issues of sexual discrimination, harassment, or equity subjects one to ridicule. There are more important issues! Urban school districts have been forced through the threat or experience of court orders to address the issue of racial inequity. Scaffolding at least has been erected, through civil rights and legal struggles, upon which to hang a banner legitimizing the issues of racial discrimination, harassment, and equity as subjects for serious concern and ongoing action. Issues of gender equity enjoy no comparable standing, although they too spring from abuses of power. Both banners should hang center stage in our concerns.

6. *Political responsibility means restructuring the organization to reflect a different vision of leadership.*

Sally Helgesen contrasts a hierarchical structure with a web structure in *The Female Advantage: Women's Way of Leadership.* In the web analogy, the leader is "in the middle" rather than "at the top" and the leader "reaches out" rather than "reaching down." According to Helgesen:

> A prime example is in information gathering. In a top-down management, information flows upward through channels; authority is established by having access to this progressively filtered information. The chain of command is broken, however, if the authority bypasses established channels in order to ask direct questions down the ladder. By contrast, being at the center, connected to every point in the whole, makes it possible to gather information directly from all sources. . . . The most important aspect of this direct contact was that there was no filter, no supervisory layer through whom "lower-downs" were expected to go.[4]

Diana Lam speaks:

During the winter and spring of 1991, severe budget constraints prompted a sweeping review of administrative positions with a goal of streamlining services. As superintendent, I proposed, and the Boston University Management Team accepted, eliminating the positions of Director of Special Education and Director of Human Services, shifting responsibility to the school site administrators and creating a new position (Director of Student

Services) who would assume some responsibilities of the former Director of Special Education and Director of Human Services. Historically, special education within and outside the district had been extremely fragmented and the rate of outside placements was above the state average. For a poor school system such as Chelsea's, the additional cost was particularly burdensome. By any measure, special education was not working and it was also extremely costly. The budget crisis presented an opportunity for restructuring.

Janis Rennie, Chelsea Public Schools Curriculum Coordinator, inspired by Helgesen's book, proposed the concept of a web in reorganizing the structure and delivery of special education services to enhance integration of all students. In the special education web ("sped web"), every school principal has primary responsibility for all students, including special education and bilingual students, within his or her school. The Director of Student Services serves as a staff resource and provides a coordinating function for implementation of more state-of-the-art procedures for integrating and educating special education students. Since this proposal deviated from state regulations, a waiver was sought and obtained from the Massachusetts Department of Education.

The "sped web" is a simple but effective example of changing the organizational structure to reflect a vision of education which draws upon a tradition of women's more inclusive leadership. The simple, but often overlooked, act of giving a name to the new structure made it more readily understood. "What do you mean?" is a legitimate question our colleagues often ask. We owe them an answer. By providing a symbol or story, the answer has momentum.

In most school systems, women have limited power, and yet they are not entirely powerless. As we move into positions of authority, whether as classroom teachers or as commissioner of education, we have a responsibility to hold the magnifying glass up to what we say and what we do. There are no extraneous gestures or comments. A ten-year-old girl may need to hear right now that she not only can become a scientist but that, when looking into the microscope, she already *is* a scientist. A principal may need to hear that her efforts to increase student achievement in mathematics are succeeding for girls and boys.

Holding up the magnifying glass can be discouraging work and we need signs of change and hope as much as anyone else. It was our own children, Stefi Campbell-Holt and Sasha Lam-Plattes, who recently reminded us we were not alone.

Stefi and Sasha are seventh-grade students at a Boston school, which until the court-ordered racial desegregation in 1974 had been all-male for over three centuries. In response to parents' requests, including our own, Stefi and Sasha are part of the first attempt to cluster students in the seventh grade in the school's history; twenty students share the same academic teachers.

Stefi arrived home one day disturbed by remarks made by their male teacher when introducing Sherlock Holmes. "It's too bad that in the first story you had to read, Sherlock Holmes was outwitted by a woman," he had joked.

Two days later, Stefi's distress had turned to anger. "Today in class he said that men are more logical than women and that there aren't any famous women mathematicians. I'm going to write a list of women mathematicians and put it anonymously on his desk."

Following a discussion on the value of signing your name to something you believed in, Stefi called a friend. Would she be willing to sign the list too?

The next day Stefi circulated the teachers' remarks to her classmates followed by a list of famous women mathematicians as well as the book titles where she had found the information.

Thirteen seventh graders, including Sasha, signed the paper which included a cover note, "This will be given to the teacher, the Headmaster, and perhaps the school newspaper." The signatures were evenly divided between boys and girls and included Hispanic, African-American, and Anglo students. One girl who initially signed the paper asked Stefi to erase her name because she was "so afraid of what the teacher would do."

When asked by his mother why he had signed the paper, Sasha replied, "At first I didn't want to sign because I didn't want Stefi to think I liked her. But I thought I should sign because you would want me to. The teacher was joking but he shouldn't have said those things."

Stefi placed the list with the names of students in the teacher's mailbox, the male Headmaster's mailbox, and the female Assistant Headmaster's mailbox. (These are the titles the school uses.)

During mathematics class, the students' names were called over the loudspeaker to report to the office. According to our children, the students were scolded for "not handling this properly" and "embarrassing" the teacher. There was no recommendation made as to how these twelve- and thirteen-year-olds should have handled this incident.

In class later that day, according to our children, the teacher, with another colleague present, told students he "had freedom of speech," that the Headmaster had "never heard of these women mathematicians," and that the students had "ruined his weekend."

This struggle was theirs and they chose not to pursue it any further. By joining together, fourteen of the youngest students in a school of 2400 had made an important point that joking about women's mathematical abilities is not funny.

"After our names were called," Stefi said later, "we were walking to the office and I asked everybody, 'Are we all together?' Everyone said yes. We hadn't done anything wrong. We were telling the truth."

Truth and justice have always been the driving force behind feminism's assertions and gains. Truth and justice alone have rarely been enough. Power, whether by persons in authority or through the voice of an organized constituency, must be exercised on behalf of female equity.

Good intentions are not enough. So many of the "bloodletting" practices in urban education—from tracking to retention to fragmented scheduling of students and teachers—stem from good intentions. We are reminded how the medical practice of "bloodletting" itself was considered state of the art for George Washington when he complained of a prolonged sore throat to his physician; the doctor with the best intentions practiced bloodletting on the first president, directly causing his death. Like Washington's doctor, we in urban schools are "bleeding" our students' minds and spirits with our insistence on clinging to past practice and thinking. Sexism is a form of bloodletting, too.

Gender equity must be put on the institutional agenda for the sake of the female and male students we serve, as well as the females and males we work with and employ. Sexism diminishes all our possibilities. If schools are a home to anything, they must be a home to human possibilities. They must be a home for us all.

Notes

1. Carolyn Heilbrun, *Writing a Woman's Life* (New York: Ballantine Books, 1988), p. 18.

2. Jonathan Hicks, "Women in Waiting," New York *Times*, Education Supplement, 3 November 1991.

3. Nora T. Mertz and Sonja R. McNeely, "Career Paths of Superintendents" (Paper presented at the Mid-South Educational Research Association meeting, Louisville, KY, November 1988).

4. Sally Helgesen, *The Female Advantage: Women's Ways of Leadership* (New York: Doubleday, 1990), p. 53.

Section Six
POWER, MULTIPLICITY, AND VOICE

CHAPTER XIII

Power and Privilege in White Middle-Class Feminist Discussions of Gender and Education

CHRISTINE E. SLEETER

In education as well as other social institutions, concerns of women often are represented as competing with concerns of racial minority groups and sometimes of low-income people. This chapter challenges that representation. Half of racial minority group members and low-income people *are* women. However, by treating race, social class, and gender as separate issues signifying discrete groups, white economically privileged women tend to benefit, and oppressed groups remain fragmented, competing against each other for scarce resources.

Issues are often framed and addressed in ways that set oppressed groups in opposition to each other and at the same time buttress the relatively privileged position of white middle- and upper-class women, while removing from scrutiny the very privileged position of white professional men. For example, African-American male academies have been proposed in several urban school districts as a way of addressing the high failure rate among African-American males. However, the concept of all-male public academies was successfully challenged in a lawsuit by the National Organization for Women on the grounds that it discriminated against girls, and particularly African-American girls.[1] This situation placed an organization dominated by white women in opposition to African-American

Christine E. Sleeter is Professor of Education in the Teacher Education Department of the School of Education, University of Wisconsin—Parkside, Kenosha, Wisconsin.

men, leaving African-American women caught in between and divided on the concept of African-American male academies. Many educators were then bewildered about what to do: Is such a school sexist? Is one being racist to oppose it?

As a second example, administrators are often encouraged to hire more "women and minorities," a phrase one encounters in everyday parlance and sometimes in institutional policies. This phrase lumps the majority of the population into what some people regard as a special interest group that then can be treated as an add-on. In addition, the phrase implicitly strips white women of their race and women of color of their sex. Similarly, many schools have created programs to encourage more "girls and minorities" to pursue mathematics, science, and computer science. Who predominates in such programs? White daughters of parents of the professional class? African-American, Latino, or Asian boys of middle- or professional-class parents? What about lower-class students (half of whom are also girls and a disproportionate number a racial minority)? The phrase "women and minorities" or "girls and minorities" lumps together everyone who is not a white male, enabling educators to believe they have diversified their hiring or their student population if they acquire a few members of that "category"—even when those they added are mainly white females. At my university, the term "diversity" increasingly replaces the phrase "women and minorities"; some white males congratulate themselves on having added "diversity" to the faculty by hiring white women. The term seems to help them to remain blind to men and women of color.

These examples illustrate the need to attend to class and race in discussions of gender. Failure to do so can divide women of color from white women, or lower-class women from economically privileged women; it can also make invisible women who are not white and who are middle- or upper-class.

Over the past twenty years, discussions of gender in education as well as in other fields have flourished, fueling activity which has helped to bring about noticeable advances for women—at least, for some women. But at the same time, much of the discourse and the political activity it supports has been criticized regularly and at times quite heatedly for the limited extent to which white middle-class women, who have dominated and profited most from this discourse and activity, usually address with seriousness the concerns and experiences of women of color and those from lower-class backgrounds.

An issue that is often discussed, for example, is the wage gap between men and women. Between 1955 and 1983, full-time working women earned an average of 59 to 64 cents for every dollar full-time working men earned. After 1983, the gap began to close steadily; by 1988, full-time working women were earning 70 cents for every dollar men earned,[2] as growing numbers of women entered jobs traditionally dominated by men. But it is important to look beyond such a statistic and ask: Were all women sharing equally in progress? The answer is No. At the same time that significant numbers of college-educated women entered fields such as law and medicine, women from low-income backgrounds found it increasingly difficult to finance a college education, the proportion of students of color entering universities fell, and low-income women increasingly entered low-paying service jobs that have traditionally employed large numbers of women. In the nation as a whole, while the gender gap in earnings narrowed, the middle class shrank, the lower class expanded, the number of female-headed households living below the poverty level grew, and the status of Americans of color—both men and women—deteriorated. The wage gap had partially reflected restricted career opportunities for middle-class women; their successful struggles for wider opportunities, however, did not advance the interests or economic status of poor women.

I use this example to argue that much feminist activity purporting to benefit women as a whole often ultimately benefits mainly white middle-class women when it does not address other forms of oppression as well. Gender issues can rarely be separated from race and class issues, and by either ignoring this or arguing that they can and should be dealt with separately, white middle-class women protect their own racial and class privilege. Ironically, the main beneficiaries are white economically privileged men, since a potentially powerful coalition does not form to challenge their control.

It is important to acknowledge that I am white and of middle-class origin. My racial consciousness developed before my feminist consciousness did; I lived and taught school for several years in and around the central area of Seattle. It was in graduate school that I began serious reading of feminist and neo-Marxist scholarship. While I was conscious that most of it was written by whites, much of the feminist scholarship I read connected so well with my own life that it was easy for me to generalize it (incorrectly) to all women. It has taken me several years, and the patience of many women friends of color, to internalize some understanding of gender issues as they are experienced and interpreted by women who are not white. And because of my limited experiences with white working- and lower-class people, I still understand class critiques mainly at an intellectual rather than "gut" level.[3]

Usually women of color must assume the task of confronting race in discussions of gender, and women from working-class backgrounds must confront class issues. Often white middle-class women assume that these are someone else's issues, and that we have addressed them when we allow women of color and women of working-class origins to join in our work and our conversations. But just as we do not allow men to marginalize gender issues this way, we should not be allowing ourselves to marginalize race and class issues, nor to ignore our own participation in a social structure stratified by race and class.

Gender, Race, and Class as Separate Topics in Education Research

Most literature about gender in education treats gender, social class, and race as additive rather than integrative forms of oppression, leaving one to choose which forms of oppression to add to one's analysis. Social class oppression, for example, may be added onto gender oppression as a separate layer.[4] In 1986 Carl Grant and I reviewed seventy-one articles in the education literature published between 1973 and 1983 that addressed race, social class, and/or gender.[5] Sixty-three of the articles addressed primarily one form of oppression; only three addressed gender and race, one addressed gender and social class, one addressed social class and race, and three addressed race, social class, and gender. Further, only one of the studies substantively integrated different forms of oppression, distinguishing among black, white, and Hispanic males and females of different social class backgrounds.[6] The rest treated these as separate (e.g., blacks and women) and additive.

It appears to be mainly white economically privileged women who consistently interrogate gender either without acknowledging race or social class relations at all, or by adding them in a supplementary fashion. The position that white women often argue is that gender is the major social division they experience as problematic; that women share common experiences resulting from their oppression, and men share common privileges; and that, while race and class oppression are also significant, discussions of gender need to stay focused on gender, as bringing in other factors would render discussions too unwieldy and dilute attention to gender.

White women are then surprised when they realize that women of color often do not share their definition of sexism. A reporter in Madison, Wisconsin, for example, talked with several white and black women on the university campus about the low participation of women of color in the city's feminist organizations. She reported: "Not unexpectedly, the white women I spoke with said there was not a significant problem." The black women saw the matter quite differently. Some charged the National Organization for Women with focusing on issues of high priority to white middle-class women but not on those of concern to women of color. Some were angry at being excluded, others were simply "not interested in the same issues as white women."[7]

I see the issue over when and whether to address race and class as a power struggle to define issues for discussion and agendas for action, more than as an academic issue about accuracy. Our analysis of gender is *never* uninformed by our racial and social class background. Every time we white economically privileged women presume to speak for all women without engaging a plurality of women in conversation, we are asserting power granted to us by virtue of our racial and social class privilege, as well as presenting a distorted picture of whatever we are speaking about. Similarly, when white professional men address equity issues mainly by supporting some demands of white professional women, race and class privileges are being protected.

Power struggles among oppressed groups are at least as old as the thirteen colonies. For example, Angela Davis described conflicts between blacks and white women over the vote, showing how white women distanced themselves from black struggles out of fear that either black men *or* white women would triumph first.[8] In the process, white women excluded black women from their definition of "women." Today's power struggles over whose voices define women's issues have very long roots; the faces and some of the terms are new, but the issues are not.[9]

A Typology of Integration

Feminist discourse has developed various analyses of how male-dominant society marginalizes women. For example, Peggy McIntosh and Mary Kay Tetreault discussed stages in the integration of content about women into the curriculum, viewing the stages as a progression from exclusion of women to full inclusion. As Tetreault described them, the stages include: male-defined curriculum, "contribution curriculum," bifocal curriculum, women's curriculum, and gender-balanced curriculum.[10] I will modify this typology to discuss levels of integrating race and class into feminist concerns. I have found this typology useful for illustrating how discussions of gender often exclude women who are not white and/or economically privileged, and how issues may be viewed much more inclusively. I do not view the levels as stages through which one must proceed, but rather as an analytic tool that roughly ranks the degree to which women of diverse racial and social class backgrounds inform any given body of discourse on gender.

Before proceeding, I must define briefly some terms that will be used.[11] Gender issues are framed quite differently depending on one's theoretical and political perspective. Liberal feminism upholds individual competition in a hierarchical society, arguing that one's sex should be irrelevant to one's chances for mobility, choice, and personal fulfillment. Radical feminism, on the other hand, argues that gender is the most fundamental social category and celebrates the biological capacities and cultural creations of women. Rather than seeking to make gender irrelevant, radical feminists advocate empowerment of women and valuing that which is feminine. Both liberal and radical feminism have been advanced mainly by white women; neither perspective gives significant attention to race or social class. Radical feminism pays more attention to sexual orientation than do other feminist perspectives.

Socialist feminism regards both gender and social class as fundamental categories for social organization, and many theorists also view race as equally fundamental. Socialist feminism analyzes how women's status is a function of patriarchy, capitalism, and racism. Nellie Wong explained:

> By feminism, I mean the political analysis and practice to free *all* women. . . . Feminism, the struggle for women's equal rights, is inseparable from socialism—but not identical to socialism. Socialism is an economic system which reorganizes production, redistributes wealth, and redefines state power so that the exploiters are expropriated and workers gain hegemony.[12]

Recently feminists have entered poststructuralist debates. Poststructuralism assumes that there is no fixed set of meanings; all symbols represent a multiplicity of meanings that depend on an individual's location in time and social structure.

LEVELS OF INTEGRATING RACE, CLASS, AND GENDER

Level 1. Issues as defined only by white economically privileged women. Writing about the male-defined curriculum, Tetreault explained that it rests "on the assumption that the male experience is universal, that it is representative of humanity, and that it constitutes a basis for generalizing about all human beings."[13] While liberal and radical feminists have strongly challenged the assumption that the male experience is universal, many assume a universal women's experience that revolves around "the minority of women in the world who are white, European, or North American, and middle- or upper-middle class."[14] As Elizabeth Spelman put it, "A measure of the depth of white middle-class privilege is that apparent straightforward and logical points and axioms at the heart of much feminist theory guarantee the direction of its attention to the concerns of white middle-class women."[15]

For example, educators often concern themselves with encouraging social interaction between girls and boys by sponsoring school dances or using cooperative learning to reduce sex segregation. In desegregated schools, most whites do not consider gender issues as a part of desegregation issues. Many girls of color do, however, and they wonder who they are expected to date if the school is predominantly white. By framing gender issues around white women's concerns, concerns of women of color are often completely ignored.

Gender issues are addressed at Level 1 when most of the women represented in the curriculum are white and middle class, or the only girls to participate in or benefit from a program for girls are white and economically privileged, or racism and classism are not discussed at the same time sexism is being discussed. Activity at this stage blatantly reproduces race and class privilege: "White women appear 'raceless' . . .[and] the distinct historical experiences of women of color, to the degree they are acknowledged, are credited solely to race."[16]

When educators analyze the history of women in education and the labor force they often discuss women as having "moved increasingly from the family sphere into the wider spheres of economic life,"[17] which is a theme based on the experiences of white women. In classrooms, when "working women" are discussed in an effort to help girls prepare for jobs or careers, the same assumption is often made—that paid labor outside the home is relatively new to women. However, this assumption holds true mainly for white economically privileged women. It certainly is not true, for example, of African-American women, who have always been highly involved in economic life, although not necessarily paid for their labor, or of white working-class women who also have an active history of wage labor.

Analyses of male benefits from sexism in the labor force suffer a similar distortion when gender is the only axis of oppression used. A discussion of the implications of men's and women's economic status for sex equity, for example, noted:

> Historically, women have experienced higher unemployment rates than men, and there is little evidence to indicate that this trend will change significantly in the near future. In 1976, for example, the unemployment rate for adult women was systematically higher than for men within racial and ethnic categories: 5.9 percent (white men) compared to 8.7 percent (white women); 16.3 percent (Puerto Rican men) compared to 22.3 percent (Puerto Rican women); and 15.9 percent (black men) to 18.9 percent (black women).[18]

The implication of the entire discussion was that men as a group accrue more benefits than women as a group. But clearly white men were the main ones experiencing the benefits, and white women were benefiting more than Puerto Ricans or blacks of either sex.

All oppressed groups must spend time and energy focusing primarily on themselves in order to examine their experiences and develop a sense of solidarity. White economically privileged women have needed to do this as much as any other group.[19] The problem arises when one group tries to generalize their experience to other groups, refusing to acknowledge the perspective of others and refusing to acknowledge one's own participation in the oppression of others. It is this arrogance of presuming the white heterosexual middle-class experience to represent *the* women's experience that has bred distrust and blocked coalition building. Level 2 presents a common attempt to "fix" the silence of Level 1 on race and social class.

Level 2. Contributions or exceptions to "the rule." Much liberal feminist discourse and many activities attempt to include women who are not white and middle class by inserting them into activities, theoretical constructs, and recommendations that originated in the experiences of white economically privileged women. Contributions to "the rule" add a few women of color; exceptions point out occasional differences between white women and women of color or lower-class women, often in a separate section near the end of the work. The main assumption is that women share experiences and perspectives that are largely similar, but that those of women of color or women from lower-class backgrounds differ in some respects. An activity, a piece of curriculum, a discussion, or a group is functioning at this level if most but not all of the women involved or referred to are white and economically privileged. Most textbooks, for example, employ a "contributions" approach to both race and gender. Cosmetically, such work is multicultural; substantively, it is not.

An example of a book in education that was structured at this level is *A Handbook for Achieving Sex Equity through Education*, which is an excellent resource for its concise synthesis of a great amount of research on gender in education.[20] However, its chapters were written almost exclusively by white liberal feminist scholars, only some of whom acknowledged diversity among women in their chapters, usually by mentioning minority women once or twice. Further, the book relegated women of color to a separate section near the end about "specific populations," assuming that discussions of women in general apply equally to all women. (The editors did acknowledge having treated women of color and women from low-income backgrounds inadequately, attributing this inadequacy to the state of research on women and girls in general.)[21] The author of chapter 19, which focused on sex equity for minority women, explained sex equity priorities of women of color:

> These priorities tend to be broad-based; they link the goal of sex equity with the goals of liberation, survival, and equity for the total target group and sometimes for oppressed people on a global scale. Moreover, minority women tend to consider various forms of inequity when attempting to achieve equity in a given arena; they do not readily isolate racial, ethnic, cultural, economic, or sex inequity.[22]

But the book implied that white women do not need to consider oppression broadly conceived, since this theme was not woven into other chapters. Even the section on "special populations" did not provide chapters about lower class white women and lesbian women; social class was mentioned occasionally throughout the text, but sexual preference was not. The book appears to advocate what Conway had described in 1974 as "an educational experience which is critical of many of the assumptions of a male-controlled culture and which takes the female as the norm rather than the deviant exception."[23] In the section on "special populations," however, the book seems to be doing just that, that is, treating women of color and women from low-income backgrounds as "deviant exceptions."

In an effort to address race or class, educators often set up false dichotomies, adding on race or class as separate. As Spelman pointed out, for example, discussions about whether racism is more important than sexism are nonsense and stem "from the erasure of black women."[24] Consider the educator who wishes to reduce effects of sex role socialization in the home, and is confronted with a child of another cultural group in which there appear to be definite sex roles. Does one defer to culture and ignore gender? There are two problems with this question. First, women belonging to the culture in question are often not consulted. Second, the question is framed in a way that ignores the group's location within American social structures of race and class. Discussions of sex role learning focus on processes within the family, such as modeling and differential treatment, and imply that the family is one of the most important sites for creating and reproducing sexism. Many educators point to Mexican-American families as prime examples of patriarchy, viewing machismo as Mexican-style patriarchy. The Anglicized version of this term ("macho") emphasizes male dominance and disrespect for women. Similarly, white male scholars have portrayed the African-American family as matriarchal, blaming it for a host of problems that African Americans experience. Focusing on gender "problems" presumed to arise from within the families of nonwhite groups neatly removes the dominant society from scrutiny.

Scholars who have examined relationships among race, class, and gender, however, view the development of sex roles quite differently. In addition to viewing sexism as a cultural phenomenon that may be transmitted through institutions such as the family, socialist feminists also argue that white wealthy men have generated over time a division of labor that relegates women of different racial and class backgrounds to different places in a stratified system of "women's work." Capitalism and caste work together with patriarchy to create or amplify sex roles, with the main beneficiaries being white wealthy men.[25] Chicanos have been employed mainly as "cheap labor," restricted to a low social and economic status. Domination of women has become for many men of color a way of gaining status within a fairly closed opportunity structure. As Alfredo Mirande and Evangelina Enríquez argued, "machismo . . . is a mechanism for shifting the focus away from Anglo oppression to alleged pathologies within Chicano culture."[26] Similarly, Paula Gunn Allen argued that

Native-American communities took on the patriarchal structure of Europeans in the process of being colonized and dispossessed of land.[27] Discussions that consider only gender or that separate sexism from racism and classism imply that sexism constitutes a relationship between men and women *within* any social class, racial, or ethnic group, rather than interrogating relations that undergird sex roles *across* social groups.

Work that adds on race and class as "contributions" or "exceptions" is clearly biased, but gives the illusion of inclusiveness. Women working at Level 2 are often puzzled when women of color or white socialist feminists show only lukewarm interest in their efforts, or criticize those efforts. I speak from experience, having worked at this level myself. To get beyond it, one must first acknowledge that race and class are already there, informing one's analysis of gender. No one and no perspective is nonracial or nonclassed. While one's own experience is a valid place to start, its limits need to be acknowledged if they are to be transcended. Hazel Carby argued, for example, that white women must come to see race as a structure within which whites participate, and which shapes white women's identity as much as it shapes black women's identity. She argued that "because the politics of difference work with concepts of diversity rather than structures of dominance, race is a marginalized concept that is wheeled on only when the subjects are black."[28] Examining and questioning one's whiteness and privilege, rather than defining these as irrelevant, are necessary for reconstructing one's understanding of gender and oppression.

Level 3. Bifocal discourse. Tetreault defined bifocal discourse as one that dichotomizes women's and men's experiences, examining how they differ and how men oppress women; it examines the interface between men's and women's experience and how gender serves as a mode of domination. Applied to the integration of race and class with gender, bifocal discourse contrasts the experiences of white, economically privileged women with the experiences of women who are oppressed on the basis of race and/or class. Rather than placing *any* group of women at the center of consideration, it examines the interfaces among women, how women oppress other women, and how different categories of women are oppressed differently. The bifocal approach "shatters the notion of a universal sisterhood. Simply stated, it permits feminist historians to discard celebration for confrontation, and allows them to explore the dynamics through which women have oppressed other women."[29]

The main theme of analysis at this level is power and domination. One is asking, "How do white economically privileged women retain their privileges over other women, and how can this relationship change?" This is very different from asking, as one does at Level 2, how to add in women of color or women who are poor. At Level 3, white economically privileged women must confront their own power and privileges. This is very hard for them to do. Usually they look for ways to avoid doing so. Spelman, for example, examined how white economically privileged feminist theorists have avoided confronting their own privileges, thereby preserving them.[30]

Consider a multiracial elementary school in which most of the teachers are white women and most of the parents with whom they have contact are women of color, many of whom are low-income women. At Level 1, a gender concern might be empowerment of the teachers in the school in relationship to the district's bureaucracy, the teachers being mainly women and the issue being framed in terms of professionalism. What remains unaddressed, however, is the relative position of the teachers and the mothers of students. Quite often teachers as professionals assume a rather patronizing stance toward mothers of lower status backgrounds, becoming concerned about teaching them how to parent better rather than sharing power with them. At Level 2, a few parent representatives would be added to a school's management team, giving mothers of color and low-income white mothers a limited voice in the school, but retaining the power of white professionals. At Level 3, the concern is for equal power sharing between white professionals and women who are not white, or who are low-income. The power differential is explicitly addressed with the aim of confronting and eliminating it. Clearly Levels 2 and 3 are very different; Level 3 is usually perceived as threatening by white professionals.

Consider another illustration, this one a program designed to help girls prepare for advanced study in computer science. At Level 1, no consideration would be given to the racial and social class status of the girls participating; if all of them were white and economically privileged, the institution would accept this as "normal." At Level 2, some extra steps would be taken to add some girls of color and perhaps some white girls from low-income homes. At Level 3, one would ask how programs such as this open up opportunities for only a segment of girls, mainly those who already enjoy the greatest opportunities; this would lead to an examination of a wide range of institutional processes in the school that stratify and serve girls as well as boys differentially, by race and social class.

Bifocal discourse represents an important step forward in integrating race and class with gender because it does not take as normative the white middle-class experience and because it grapples directly with unequal relations of power and privilege among women. It is limited, however, in its bifurcation of the world of women into relatively undifferentiated dominant and subordinate groups. For example,

> The framework itself leads the historian to focus her examination on the relation between a powerful group, almost always white women, and minority women, the varieties of whose experiences are too often obscured. In other words, the historical emphasis is on white power, and women of color have to compete for the role of "other." The historical testimonies of women of color thus tend to be compacted into a single voice.[31]

Upper, middle, and lower class women of diverse racial and ethnic memberships are lumped together; poor white women are lumped with women of color, many of whom are middle or upper class. For this reason, Level 3 is insufficient, even though it presents an important step forward.

Level 4. Discourse about and by women who are not white and economically privileged. Just as much of the scholarship on women starts with the experiences of women rather than men, many feminist scholars of color and scholars from lower-class backgrounds start with experiences of women like themselves. Such work does not attempt to enlarge the discourse defined mainly by white economically privileged women as much as it regards that discourse as either peripheral or irrelevant. Women who are not white and middle or upper class are at the center rather than in the margins. In the preface to her book about the history of black women, Paula Giddings explained:

> For despite the range and significance of our history, we have been perceived as token women in black texts and as token blacks in feminist ones. . . . Black women have a history of their own, one which reflects their distinct concerns, values, and the role they have played as both Afro-Americans and women. And their unique status has had an impact on both racial and feminist values.[32]

Rich bodies of literature have been produced by women from a variety of racial and social class groups and sexual orientations. Most of it exists outside the field of education, but it is relevant to educators because it reframes questions and practices in education. Literature by and about women of color and/or women of lower-class origins can roughly be classified into three categories: critiques of white liberal and radical feminism,[33] discussions of the subjective experience and theoretical position of one's own group,[34] and investigation of an issue or development of a line of inquiry based on the experiences and perspective of one's own group.[35]

For example, in an attempt to add Indian women to the curriculum, well-intentioned white feminists (working at Level 2) may simply assume Indian women were subordinate to men in the past, select heroines who are different from those whom Indian women admire, focus on assimilation of Indian women into industrial society rather than the preservation and strengthening of Indian communities, or add some Indian women to a white feminist curriculum rather than acknowledging the "red roots of white feminism."[36] In contrast, Paula Gunn Allen discussed the processes of self-definition that put her own experiences and world view as a Native-American woman at the center, and of reconstructing what she had learned about Indian women from outside sources:

> Whatever I read about Indians I check out with my inner self. Most of what I have read—and some things I have said based on that reading—is upside down and backward. But my inner self, the self who knows what is true of American Indians because it *is* one, always warns me when something deceptive is going on.[37]

She framed her work around the themes of Indians as survivors, Indian cultures as woman-centered, white colonization of Indians as stemming from fear of women's power, and Indian cultures as similar to many other tribal cultures around the world that Europeans have attempted to destroy. While not all Native Americans agree with all of her ideas (indeed, no individual speaks completely for a whole group), she does present a very different perspective from that which non-Indians typically take.

On many university campuses today, it is fashionable to study women of color. While at first glance this would seem to encourage white women to immerse themselves in other women's oppression, Hazel Carby has noted how easily many white women plunge into literature by and about women of color without coming to grips with their own participation in a racist social structure. They define women of color as "other" and different, living in a world that is strangely detached from the white world. In the process they do not hear the rage of women of color against racial oppression or recognize that white women accept racism and socialize their children as racists.[38] Several years ago a white student was completing an independent study under my direction, focusing on inclusion of literature by black women writers in the high school curriculum. After reading several pieces of literature, she commented to me that it expresses much anger and pain and will be better literature once black women get past their anger and pain, the causes of which she assumed to be historical only. I redirected her to examine what they might be angry about today, and what our role as whites continues to be in maintaining reasons for anger.

As white middle-class women, we wish men to stand in our shoes and view patriarchy from our perspective, but we experience great difficulty viewing race, class, and ourselves from the perspectives of women in whose oppression we participate. As Johnnella Butler put it,

> White women function both as women who share certain similar experiences with women of color and as oppressors of women of color. This is one of the most difficult realities to cope with while maintaining valuable dialogue among women and conducting scholarship. White women who justifiably see themselves as oppressed by white men find it difficult to separate themselves from the effects of shared power with white men.[39]

Level 5. Multicultural emancipatory discourse. Tetreault defined a gender-balanced curriculum as one which recenters knowledge in the disciplines in a way that draws on the experiences and scholarship of both men and women equally, and in the process transforms our understanding of the social world.[40] Here, I am applying her idea to mean a broadly based, multicultural discourse about education and society that is rooted in the experiences of many groups and that is politically oriented toward equality and emancipation. No one group's perspectives would dominate, and no one group would consistently benefit. For example, only about one-fifth of the people, experiences, and viewpoints in curricula would be drawn from the white experience, rather than half to four-fifths, as is currently the case. Power in a school district would substantively be shared; white professionals would not retain "last say" on matters.

Further, a multicultural emancipatory discourse about gender would explore how some groups of men are oppressed partly on the basis of gender. Gay men, for example, do not experience the same advantages and privileges as heterosexual men; their oppression is clearly sexual. As Barbara Smith pointed out, "Recent studies indicate that 30 percent of youth suicides can be attributed to turmoil about sexual orientation and the fear or actual experience of homophobia."[41] One can argue that oppression of either sex based on sexual preference is a consequence of patriarchy, an effort to keep men "men" and women "women."[42]

Young African-American men experience oppression that cannot simply be reduced to race or class, since young women of their race and class fare somewhat better on many indicators: African-American women attend college in greater numbers than African-American men, are much less likely to be killed or incarcerated, and live longer. Many whites fear the potential power of African-American men, and in response castrate them, either literally or figuratively. Images of violence and rape that whites associate with African-American men distinctly revolve around gender, and are evoked periodically to play on white racial and sexual fears, such as during the Bush-Dukakis presidential race. Among other things, this sexual oppression helps maintain a wedge between whites and African Americans, which in turn maintains divisions among oppressed groups who might otherwise work together to challenge the social order.

Poststructuralism offers a theoretical perspective which some scholars view as important to the development of multicultural emancipatory work, although others are more skeptical. Some theorists view poststructuralism's emphasis on multiple voices and experiences as an advance—as a movement away from the tendency to construct a "one size fits all" theory of women's experience. For example, Nancy Fraser and Linda Nicholson wrote that,

> Postmodern-feminist theory would dispense with the idea of a subject of history. It would replace unitary notions of woman and feminine gender identity with plural and complexly constructed conceptions of social identity, treating gender as one relevant strand among others, attending also to class, race, ethnicity, age, and sexual orientation.[43]

Others are skeptical about the usefulness of poststructuralists' fragmenting of oppressed groups (such as people of color) into multiple subgroups, and in the process minimizing attention to systemic power relations. Nancy Hartsock, for example, asked,

> Why is it that just at the moment when so many of us who have been silenced begin to demand the right to name ourselves, to act as subjects rather than objects of history, that just then the concept of subjecthood becomes problematic? Just when we are forming our own theories about the world, uncertainty emerges about whether the world can be theorized.[44]

At present, I see the value of poststructuralism as its renouncing of one voice, one theory, and one experience, and its emphasis on listening to many voices. Colleen Capper has recently applied a poststructural analysis to issues of concern to educational administrators.[45] In addition to explicating some main ideas of poststructuralism, her volume discusses administrative and policy concerns from a multiplicity of perspectives.

When I have presented this typology to groups, listeners who like Level 5 often ask questions such as, "Which textbooks are at this level?" or "How would you resolve such-and-such a problem in my school at this level?" Such listeners usually wish to bring back to their schools an answer that will solve a problem, a desire with which I can sympathize. However, Level 5 demands some considerations that are difficult and often avoided. First, power is to be shared, and shared with people who usually have been excluded. One person does not hand down "the" answer; answers emerge from collective work. Second, there is no one textbook, curriculum, program, or set of recommendations that can be transferred intact from one setting to another. The curriculum or school program must fit the particular people in a school and must reflect their concerns and input. One might offer models, but good models cannot simply be imposed. Third, in order to function at Level 5 any professional, and particularly any white professional, must come to grips with her or his own privileged position that results from one's racial, social class, and/or gender status. Without doing so, one will still be functioning in an "add and stir" mode—Level 2—without realizing it.

Building a multicultural emancipatory discourse rests on bridges and coalitions, the building of which requires much work. Albrecht and Brewer's book, *Bridges of Power: Women's Multicultural Alliances*, speaks directly to the politics of building a multicultural emancipatory discourse.[46] The book emerged from discussions in the 1988 National Women's Studies Association Conference, and grapples directly with the work of building alliances among women of different racial and ethnic groups, social class origins, religions, and sexual orientations, and further alliances with men who are oppressed on the basis of race, class, and sexual orientation. Ironically, at the 1990 National Women's Studies Association Conference, women of color seceded following confrontations with white women over race. Bridges are fragile, indeed.

Conclusion

Ultimately, we should be working toward the emancipation of all oppressed people, but this cannot be done without directly confronting power differences among oppressed groups. Power differences are difficult to confront and acknowledge before oppressed groups have separately articulated their own experiences, concerns, and agendas, and developed their own internal networks, theoretical constructs, leadership styles, and so forth. For white economically privileged women, participating in multicultural emancipatory discourse will mean learning to renounce their racial and social class privileges and work in coalitions in which they are in the minority. This means facing fears of what they might lose in order to recognize what they gain in the process.

I am grateful to the editors of this volume, Sari Knopp Biklen and Diane Pollard, and to Clara New, Lana Rakow, Barbara J. Shade as well as to the anonymous reviewers for their comments and suggestions on an earlier draft of this chapter.

Notes

1. Patricia A. Jones, "Educating Black Males: Several Solutions, but No Solution," *Crisis* 98, no. 8 (1991): 12-18.

2. U. S. Bureau of the Census, *Statistical Abstract of the United States 1990*, 110th ed. (Washington, D.C.: U. S. Government Printing Office, 1990), p. 409.

3. Other white women, such as Michelle Fine, Renee Martin, Elizabeth Swadener, and Lois Weis, also address race and class issues seriously. I suspect the main reasons we do so is our sustained life experience with people outside our own race and class status—experience that includes conversations about different experiences with and perceptions of gender. I have not, however, studied this issue systematically.

4. Cameron McCarthy and Michael W. Apple, "Race, Class, and Gender in American Educational Research: Toward a Nonsynchronous Parallelist Position," in *Class, Race, and Gender in American Education*, edited by Lois Weis (Albany, NY: SUNY Press, 1989), pp. 24-25.

5. Carl A. Grant and Christine E. Sleeter, "Race, Class, and Gender in Education Research: An Argument for Integrative Analysis," *Review of Educational Research* 56, no. 2 (1986): 195-211.

6. Russell W. Rumberger, "Dropping Out of High School: The Influence of Race, Sex, and Family Background," *American Educational Research Journal* 20 (1993): 119-220.

7. Amy J. Arntsen, "Feminist Organizations Called Subtly Racist," *The Cardinal* (Madison, WI), 22 February 1984, p. 11.

8. Angela Y. Davis, *Women, Race, and Class* (New York: Random House, 1981).

9. Barbara J. Shade drew my attention to the importance of acknowledging the long history of power conflicts surrounding race, gender, and class.

10. Peggy Means McIntosh, "Curricular Revision: The New Knowledge for a New Age," in *Educating the Majority: Women Challenge Tradition in Higher Education*, edited by Carol S. Pearson, Donnal L. Shavlik, and Judith G. Touchton (New York: Macmillan, 1987), pp. 400-412; Mary Kay Thompson Tetreault, "Integrating Content about Women and Gender into the Curriculum," in *Multicultural Education: Issues and Perspectives*, edited by James A. Banks and Cherry A. McGee Banks (Boston: Allyn and Bacon, 1989), pp. 124-144; Ellen Carol DuBois and Vicki L. Ruiz, *Unequal Sisters* (New York: Routledge, 1990).

11. Alison M. Jaggar, in *Feminist Politics and Human Nature* (Totowa, NJ: Rowman and Allanheld, 1983) distinguished among four feminist epistemologies: liberalism, Marxism, radical feminism, and socialist feminism. In *Feminist Practice and Poststructuralist Theory* (Oxford: Basil Blackwell Ltd., 1987), Chris Weedon distinguished among liberalism, radical feminism, socialist feminism, and poststructuralist feminism.

12. Nellie Wong, "Socialist Feminism: Our Bridge to Freedom," in *Third World Women and the Politics of Feminism*, edited by Chandra Talpade Mohanty, Ann Russo, and Lourdes Torres (Bloomington, IN: Indiana University Press, 1991), p. 290.

13. Tetreault, "Integrating Content about Women and Gender into the Classroom," p. 125.

14. Hazel V. Carby, "The Politics of Difference," *Ms: The World of Women* 1, no. 2 (1990): 84.

15. Elizabeth V. Spelman, *Inessential Woman* (Boston: Beacon Press, 1988), p. 4.

16. DuBois and Ruiz, *Unequal Sisters*, p. xi, 5.

17. Maxine Greene, "Sex Equity as a Philosophical Problem," in *Handbook for Achieving Sex Equity through Education*, edited by Susan S. Klein (Baltimore: Johns Hopkins University Press, 1985), p. 33.

18. Glen Harvey and Elizabeth Noble, "Economic Considerations for Achieving Sex Equity through Education," in *Handbook for Achieving Sex Equity through Education*, edited by Susan S. Klein (Baltimore: Johns Hopkins University Press, 1985), p. 20.

19. Barbara Grizzuti Harrison discussed this idea well in *Unlearning the Lie: Sexism in School* (New York: Liveright, 1973).

20. Susan S. Klein, ed., *Handbook for Achieving Sex Equity through Education* (Baltimore: Johns Hopkins University Press, 1985).

21. Saundra Rice Murray, "Sex Equity Strategies for Specific Populations," in *Handbook for Achieving Sex Equity through Education*, edited by Susan S. Klein (Baltimore: Johns Hopkins University Press, 1985), p. 361.

22. Shelby Lewis, "Achieving Sex Equity for Minority Women," in *Handbook for Achieving Sex Equity through Education*, edited by Susan S. Klein (Baltimore: Johns Hopkins University Press, 1985), p. 366.

23. Jill Conway, "Coeducation and Women's Studies: Two Approaches to the Question of Women's Place in the Contemporary University," *Daedalus* 103, no. 4 (1974): 241.

24. Spelman, *Inessential Woman*, p. 120.

25. See, for example, Nancy A. Hewitt, "Beyond the Search for Sisterhood: American Women's History in the 1980s," in *Unequal Sisters*, edited by Ellen DuBois and Vicki L. Ruiz (New York: Routledge, 1990), p. 1.

26. Alfredo Mirande and Evangelina Enriquez, *La Chicana* (Chicago: University of Chicago Press, 1979), p. 242. See also, Maxine Baca Zinn, "Mexican-American Women in the Social Sciences," *Signs: Journal of Women in Culture and Society* 8 (1982): 263.

27. Paula Gunn Allen, *The Sacred Hoop* (Boston: Beacon Press, 1986).

28. Carby, "The Politics of Difference," p. 85.

29. DuBois and Ruiz, *Unequal Sisters*, p. xii.

30. Spelman, *Inessential Woman.*

31. DuBois and Ruiz, *Unequal Sisters*, p. xii.

32. Paula Giddings, *When and Where I Enter: The Impact of Black Women on Race and Sex in America* (New York: Bantam Books, 1984), pp. 5-6.

33. See, for example, Carby, "The Politics of Difference."

34. See, for example, Gloria Anzaldua, *Borderlands/La Frontera* (San Francisco: Spinsters/Aunt Lute, 1987); bell hooks, *Yearning* (Boston: South End Press, 1990); Trinh T. Minh-ha, *Woman Native Other* (Bloomington: University of Indiana Press, 1989).

35. See, for example, Allen, *The Sacred Hoop*; Giddings, *When and Where I Enter*; Nancy Hartsock, *Money, Sex, and Power* (New York: Longman, 1983); Mirande and Enriquez, *La Chicana.*

36. Allen, *The Sacred Hoop*, p. 209.

37. Ibid., pp. 6-7.

38. Carby, "The Politics of Difference."

39. Johnnella E. Butler, "Transforming the Curriculum: Teaching about Women of Color," in *Multicultural Education: Issues and Perspectives*, edited by James A. Banks and Cherry A. McGee Banks (Boston: Allyn & Bacon, 1989), p. 148.

40. Tetreault, "Integrating Content about Women and Gender into the Curriculum."

41. Barbara Smith, "The NEA Is the Least of It," *Ms: The World of Women* 1, no. 3 (1990): 67.

42. Lana Rakow, personal communication.

43. Nancy Fraser and Linda J. Nicholson, "Social Criticism without Philosophy: An Encounter between Feminism and Postmodernism," in *Feminism/Postmodernism*, edited by Linda J. Nicholson (New York: Routledge, 1990), pp. 34-35.

44. Nancy Hartsock, "Foucault on Power: A Theory for Women?" in *Feminism/ Postmodernism*, edited by Linda J. Nicholson (New York: Routledge, 1990), p. 163.

45. Colleen Capper, ed., *Administration in a Pluralistic Society* (Albany, NY: SUNY Press), in press.

46. Lisa Albrecht and Rose M. Brewer, *Bridges of Power: Women's Multicultural Alliances* (Santa Cruz, CA: New Society Publishers, 1990).

CHAPTER XIV

Gender, Multiplicity, and Voice

MAXINE GREENE

This is a time of suddenly acknowledged multiplicity and diversity. Voices long ignored or long repressed are making themselves heard, many of them demanding that we look at things from their perspectives and recognize how numerous are the ways of defining what is "real." At once, and more and more frequently, we in education are being challenged to look through unaccustomed lenses at life in classrooms: for example, the lens of gender, so seldom utilized in educational history. Gender, we now realize, must be understood as a social construct or a cultural construct, referring to the meanings attached to the biological division of the sexes. More simply, gender identifies the implications of what it means in different contexts to be born a girl or a boy. It has to do with the mannerisms taught or adopted, and the expectations internalized, the modes of perceiving others and being perceived.

For more than a century after the founding of American public schools, most histories of education were written by men and focused largely on what male leaders said and did in the field. Granted, most children were taught by women; but their practice was screened and interpreted by males viewed as spokespeople out in the public realm. No attention was paid to gender practices, for example, to the ways in which existing modes of differentiation diminished girls' and women's opportunities to explore all their potentialities, to take risks, to act on their freedom in the world. The school, after all, was assumed to be a *common* school; conducted in accord with natural law and universal moral principles, the school reformers said, it offered the same opportunities to everybody. One of its stated aims, of course, was (as Horace Mann put it) "to equalize the conditions of men."[1] If he were asked, however, he would have asserted that "men" was a generic term, as it was in the Declaration of Independence. At once, he never

---

Maxine Greene is Professor in the Division of Philosophy, the Social Sciences, and Education at Teachers College, Columbia University.

hesitated to underline the gentle, motherly qualities of women, including teachers. Nor would he have consented to giving the young, poorly trained women in the classrooms a status equal to supervisors, principals, or superintendents. Those usually humble, dependent, unmarried persons had their particular functions. Not only were they to equip the children with the basic skills of literacy; they were to embody the moral stability all women were counted upon to provide in a country tumultuous with the pursuit of wealth or land, or simply with ways to survive.

In 1837, this was still the "new world." As F. Scott Fitzgerald was to write in the next century, it "pandered in whispers to the last and greatest of all human dreams."[2] We know how many of them were dreams of power and control, patriarchal dreams. In the Jacksonian moment, an awareness of that gave rise to fears of violence and anarchy; there had to be ways of tamping down the energies released, the huge desires for gain. The school, therefore, had two contrasting missions: to prepare people to pursue wealth, either by serving those who could take initiatives, or by establishing themselves as masters and shapers, and, at once, accede to social control and compliance with the moral law. The women's task was to assuage or to provoke guilt after excesses; women were to be "angels" of a hearth, pulling, beckoning, keeping conscience alive.

In another place in his *Reports*, Mann asked his readers to imagine a model teacher "whose language is well selected, whose pronunciation and tones of voice are correct and attractive, whose manners are gentle and refined, all whose topics of conversation are elevating and instructive, whose benignity of heart is constantly manifested in acts of civility, courtesy, and kindness, and who spreads a nameless charm over whatever circle may be entered."[3] Such a person, he said, should be the teacher in every common school. Not long after, writing about education as the machinery "by which the 'raw material' of human nature can be worked up into inventors and discoverers, into skilled artisans and scientific farmers, into scholars and jurists, into the founders of benevolent institutions, and the great expounders of ethical and theological science," he went on to offer as examples college presidents, school superintendents, artists, judges, leaders of armies, and "that best of all heroes, who will secure the glories of a peace unstained by the magnificent murders of a battlefield."[4]

Every possibility Mann listed, of course, was closed to women. Moreover, none of the virtues implicit in his portrait of the ideal teacher appears in his celebration of what the school could achieve. It is obvious that the exclusiveness, what we might call the sexism of such a point of view, would never have occurred to the great school reformer. Sanctioned as they supposedly were by the moral law and the wisdom of righteous men like himself, the schools were to do what it was assumed schools *should* do. Why would it occur to the schoolmen of that time that a singling out of what are now called sex-typed jobs and professions would implicitly discourage young girls, especially those with leadership potential, or those who had the capacity to judge others appropriately? Looking back at this from an ethical point of view, we might recognize that the approach was arrantly unfair and wrong because of what it did to deprive young women of the choice of options for themselves. How does *this* relate to the American Dream, "the last and greatest of all human dreams"?[5] It is not irrelevant to recall, with Fitzgerald in mind, Daisy Buchanan (in *The Great Gatsby*) confiding in Nick Carraway what she said when her baby girl was born: " 'I woke up out of the ether with an utterly abandoned feeling and asked the nurse right away if it was a boy or a girl. She told me it was a girl, and so I turned my head away and wept. 'All right,' I said, 'I'm glad it's a girl. And I hope she'll be a fool—that's the best thing a girl can be in this world—a beautiful little fool.' "[6]

Back in the early nineteenth century, there was an almost perfect match, when it came to the conceptualization of women, between the views of Mann and Ralph Waldo Emerson, in most cases bitterly at odds. The great glowing center of Emerson's Phi Beta Kappa address, "The American Scholar," is the section on "Man Thinking."[7] That man is the self-reliant scholar who never defers to popular opinion.

> He is the world's eye. He is the world's heart. He is to resist the vulgar prosperity that retrogrades ever to barbarism, by preserving and communicating heroic sentiments, noble biographies, melodious verse, and the conclusions of history. Whatsoever oracles the human heart, in all emergencies, in all solemn hours, has uttered as its commentaries on the world of actions—these he will receive and impart. And whatsoever new verdict Reason from her inviolable seat pronounces on the passing men and events of today, this he shall hear and promulgate.[8]

Objecting to crowds and categories, Emerson was addressing his "brothers and friends," telling them: "We will walk on our own feet; we will work with our own hands; we will speak our own minds. . . . A nation of men will for the first time exist, because each believes himself inspired by the Divine Soul which also inspires all men."[9]

This is the romantic speaking, the transcendentalist sure that he is expressing himself in universal terms. "Man," for him, was also a generic term; but the images of the free-swinging ego, the being with an almost infinite entitlement, evoke once again everything a woman (at that time) could never be. And indeed, Emerson did not himself believe she could be any of those things. He changed his position now and then about home and family (which he sometimes thought interfered with male development and further growth); but he did say that "man represents Intellect whose object is Truth, woman Love whose object is Goodness. Man loves Reality, woman order; man power, woman grace. Man goes abroad in the world and works and acquires. Woman stays at home to make the house beautiful."[10] We might well ask ourselves how the local housewife, or milkmaid, or mill girl would respond to that? How would Nathaniel Hawthorne's Hester Prynne respond (if transported out of the fictional domain)?

Emerson and Mann were not deliberately intending to discriminate or exclude, at least in the context of their own understandings. The differences between their world views were vast; but they both acceded to the taken-for-granted notions about men and women. What they assumed in their benevolence and imaginativeness became more and more unshakable as industry expanded in the United States. The gulf continued to widen between the spheres of the private and public and of the domestic undertakings and "work" in the meeting house or the factory or out at sea. Yes, there were woman laborers; but, as in the case of the Lowell cotton mills, they were scrupulously contained, even as they were cruelly exploited, and were presented to outside observers as nice little girls in schools. Herman Melville, in "The Tartarus of Maids," may have exposed what this implied most significantly in describing a New England paper mill. It is a place with iron frames, pistons, all worked by pale girls handling sheet-white paper at the end of a chill, unending process in which all are involved. The narrator asks the factory's proprietor why female operatives like his are indiscriminately called girls, never women. "We want none but steady workers," says the proprietor, "twelve hours to the day, day after day, through the three hundred and sixty-five days, excepting Sundays, Thanksgiving, and Fast-days. That's our rule. And so, having no married women, what females we have are rightly enough called girls."[11]

The infantilized and dependent young women existed, it is clear, in a peculiar extension of home and hearth. Around them there was competition of various sorts that never included them, except as laborers themselves or objects in the form of prizes. There were striving and contract making and self-sufficiency and swagger, assumed to be normal if not admirable. Back in the more prosperous homes, there were family dining tables and conversations; there were quilting bees and charitable undertakings. Sometimes, in the more emancipated homes, there were reform projects, now and then verging on political talk. Those were the places where the values of connectedness and compassion were nurtured (even against the repressed grumblings of frustration and despair). For many men, homes could not but be thought of as havens, refuges from an increasingly impersonal and heartless world. In popular literature and conventional thought, they were rendered as sanctuaries of virtue, civility, and morality. The *paterfamilias*, loving or not, devoted or not, was spoken of as defender, guardian against the impinging wilderness outside.

When Catherine Beecher began to dignify the domestic virtues and write of the dignity of women's "separate sphere,"[12] she did so partly to convince women of the impropriety of factory life for them and for the young persons who might otherwise have served them. But a Catherine Beecher could not respond to the needs of a brilliant, restless "bluestocking" like Elizabeth Peabody (or a radical thinker like Frances Wright, or a pioneer for women's rights like Susan B. Anthony, or any other of the outraged women intellectuals of the time). It is painful to note that Elizabeth Peabody worried about what she thought might be unseemly in her friendship for the widowed Horace Mann. She thought there was something wrong about the intensity of her feelings; and, when her sister Mary finally married Mann, she said that Mary's "humility and sweetness—and self-sacrifice"[13] were to be preferred to her sister's intellectuality. It becomes more and more obvious that the accepted or the official definitions not only frustrated the development of many women but forced them into repression and many sorts of illness. They partially account for the persisting silences, and long-lasting "invisibility" of women in American history. (The image of the woman in Charlotte Perkins Gilman's "The Yellow Wallpaper" surges up—the woman subdued into sickness by her husband, imagining the women behind the bars of the wallpaper in her closed room, women creeping out all together, moving into the light.)

And the "good" women, the "good" and nurturant teachers continued to be commended for their lack of ambition, their frugality, their docility. They were like devoted daughters to their superiors;

they were like mothers (unmarried, to be sure) to the children. Unlike Gilman's heroine, they gave no evidence of a need to tell about it, to write it down. Of course there were women like Margaret Fuller, who *did* write. Indeed, in her *Woman in the Nineteenth Century*, she tried to provide a philosophical justification for the right of woman to grow intellectually, to unfold her powers, to be free.[14] Only if she were as free as a man, she thought, could there be the kind of harmony between the sexes that might insure the excellence of the race. She wanted, at various times, to provoke women to build lives of thought grounded in lives of action. Frances Wright went further: she worked to persuade her sisters to free themselves by joining movements for political reform. Working with Robert Dale Owen, she raged against religious authoritarianism, tried prematurely to build workers' parties, understood in some fashion the oppressive effect of social structures on women's lives. But there were the unrecorded women who survived the looms, the whirling factory wheels, the choking dust, and who made their own songs, told their own tales. There were those who handled their husbands' chores when they were at sea or seeking new homesteads on the frontiers. There were those who took responsibility for fisheries or for farming or (later on) for ranches far in the west.

There were thousands of black women who could never submit to being humble or sweet, not if they were to survive and enable their families to survive. In fact, we have only recently begun to hear the strength of Harriet Tubman's voice and Sojourner Truth's and tens of other long unknown black women leaders. There were as well women like the Grimke sisters who fought for and with their black sisters in the slave houses, on the auction blocks. And there were those who went on to struggle for women's rights, writing their own Declaration of Independence, struggling more than a century ago for the franchise. What is called humanist feminism was expressed in the often pain-ridden demands for some elementary equality. American women, by degrees and often silently, were beginning to see themselves condemned to the limitation of their possibilities in a society ostensibly dedicated to freedom. Some were able to confront the fact that theirs was a society oriented to the self-development of men. What certain kinds of women yearned for, at the very least, was a modicum of equal opportunity: the right to take their chances in accord with the conventions and values governing the lives men lived out in the public spaces of the world.

But there were thousands of others: the submerged ones, the enmeshed ones—infantilized, smothered, defined by patriarchy. The incompleteness of our understanding of these, even today, may be clarified through encounters with American fiction, novels read from perspectives unknown in earlier days. Hawthorne's *The Scarlet Letter*, for one, sheds a startling light on women's predicaments if it can be read as an open text, no longer closed by pious words about adultery or secret guilt or even Puritanism. Yes, Hester Prynne lives in Puritan times—or, let us say, a constructed Hester lives her "as if" life in an unreal but plausible theocratic colony in seventeenth century Massachusetts. And that is but a sketch of a beginning.

The vantage point is the nineteenth century's Jacksonian moment; and it is defined by a discovery in a customs house of a rag with a letter 'A' embroidered on it. The narrator goes in search of the referent of that 'A', continually teasing, reaching beyond wherever imagination leads. Reading the novel without an expectation of predetermined meanings, we realize that we as readers are obligated to achieve meaning as we work to bring the book to life as an object of our experience. This means shaping the stuff of memory, stored images, sedimented beliefs in accord with the story as it reveals itself and in accord with the demands of its world. The contradictions and paradoxes in many women's lives come clear when Hester dares to assume "a freedom of speculation which our forefathers, had they known of it, would have held to be a deadlier crime than that stigmatized by the scarlet letter."[15] Yes, the lens held up was that of a male writer; but something deeply significant is encountered here when we realize the dread aroused when the oppressed begin thinking critically. Something is happening to Hester Prynne that goes beyond the effects of ostracism and social subordination. In fact, it places her in a marginal position with respect to her community. ("The world's law was no law for her mind.")[16] She looks "as if through the eyes of a wild Indian" at the institutions of the town. And yet she acts as Samaritan within the town; she cannot abandon the community. After some years, however, she tries to provoke her lover, the afflicted Reverend Dimmesdale, to pursue his own freedom by moving into the wilderness or taking the "broad pathway of the sea" away from "all these iron men, and their opinions."[17] He turns out to be the one who is powerless to move, who says "I dare not quit my post . . .," his post as elder, acclaimed speaker for the community.

When we as readers attend to Hester's surge of existential courage in the square when Dimmesdale dies, when we watch her disappear from view and later (years afterward) reappear, we cannot but lend her some of our own lives. Her choosing, on some level, becomes our choosing. Engaging with her, we cannot but discover facets in our experience that habit and taken-for-grantedness may long have obscured. When she does come back, she takes on the responsibility of comforting lost and wretched women. Also, she ponders lost dreams of becoming the prophetess of a "brighter period, when the world should have grown ripe for it." What feminist has not, at some point, dreamed of being leader or saviour, and then retreated in the face of her own internalized shame? Who has not, ironically, sometimes tragically, found new shadings and contours in her own experience simply by looking through someone else's eyes?

Confronting the Hester grasped by our consciousness, we find nothing "essentially" feminine about her, if we indeed believe that it is the "essence" of women to be compassionate, caring, and concerned. We may be compelled to question the familiar dichotomies, even the opposition between "she" and "he." We may find ourselves coping with particularities of startling kinds, contradictions, tensions that cannot be resolved. Depending upon our own involvements (with postmodernism, say, or later phases of feminism)[18] we may be drawn to revisions of our notions of difference, our concepts of diversity. At once, we may find ourselves redefining subjectivity and even maternality. There are many ways of being women, many ways of being in the world. Having recognized this, we may begin envisaging a world grown "ripe," in Hawthorne's words, a new truth revealed, "in order to establish the whole relation between man and woman on a surer ground of mutual happiness."[19] This implies something more than acceptance, either as equal or as different in a patriarchal world. To grow "ripe" may mean moving beyond the patriarchal and the matriarchal. There may be a hidden call for transformations reaching beyond Wright, Fuller, the Grimkes, Mann, Emerson, and Hawthorne himself.

As far as we know, apart from the journals and recovered letters here and there, there were few contemporary attempts in the nineteenth century to explore the full complexity of women's existence—or to venture into the lived worlds of working women (like the Lowell mill girls, or Melville's pallid operatives) or slave women and freedwomen (whose lives Alice Walker and Toni Morrison were to tap in years to come). The great canonical writers wrote affirmatively or tragically about the industrialization of Eden, about the Janus faces of progress, about prairies and ponds and mountain peaks and trout streams and whaling ships. There were no women present in such places—no women on Huck's raft nor on the Pequod nor at Walden Pond. If they existed in their absence, they were waiting, keeping the houses in order, pacing the widow's walks, shielding the firelight, or (only occasionally acknowledged) beckoning, whispering in shadows on run-down city streets. Most readers at the time preferred romance novels, genteel novels. What they found in them, more often than not, overlapped and confirmed conventional views of the "normal," the "proper," the respectable. It would take many alternative visions of history and customs to defamiliarize the taken-for-granted sufficiently so that readers would actually "see" what they were being made to believe. Few were offered opportunities or sought out opportunities to look from the standpoints of freedmen and articulate African-American spokespeople (Sojourner Truth, Frederick Douglass, W.E.B. Dubois). If they did open themselves to such viewpoints, some women at least might have questioned what surrounded them and swathed so many injustices in the normal, the comforting, and the safe. Schools and colleges, however, did not prompt people to look through any but canonical lenses. Gender lenses, or those made available by black poets and story-tellers, were not taken into account. Nor were those presented by the experiences of Native Americans, forced to abandon their sophisticated settlements, driven repeatedly down hostile roads.

A paragraph near the beginning of E. L. Doctorow's *Ragtime* offers some idea of the denials, the decorous surfaces on which the American majorities thought they lived.

> Patriotism was a reliable sentiment in the early 1900s. Theodore Roosevelt was President. The population customarily gathered in great numbers either out of doors for parades, public concerts, fish fries, political picnics, social outings, or indoors in meeting halls, vaudeville theatres, operas, ballrooms. There seemed to be no entertainment that did not involve great swarms of people. Trains and steamers and trolleys moved them from one place to another. That was the style, that was the way people lived. Women were stouter then. They visited the fleet carrying white parasols. Everyone wore white in summer. Tennis racquets were hefty and the racquet faces were elliptical. There was a lot of sexual fainting. There were no Negroes. There were no immigrants.[20]

A bit later, Doctorow tells of the murder of the architect Stanford White by Harry K. Thaw, scion of a railroad fortune and husband of Evelyn Nesbit: "Her underclothes were white. Her husband habitually whipped her. She happened once to meet Emma Goldman, the revolutionary. Goldman lashed her with her tongue. Apparently, there *were* Negroes. There *were* immigrants. And though the newspaper called the shooting the Crime of the Century, Goldman knew it was only 1906 and there were ninety-four years to go."[21] There were women too, it turned out, in a grand confusion. Diverse women from a great range of countries lived on the lower East Side of the city, in the uptown mansions, in the settlement houses, in the schools. There were those who supported the great charities, those who took classes in Italian opera at educational centers, those who worked at sewing machines, those who sponsored and those who slaved and those who peddled on the streets. Doctorow's date, 1906, could signify a summing up, a period, or a beginning. The diversity denied remained, as most Americans continued to cling to the reassuring and excluding constructs. Lenses were and are required; lenses and the ability to perceive the tears in the country's fabric, deficiencies that called out for repair.

Since late in the nineteenth century there have been moments of resistance to pressures and deprivations that have brought women into unexpected visibility: strikes in the garment industry; industrial accidents; suffrage actions. In John Irving's *The Cider House Rules*, we are made to recall the carnage caused by illegal abortions in the South End of Boston, women with their underwear safety-pinned to their shoulders, a place "mercilessly full of evidence of uncharitableness towards the erring."[22] The "erring" were women, visible too often in their suffering, now and then in their outrage. Considering them, we find the monological mode of sense-making breaking open; it becomes harder to "other," harder to make objects of those we keep at a distance from ourselves. Taking a dialogical approach, we begin to become aware of a plurality of consciousnesses, each with her own right to attentiveness and regard. The emergent awareness of plurality partly accounts for the uncovering of women's texts unknown and unheeded in the past. They are read today because of the ways in which Women's Studies courses, women's journals, women's literary criticism drew attention to them; and they have, even though some were written a century ago, a hauntingly contemporary feel. Most of us know Kate Chopin's *The Awakening* by now, Louisa May Alcott's *Work*, the Gilman works, and Rebecca Harding Davis's *Life in the Iron Mills*, that disclosure of the "vast machinery of the system" crushing lives.[23]

The Awakening, well known by now, has much to do with a woman unable to break with the terrible dichotomies strangling so many female lives, even as she does awaken to her consciousness of her self. She feels trapped; she thinks, when she swims to her death, of the choice between the "soul's slavery" of domesticity and what she can only anticipate as a life of promiscuity.[24] She cannot, though, (because of a sterile education, a repressive family history, infantilization by her Creole husband) even imagine what life would be like without a man. Like many women's novels, novels written on the margins, the text raises more and more unanswerable questions. How much of the tragedy is due to Edna's innocence and ignorance? How much to the culture's pressures and demands? Under what circumstances can a woman like Edna—comfortable, protected, talented—break free? What of Edna as mother, lover, wife, manager, child? What of the language available, a language that gave rise to its own peculiar transgressions and treacheries? Like the film, *Thelma and Louise*, so many years later, whatever ironic "awakening" there has been opens the road to death.

Edith Wharton's *House of Mirth*, the tale of a woman whirling through a crowded world of social entertainment and pleasure, acquiescing, then cast out until she is an "organism as helpless out of its narrow range as the sea anemone torn from the rock,"[25] is one of several texts rendering women as cogs, women as things. There is Harriette Arnow's *The Dollmaker*, telling how economic and moral systems together conspire to erode the strength of a powerful mountain woman who carves dolls from wood and struggles a lifetime to release a head of Christ from a tree trunk that travels with her from the Kentucky hills to the tenements of Detroit.[26] There is Maya Angelou explaining how she sentenced herself to muteness after she was raped as a child, and the rapist was mysteriously killed. "When I refused to be the child they knew and accepted me to be, I was called impudent and my muteness sullenness."[27] There is Tillie Olsen, in *Tell Me a Riddle*, rendering the dying days of a woman prevented from moving to her own rhythms, singing her own songs, reading her own books, by husband and children through a lifetime of repression. There is Jamaica Kincaid, in *Lucy*, enabling us to experience what it is for a young woman to come from Antigua and try to hold on to her identity as an *au pair* girl in New York. And so many other texts to supplement what we know of history and, yes, of education. They have the power to engage us with concrete cases of subordination, with particular lives of suffering and sensuality and savagery and joy.

Also, texts like these offer us new modes of revisioning, not only what we have read in the past, but the texts of our own lived lives. Surely we know by now that there is no category—be it female or "womanist" or gender-specific—into which all girls and women can be thrust. We read of the Chinese woman's mythic quests in Maxine Hong Kingston's *The Woman Warrior*, of the weight of a previous generation's memories in Amy Tan's *The Joy Luck Club*, of the picaresque life of a Chilean Scheherazade in Isabel Allende's *Eva Luna*, of the struggles of a Hindu woman in Iowa in Baraka Mukerjee's *Jasmine*, of a Holocaust survivor on the knife edge of her sanity in Cynthia Ozick's *The Shawl.* Different women, women leaving different thumbprints. But there are connections; there are concerns. And we know there is something that links women's lives together, something absent in the patriarchal world.

To come to terms with the endlessly unfolding scrolls rendering diversity is not merely to acknowledge it, to encourage the spinning of more and more narratives. It is to recognize how the very shaping of stories pulls us to different modes of seeing and feeling. Toni Morrison has made us feel the impact of the "master story" by telling us the tale of Pecola Breedlove in *The Bluest Eye*. Overwhelmed by the culture's myth (or metanarrative) about the wonder of a blue-eyed Shirley Temple, unloved little Pecola is at length driven mad. She cannot break with what dominates her and weighs down upon her; she is not loved enough or articulate enough to tell her own story. And, in any case, the land around is barren when it comes to the nurture of little black girls. In Morrison's *Sula*, on the other hand, Sula tells her friend Nel: "I'm going down like one of those redwoods. I sure did live in this world." Nel responds: "Lonely, ain't it?" And Sula says, "Yes, but my lonely is *mine*."[28] Yes, we might well affirm, "my lonely is mine"; "my experience with mothering is mine"; "my search for meaning is mine, all mine." Saying that, we think we know what we mean. And then we open texts again.

We might think of Gertie Nevels in *The Dollmaker*, seeing her child Cassie running after her imaginary playmate, run over by a train. Gertie, out of self-protection and protection of her child in the slum alleys of Detroit, has tried to discourage her belief in Callie Lou. But there is no substitute; there is no place for Cassie, and she dies. We might think of Sethe in Morrison's *Beloved*, thinking helplessly of the seven children sold away from her when they were young, and about never knowing how they grew up, what their hands looked like, how they walked, what they liked to eat. Few of us have suffered the losses of children as Gertie and Sethe did; but we *know*, and reading of them, lending them our lives, we have come to know more. We are connected with them through our own struggles to keep children alive and growing; we are related through the losses even we have known.

To recognize this is to feel the urgency of breaking the hold of the canonical and, yes, the phallocentric. To recognize it is to find ourselves throbbing with new questions with regard to customary renderings of the way women are supposed to be. We may have to set aside persisting notions of "essence," to orient ourselves to all sorts of open possibilities where identity and communion are concerned. Expectations have to widen. A range of new experiences, many of them contradictory and painful, have to be risked and, in time, explored. They are not the kinds of experiences that can be provided through the descriptions and generalizations of the social sciences, important though they may be. They are the kind that require leaps of imagination and insistent looking through the windows of the actual. They require the relational thinking we associate with "women's ways of knowing."[29] They require, too, the sense of presentness and responsibility that accompanies the realization of constructing knowledge from situated vantage points in the world. There has to be pondering, wondering, thinking in terms of networks and textures, thinking resembling Whitney Otto's "quilt-making," with its multiple patterns, its randomized realities.

Only the gender lenses we have spoken of can disclose the cruel artifices of exclusion and suppression. Only through the breaks with the everyday that literature makes possible can we feel the bite of those artifices, feel the particularity of humiliation and alienation and remembered pain. Through a coming together in our difference, and with our memories and our stories, we may bring a new generative power into being. Refusing the "normal," we may even create generative schools with open spaces where diverse persons can invent projects of their own and, by doing so, choose themselves. In her poem, "Kathe Kollwitz," Muriel Rukeyser wrote:

> I am in the world
> to change the world
> my lifetime
> is to love to endure to suffer the music[30]

To do that is to make the questions dangerous. "To love, to endure, to suffer the music . . ." may involve reweaving, renewing a community, making lives liveable, some for the first time. This may be the way we find for confronting, in their power and their resonance, the realities of gender and diversity.

Notes

1. Horace Mann, *The Republic and the School: Horace Mann on the Education of Free Men*, edited by Lawrence A. Cremin (New York: Teachers College Press, 1979), p. 87.

2. F. Scott Fitzgerald, *The Great Gatsby* (New York: Charles Scribner, 1974), p. 177.

3. Mann, *The Republic and the School*, pp. 87-88.

4. Ibid., p. 79.

5. Fitzgerald, *The Great Gatsby*, p. 177.

6. Ibid., p. 17.

7. Ralph Waldo Emerson, "Self-Reliance" and "The American Scholar," in *Emerson on Education*, edited by Howard M. Jones (New York: Teachers College Press, 1966), pp. 90-96.

8. Ibid., p. 91.

9. Ibid., pp. 100-101.

10. Robert E. Spiller et al., editors, *The Early Lectures of Ralph Waldo Emerson* (Cambridge, MA: Harvard University Press, 1972), p. 62.

11. Herman Melville, "The Tartarus of Maids," in *Selected Writings: Complete Short Stories* (New York: Modern Library, 1952), p. 210.

12. Nancy Hoffman, *Woman's "True" Profession: Voices from the History of Teaching* (Old Westbury, NY: Feminist Press, 1981), p. 52.

13. Anne C. Rose, *Transcendentalism as a Social Movement* (New Haven: Yale University Press, 1981), p. 179.

14. Margaret Fuller, *Woman in the Nineteenth Century*, and *Kindred Papers Relating to the Sphere, Condition, and Duties of Women*, edited by Arthur B. Fuller (New York: Greenwood Press, 1968).

15. Nathaniel Hawthorne, *The Scarlet Letter and Selected Tales* (New York: Penguin Press, 1969), p. 183.

16. Ibid., p. 182.

17. Ibid., pp. 214-215.

18. Jane Flax, *Thinking Fragments* (Berkeley: University of California Press, 1990); Barbara Herrnstein Smith, *Contingencies of Value* (Cambridge, MA: Harvard University Press, 1988).

19. Hawthorne, *The Scarlet Letter*, p. 275.

20. E. L. Doctorow, *Ragtime* (New York: Random House, 1974), p. 3.

21. Ibid., p. 46.

22. John Irving, *The Cider House Rules* (New York: William Morrow and Co., 1985), p. 69.

23. Rebecca Harding Davis, "Life in the Iron Mills," in *Four Stories by American Women*, edited by Cynthia G. Wolf (New York: Penguin Books, 1990), p. 15.

24. Kate Chopin, *The Awakening* (New York: Avon Books, 1972), p. 189.

25. Edith Wharton, *The House of Mirth* (New York: New American Library, 1964), p. 311.

26. Harriette Arnow, *The Dollmaker* (New York: Avon Books, 1972).

27. Maya Angelou, *I Know Why the Caged Bird Sings* (New York: Bantam Books, 1971), p. 73.

28. Toni Morrison, *Sula* (New York: Bantam Books, 1975), p. 123.

29. Mary Belenky, Blythe Clinchy, Nancy Goldberger, and Jill Tarule, *Women's Ways of Knowing: The Development of Self, Voice, and Mind* (New York: Basic Books, 1986).

30. Muriel Rukeyser, "Kathe Kollwitz," in *by a Woman writt*, edited by Joan Goulianos (New York: Bobbs Merrill, 1973), p. 374.

Name Index

Subject Index

INFORMATION ABOUT MEMBERSHIP IN THE SOCIETY

Membership in the National Society for the Study of Education is open to all who desire to receive its publications.

There are two categories of membership: Regular and Comprehensive. The Regular Membership (annual dues in 1993, $30) entitles the member to receive both volumes of the yearbook. The Comprehensive Membership (annual dues in 1993, $55) entitles the member to receive the two-volume yearbook and the two current volumes in the Series on Contemporary Educational Issues.

Reduced dues (Regular, $25; Comprehensive, $50) are available for retired NSSE members and for full-time graduate students *in their first year of membership.*

Membership in the Society is for the calendar year. Dues are payable on or before January 1 of each year.

New members are required to pay an entrance fee of $1, in addition to annual dues for the year in which they join.

Members of the Society include professors, researchers, graduate students, and administrators in colleges and universities; teachers, supervisors, curriculum specialists, and administrators in elementary and secondary schools; and a considerable number of persons not formally connected with educational institutions.

All members participate in the nomination and election of the six-member Board of Directors, which is responsible for managing the affairs of the Society, including the authorization of volumes to appear in the yearbook series. All members whose dues are paid for the current year are eligible for election to the Board of Directors.

Each year the Society arranges for meetings to be held in conjunction with the annual conferences of one or more of the major national educational organizations. All members are urged to attend these sessions. Members are also encouraged to submit proposals for future yearbooks or for volumes in the series on Contemporary Educational Issues.

Further information about the Society may be secured by writing to the Secretary-Treasurer, NSSE, 5835 Kimbark Avenue, Chicago, IL 60637.

RECENT PUBLICATIONS OF THE NATIONAL SOCIETY FOR THE STUDY OF EDUCATION

1. The Yearbooks

Ninety-second Yearbook (1993)

Part 1. *Gender and Education.* Sari Knopp Biklen and Diane Pollard, editors. Cloth.

Part 2. *Bilingual Education: Politics, Practice, and Research.* M. Beatriz Arias and Ursula Casanova, editors. Cloth.

Ninety-first Yearbook (1992)

Part 1. *The Changing Contexts of Teaching.* Ann Lieberman, editor. Cloth.

Part 2. *The Arts, Education, and Aesthetic Knowing.* Bennett Reimer and Ralph A. Smith, editors. Cloth.

Ninetieth Yearbook (1991)

Part 1. *The Care and Education of America's Young Children: Obstacles and Opportunities.* Sharon L. Kagan, editor. Cloth.

Part 2. *Evaluation and Education: At Quarter Century.* Milbrey W. McLaughlin and D. C. Phillips, editors. Paper.

Eighty-ninth Yearbook (1990)

Part 1. *Textbooks and Schooling in the United States.* David L. Elliott and Arthur Woodward, editors. Cloth.

Part 2. *Educational Leadership and Changing Contexts of Families, Communities, and Schools.* Brad Mitchell and Luvern L. Cunningham, editors. Paper.

Eighty-eighth Yearbook (1989)

Part 1. *From Socrates to Software: The Teacher as Text and the Text as Teacher.* Philip W. Jackson and Sophie Haroutunian-Gordon, editors. Cloth.

Part 2. *Schooling and Disability.* Douglas Biklen, Dianne Ferguson, and Alison Ford, editors. Cloth.

Eighty-seventh Yearbook (1988)

Part 1. *Critical Issues in Curriculum.* Laurel N. Tanner, editor. Cloth.

Part 2. *Cultural Literacy and the Idea of General Education.* Ian Westbury and Alan C. Purves, editors. Cloth.

Eighty-sixth Yearbook (1987)

Part 1. *The Ecology of School Renewal.* John I. Goodlad, editor. Paper.

Part 2. *Society as Educator in an Age of Transition.* Kenneth D. Benne and Steven Tozer, editors. Cloth.

Eighty-fifth Yearbook (1986)

Part 1. *Microcomputers and Education.* Jack A. Culbertson and Luvern L. Cunningham, editors. Cloth.

Part 2. *The Teaching of Writing.* Anthony R. Petrosky and David Bartholomae, editors. Paper.

Eighty-fourth Yearbook (1985)

Part 1. *Education in School and Nonschool Settings.* Mario D. Fantini and Robert Sinclair, editors. Cloth.

Part 2. *Learning and Teaching the Ways of Knowing.* Elliot Eisner, editor. Paper.

Eighty-third Yearbook (1984)

Part 1. *Becoming Readers in a Complex Society.* Alan C. Purves and Olive S. Niles, editors. Cloth.

Part 2. *The Humanities in Precollegiate Education.* Benjamin Ladner, editor. Paper.

Eighty-second Yearbook (1983)

Part 1. *Individual Differences and the Common Curriculum.* Gary D Fenstermacher and John I. Goodlad, editors. Paper.

Eighty-first Yearbook (1982)

Part 1. *Policy Making in Education.* Ann Lieberman and Milbrey W. McLaughlin, editors. Cloth.

Part 2. *Education and Work.* Harry F. Silberman, editor. Cloth.

Eightieth Yearbook (1981)

Part 1. *Philosophy and Education.* Jonas P. Soltis, editor. Cloth.

Part 2. *The Social Studies.* Howard D. Mehlinger and O. L. Davis, Jr., editors. Cloth.

Seventy-ninth Yearbook (1980)

Part 1. *Toward Adolescence: The Middle School Years.* Mauritz Johnson, editor. Paper.

Seventy-eighth Yearbook (1979)

Part 1. *The Gifted and the Talented: Their Education and Development.* A. Harry Passow, editor. Paper.

Part 2. *Classroom Management.* Daniel L. Duke, editor. Paper.

Seventy-seventh Yearbook (1978)

Part 1. *The Courts and Education.* Clifford B. Hooker, editor. Cloth.

Seventy-sixth Yearbook (1977)

Part 1. *The Teaching of English.* James R. Squire, editor. Cloth.

The above titles in the Society's Yearbook series may be ordered from the University of Chicago Press, Book Order Department, 11030 Langley Ave., Chicago, IL 60628. For a list of earlier titles in the yearbook series still available, write to the Secretary, NSSE, 5835 Kimbark Ave., Chicago, IL 60637.

2. The Series on Contemporary Educational Issues

The following volumes in the Society's Series on Contemporary Educational Issues may be ordered from the McCutchan Publishing Corporation, P.O. Box 774, Berkeley, CA 94702-0774.

Academic Work and Educational Excellence: Raising Student Productivity (1986). Edited by Tommy M. Tomlinson and Herbert J. Walberg.

Adapting Instruction to Student Differences (1985). Edited by Margaret C. Wang and Herbert J. Walberg.

Aspects of Reading Education (1978). Edited by Susanna Pflaum-Connor.

Choice in Education (1990). Edited by William Lowe Boyd and Herbert J. Walberg.

Colleges of Education: Perspectives on Their Future (1985). Edited by Charles W. Case and William A. Matthes.

Contributing to Educational Change: Perspectives on Research and Practice (1988). Edited by Philip W. Jackson.

Early Childhood Education: Issues and Insights (1977). Edited by Bernard Spodek and Herbert J. Walberg.

Educational Environments and Effects: Evaluation, Policy, and Productivity (1979). Edited by Herbert J. Walberg.

Educational Leadership and School Culture (1993). Edited by Marshall Sashkin and Herbert J. Walberg.

Effective School Leadership: Policy and Prospects (1987). Edited by John J. Lane and Herbert J. Walberg.

Effective Teaching: Current Research (1991). Edited by Hersholt C. Waxman and Herbert J. Walberg.

From Youth to Constructive Adult Life: The Role of the Public School (1978). Edited by Ralph W. Tyler.

Improving Educational Standards and Productivity: The Research Basis for Policy (1982). Edited by Herbert J. Walberg.

Moral Development and Character Education (1989). Edited by Larry P. Nucci.

Motivating Students to Learn: Overcoming Barriers to High Achievement (1993). Edited by Tommy M. Tomlinson.

Psychology and Education: The State of the Union (1981). Edited by Frank H. Farley and Neal J. Gordon.

Reaching Marginal Students: A Prime Concern for School Renewal (1987). Edited by Robert L. Sinclair and Ward Ghory.

Research on Teaching: Concepts, Findings, and Implications (1979). Edited by Penelope L. Peterson and Herbert J. Walberg.

Restructuring the Schools: Problems and Prospects (1992). Edited by John J. Lane and Edgar G. Epps.

Selected Issues in Mathematics Education (1981). Edited by Mary M. Lindquist.

School Boards: Changing Local Control (1992). Edited by Patricia F. First and Herbert J. Walberg.